Impossible Purities

Jennifer DeVere Brody

IMPOSSIBLE PURITIES

Blackness, Femininity, and

Victorian Culture

Duke University Press   Durham and London

1998

Designed by C. H. Westmoreland

Typeset in Berthold Bodoni with Miehle Classic Condensed

display by Tseng Information Systems, Inc.

Library of Congress Cataloging-in-Publication

Data appear on the last printed page

of this book.

I dedicate this book to Nathan and

Erness Bright Brody, without whom this work

truly would have been impossible.

Contents

Illustrations

Acknowledgments

I wish to thank all those who, in the words of Dorian Gray, "stirred in [me] the passion for impossible things," including: Anthony Wohl, who taught me much about Victorian prejudice and policy as organizer of Vassar College's Victorian Studies major; Beth Darlington, Cyrus Vakil, Hazel Carby, Ann duCille, Robert G. O'Meally, Marshall Hyatt, Charles Rowell, and Clarence Walker; my friends and colleagues from graduate school, Elizabeth Alexander, Lindon Barrett, Ann Cubilié, Nicole King, Carol Neuman, Barbara Kigozi, and Amy Robinson; and my dissertation advisers at the University of Pennsylvania, Peter Stallybrass and Dan Bivona. My main adviser, Nina Auerbach, deserves special mention for her guidance.

The 1993 Contested Boundaries in African American Studies conference at the University of California, Irvine facilitated conversations with Phillip Brian Harper, Arthur Little, and most significantly, Kim Hall, whose work on race, gender, and the Renaissance has been invaluable for this project. More recently, J. S. Bratton, Derek Forbes, Lorraine O'Grady, Howard Malchow, Steven Small, Paul Simon, and Robyn Wiegman shared valuable material with me. Jill Dolan, Kate Davy, Stacy Wolf, and others associated with the Women and Theater Program provided me with an important intellectual community. I learned much from a seminar with Homi K. Bhabha at the School of Criticism and Theory at Dartmouth. Jonathan Arac, Ronald Judy, Carol Kay, and Toi Derricotte influenced my thinking during my postdoctoral fellowship at the University of Pittsburgh.

At the University of California, Riverside, my home institution, I thank the former and current chairs of the English department, Steve Axelrod and John Ganim, as well as Philip Brett, Piya Chatterjee, Emory Elliott, George Haggerty, Tiffany Lopez, Kathleen McHugh, Katherine Kinney, Nancy Rettig, Sally Ness, Ray Kea, Sterling Stuckey, Marguerite Waller, and Traise Yamamoto. For true friendship, daily fellowship, and other generous acts, I am indebted to Carole-Anne Tyler, Rick Keane, Ethan Nasreddin-Longo, and Parama Roy. Students in various seminars added to the project, notably Kimberly Lutz, Julia Gardner and

Stefanie Dunning. Jennifer Itatani and Janet O'Shea provided excellent editorial assistance. Martin L. White completed the index.

The Society for Theatre Research in Great Britain awarded me a grant to complete the primary research for this book. Lisa Libby at the Huntington Library and staff members at the British Library, the Stowe-Day Library, the Parrish Collection in the Firestone Library at Princeton University, the Theatre Museum in Covent Garden, the University of California—Riverside Photographic Services, and the London Library assisted me greatly. Richard Morrison, Paula Dragosh, and the rest of the staff at Duke University Press were wonderfully attentive. I am grateful to Ken Wissoker for his patience, insight, and invaluable contributions. The readers selected to review this work, especially Joseph Roach, gave me superb advice—indeed, any remaining mistakes are my own. I thank my family—Alan, Melinda, and Aidan Brody; Georgine Willis; John Simmons; and Michael Watkins—for sustaining me in multiple, always meaningful ways. The last acknowledgment belongs to my first and best friends, my parents, Nathan and Erness Bright Brody.

My first desire is always boundless;

my first impulse is always towards the impossible.

—Alexandre Dumas

But what is impossible to think,

and what kind of impossibility are we faced with here?

—Michel Foucault

Prologue
COMPLICATING CATEGORIES

Fee, Fie, Fo, Fum—I smell the blood of an Englishman!
—*Jack and the Beanstalk*

"A True-Born Englishman: A Satyr [*sic*]"

Thus from a Mixture of all kinds began,
That Het'rogeneous Thing, *An Englishman:*
In eager Rapes, and furious Lust begot,
Betwixt a Painted *Britton* and a *Scot:*
Whose gend'ring Offspring quickly learnt to bow,
And yoke their Heifers to the *Roman* Plough:
From whence a Mongrel half-bred Race there came,
With neither Name nor Nation, Speech or Fame.
In whose hot Veins new Mixtures quickly ran,
Infus'd betwixt a *Saxon* and a *Dane.*
While their Rank Daughters, to their Parents just,
Receiv'd all Nations with Promiscuous Lust.
This Nauseous Brood directly did contain
The well-extracted Blood of Englishmen.

The odor of an impossible substance—the well-extracted blood of a true-born Englishman—lingers in xenophobic references to a pure and unified British nation.[1] In his poem's title, Daniel Defoe uses a pun, satyr/satire, to articulate the miscegenated and impure foundations of Englishness.[2] The subject of impurity is replicated in the poem's impure forms. The repetition of the words *betwixt, mixture, quickly,* and *lust,* along with the preponderance of *x*'s, points to the "hybrid," crossbred nature of pure origins in two senses: the very concept of hybridity presupposes pure forms that can be mixed, and the reproduction of purity requires the erasure of hybridity.

Defoe's "couplets" yoke together disparate figures miming artificial constructions of the Englishman himself.[3] The central "couplet" proclaims, "From whence a Mongrel half-bred Race there came, / With neither Name nor Nation, Speech or Fame." The four words that seem to be essential in forming a racialized identity are connected intimately with language and signs. The requirements of nationness include a name, a nation (geographic space), speech (a native tongue), and fame (a history, events, and "others" to recognize this fame). As the lines "this Nauseous Brood directly did contain / The well-extracted Blood of Englishmen" suggest, the blood (ancestry) of the Englishman has been *made* pure by extraction—a taking away of desired elements, or an erasure, perhaps, of complicated and corrupting sources.

The text begins with the statement, "A True-born Englishman's a contradiction, in speech and irony / fact and fiction . . . a metaphor to express / a man a-kin to all the universe." The metaphor of kinship is replaced in later accounts of the Englishman's origin by a model of the Englishman as metonym for (Western) man. Defoe argues that

While every nation that her powers reduced
Their languages and manners some infused
. . . From these mixed relics our compounded breed
By spurious generation did succeed.
Making a race uncertain and uneven
Derived from all nations under heaven . . .
All these their barb'rous offspring left behind
the dregs of armies, they of all mankind
Blended with Britons.

The British race, "uncertain and uneven," absorbed, amalgamated, and assimilated all other nations. Thus, the Englishman could be the "offal, out-cast progeny of Europe's sink, / [and] From this amphibious ill-born mob began / That vain ill-natured thing, an Englishman." Hippolyte Taine noted nearly 150 years after Defoe that "the Saxon Barbarian has been transformed into the Englishman of today."[4] Defoe's poem exposes this unseemly process of transformation, in which the "true-born," virtuous, and pure Englishman is *made* out of the impure vices that produce the "false" or ill-born.

Dramatizing the growth from "An Englishman" to "Englishmen," the poem references the desire for a collective national identity that must be made repeatedly. The creation of a modern nation of Englishmen is prefigured in the poem's statement that

. . . England, modern to the last degree
Borrows or *makes* her own nobility
And yet, boldly boasts of pedigree
Repines that Foreigners are put upon her
And tells of her antiquity and honour;
Her Sackvilles, Saviles, Capels, De la Mares,
Mohuns, and Montagues, Darcy's and Veres,
Not one have English names, yet all are English peers.

.   .   .   .

Then let us boast of ancestors no more,
Or deeds of heroes done in days of yore,
In latent records of the ages past,
Behind the rear of time, in long oblivion placed.
For if our virtues must in lines descend,
The merit with the families would end,
And intermixtures would most fatal grow;
For vice would be hereditary too;
The tainted blood would of necessity
Involuntary wickedness convey.
(italics added)

When the speaker of the poem suggests that the English should "boast of ancestors no more, or deeds of heroes done in days of yore," he notes that the past is impure and that it is the viscous substance of blood itself that conveys both virtue and vice. The poem emphasizes England's contradictory, mongrelized roots and is never clear about the exact origins of the Englishman (he uses half-breed and then goes on to mention Britons, Scots, Romans, Saxons, and Danes). Although satirical, "Defoe's uncompromising insistence on the ethnic diversity of England, its early exposure to successive invasions from continental Europe, and the constant intermingling of its peoples with the Welsh and Scots, was fully justified in historical terms."[5]

The genre (satire) is named in the title of Defoe's poem, which also

introduces a satyr that is native to English soil. The poem is addressed
not to a muse, but to the satyr himself, who is invoked in phrases such
as, "Speak, Satyr, for none like thee can tell," and "Satyr, be kind, and
draw a silent veil / Thy native England's vices to conceal." A leitmo-
tiv, satyrs are referenced frequently in various forms of English literature and culture, illustrating an obsession with impurity, impropriety,
and the impossible. How might we explain English culture's preoccupation with this and other hybrid, miscegenated figures?[6] Why should
a satyr, a fabled hybrid man-beast, serve as England's native infor-
mant?

Certainly, Defoe's use of the satyr to veil the vices of the hybrid nation
carries with it a reference to satire, which is a hybrid, double-voiced
genre; retrospectively speaking, however, it seems to be prescient in that
Britain would be the birthplace of the modern biological sciences, such
as psychology, that transformed men into animals—most famously, in
Charles Darwin's work. Defoe suggests that the satyr cannot veil vices
completely, and implores, "if that task's impossible to do, / At least be
just and show her virtues too." The impure legacies of the enlightened
West are implicated in such injunctions. In Defoe's satirical recounting
of the birth of the true-born Englishman, the path of virtue inevitably
crosses the path of vice. This cultural contradiction, contained in and
by the citation of the satyr/satire, is also an icon of an impossibly mixed
situation—literally, figuratively, and ethically. Defoe's poem therefore
exemplifies Walter Benjamin's thesis that "There is no document of
civilization which is not at the same time a document of barbarism."[7]

A True-Born Englishman: A Satyr highlights the violent, haphazard,
and chaotic birth of English*men,* and expresses concern with the purity
of male bloodlines.[8] Defoe's poem emphasizes that it is "Rank" [as in
carefully placed, and strong and offensive] *daughters* who "Receiv'd
all Nations with Promiscuous Lust." This line suggests that the female
becomes the main vessel through which contamination occurs, even
though "rape" has been mentioned earlier. Such feminized penetrated
figures are the vehicles of impurity. The English preoccupation with
the problem of purity has been seen as a problem not only of morality,
or even "race," but also of "gender." As figures "vestibular to culture," women have played a particular role in national (re)productions.[9]
The supposed instability, plasticity, and variableness of the feminine

"woman" generates contradictory narratives of her value and power, as well as prescriptive tracts detailing strategies for her control.

A frequently referenced figure of monstrous femininity is the young heroine of Lewis Carroll's Victorian classic, *Alice's Adventures in Wonderland* (1866). The chapter in the book entitled "A Caucus Race and a Long Tale," plays with ideas about the history of the English race. It relays a long tale of the Normans, the Earls of Mercia, and the "patriotic Archbishop of Canterbury."[10] While telling the long tale of English peers and personages, the dodo bird is accused of not knowing the meaning of the English words he speaks. Alice tells him, "You're all wet!" The dodo responds in an "offended tone" to this charge by stating, "the best thing to get us dry would be a Caucus race."[11] Although most critics have read the reference to "race" as an event—a kind of game—it might also connote the idea of racialist "races."[12] The "Caucus race," in which the characters run around in circles without a clear beginning and every participant wins a prize at the arbitrary conclusion, can be (mis)understood to also suggest the falsely won (one) category of racial designation. Carroll's clever conceit suggests the circular, artificial origins of the Caucasian race.

Similarly, Salman Rushdie's brilliant novel, *The Satanic Verses*, may be read in part as an extended satirical meditation on Englishness. Resonating with ideas presented by both Defoe and Carroll (not to mention H. G. Wells, Charles Dickens, and others), the more anglicized of the novel's protagonists, Saladin Chamcha, turns into a satyr when he is arrested by the police.[13] In this postcolonial encounter, the beastly British police unleash their brutality on the animalized "foreigner," who is shocked to find he is not the civilized gentleman he was in India. *The Satanic Verses* cannily returns to constructions of Englishness and English history by stating: "The trouble with the Engenglish is that their hiss hiss history happened overseas, so they dodo don't know what it means" (p. 343). The orthography here could not be more telling—the stuttering reflects the effort involved in constructing Englishness. The sentence echoes Carroll's dodo, who does not know the meaning of English history that happened "over seas" (a reference to Britain's naval prowess). The idea of a land-locked island of Albion free from contact and contamination is an impossibly maintained fiction. So too, it is significant that the word history is preceded with "hissing," because it so neatly combines gender with derision. The phrase suggests that the Englishman does not know (and perhaps does not wish to know) the various meanings of his origins.

Rushdie, Carroll, and Defoe each privilege a "wet" version of English history, where "wet" means muddied, muddled, and meddled with (hence impure), and "dry" means officially sanctioned and purified.[14] The problem of English purity is also the focus of this book, which seeks to unveil the "hidden" roots of an English identity that, quite possibly, are impossible, as Defoe's *True-Born Englishman* implies. Relatively speaking, rather than emphasize connectedness, contact, or commonality, English texts often stress the nation's continual covering over, absorption, or exaggeration of differences. Repeated ruptures in the narration of the nation are smoothed by sanitized, sanctified versions of history. This project focuses on the struggle to maintain the myth of a stable English identity that seemed to disintegrate as a result of "external" geopolitical and socioeconomic pressures.

Impossible Purities explores the pitfalls and possibilities of performing various forms of critical (in both senses of the word) "miscegenation." The book mines the intersection of the supposedly distinct fields of Victorian studies and African American studies. By intervening at the interstices of these institutionally sanctioned and organized areas of research, the book analyzes discursive formations that reproduce cultural categories as discrete. The usually aporetic relationship between Victorian studies and African American studies is refigured so that the putative "objects and subjects" of these disciplines, which are thought to be distinct and mutually exclusive, are read together. In an effort to rethink connections among and between bodies, boundaries, and binary oppositions, the book historicizes and reconnects fields "born" of a segregated academy.

There are several ways to challenge the discrete boundaries between "Victorian" and "African *American*" or "Black" studies.[15] Recently, Paul Gilroy has theorized the traffic of the "black Atlantic."[16] Gilroy's project reimagines the geopolitical borders among Africa, Europe, Britain, and the Americas in a manner analogous to anthropologists' (not to mention economists') understanding of the Pacific Rim. A comparable idea comes from Joseph Roach's conception of a "circum-Atlantic world," which insists on the centrality of the diasporic and genocidal histories of Africa and the Americas, North and South, in the creation of the culture of modernity. In this sense, a New World was not discovered in the Caribbean, but one was truly invented there. Newness enacts a kind of surrogation—in the invention of a new England or a new France out of the memories of the old—but it also conceptually erases indigenous populations, contributing to a mentality conducive to the practical implementation of the American Holocaust. While a great deal of the unspeakable violence instrumental to this creation may have been officially forgotten, circum-Atlantic memory retains its consequences, one of which is that the unspeakable cannot be rendered forever inexpressible: the most persistent mode of forgetting is memory imperfectly deferred.[17]

Such a reconfigured genealogy allows scholars to discuss Frederick Douglass's and Ida B. Wells's famous lectures in England, reactions to American Ira Aldridge's Shakespearean performances at Drury Lane, the highly acclaimed Fisk Jubilee singers in various London venues, or to focus on Charles Dickens's and Oscar Wilde's American tours, as well as the fact that Harriet Beecher Stowe's *Uncle Tom's Cabin* created a sensation on both sides of the Atlantic. These historical connections between England and America begin to realign national and rhetorical borders by revealing the tenuousness of such sociopolitical, ideological, and even economic boundaries.

This work brings to the recent study of "black Atlantic" cultural traffic a sustained discussion of gender and sexuality focused on the utility of "black" women (mulattas, octoroons, prostitutes) for the (re)production of certain forms of English subjectivity. Through readings of literary, visual, and theatrical texts, the book shows how "black" (racialized and sexualized) women were indispensable to the construction of Englishness as a new form of "white" male subjectivity. More specifically, this work studies constructions of what might be the nineteenth century's most important "miscegenated" coupling: black women and white men.[18] Historically, actual alliances and encounters between white English men and black women took place on distant shores and under colonial rules, institutional regimes, and structural arrangements such as the tea, sugar, cotton, and coffee plantations throughout Africa, the Americas, and India.[19] A specific aspect of the "black Atlantic" surveyed here is the importation of "black" American figures, especially black female figures along with figurations of the black feminine, to England.[20]

Unlike the 1960s' *Guess Who's Coming to Dinner* images that cast a white woman and a black man as the quintessential miscegenated couple, in the 1860s, the image of miscegenation promoted by a range of discourses was that of the black woman and the white man. This couple's coherence was sustained by sexual theories that labeled the prior union (between black man and white woman) sterile and literally "impossible," and the latter (between white man and black woman) fecund and, in some cases, not only possible but desirable—especially for economic gain.

An example of this theory appears in Paul Broca's tract on human hybridity, *On the Phenomena of Hybridity in the Genus Homo.*[21] Broca, who has a more complicated reading and does not believe in the sterility of such unions, nevertheless quotes anthropologist Theodore Waites as saying that "the children of a European woman and a Negro are rarely vigorous" (p. 29). So, too, he cites a Professor Serres, who states:

The union of the Caucasian man with an Ethiopian woman is easy and without any inconvenience for the latter. The case is different in the union of the Ethiopian with a Caucasian woman, who suffers in the act, the neck of the uterus is pressed against the sacrum, so that the act of reproduction is not only painful, but frequently non-productive. (p. 28)

This racist reversal recasts the frequent rape of black women as "inconsequent" and "easy" sex, while it also definitively labels sexual relations between white women and black men as painful (the uterus is pressed; the woman suffers). In other words, the dominant (and dominating) ideology of the day allowed Englishmen to populate and maintain power over most women, black and white. At the same time, this concept permitted such men to maintain the fantasy that white women not only *would* not, but more important, *could* not procreate with black men—an act that might result in complicating the white man's already unstable power of paternity. Such a construction of the difference between these divergent mergers serves to safeguard certain forms of white male power.[22]

The chapters that follow seek to unmask the performative nature of whiteness that too often has been "seen" as the unmarked, unchallenged normative site of power. By exposing the construction of the supposedly pure white, English characters whose origins, like all origins, are hybrid, it is hoped that new readings of Victorian culture will emerge. Moreover, this study will add to the growing scholarship on "race" in Victorian studies by interpreting nineteenth century white, male bodies as e-raced and gendered subjects. "Whiteness," "heterosexuality," and "masculinity" are concepts that need to be historicized further. As Kobena Mercer posits, the "real challenge . . . is to make whiteness visible as a culturally constructed ethnic identity historically contingent upon the disavowal and violent denial of difference."[23]

Such an inquiry requires us to examine the construction of Englishness as a "white" identity. How and why did the English become "white"? Or rather, how did Victorian texts construe Englishness as "masculine," "white," and "pure"? In order to answer this question, *Impossible Purities* looks at a range of Victorian cultural products, many of which ironically reference tropes of blackness and femininity as the "disavowed and violently denied differences." The book reads nineteenth-century texts through a black feminist lens that colors conventional readings of the texts as pure, perfect abstractions, recoding them as "mere" cultural artifacts that, along with other cultural detritus, may be seen as expressing popular anxieties about race, gender, sexuality, class, and nationalism.

Black feminist theory, a form of *cultural criticism* that reads "race," class, gender, and sexuality as overlapping discourses,[24] is a useful tool for this project. Black feminist theorists such as Valerie Smith, Hazel Carby, and others have long offered interpretations that account for "intersectionality," to use critical legal studies professor Kimberle Crenshaw's term.[25] By locating the black woman at the nexus of race and gender, her interstitial placement is highlighted and critiqued.[26] In this critical praxis, the salient components of identities are not conceived "sequentially" (one is first this, then that), but rather, synchronically. All identities can be understood as imbricated and intersubjective in order to work against ideas of identities as ossified categories reproduced in hegemonic discourse. Race and gender, the tame and the wild—or even the human and the animal—are not "conflicting" categories; they are mutually constitutive as well as always already divided and divisive terms. This thesis grounds the following discussions of Victorian English gentlemen.

Impossible Purities examines Victorian representations that are located at the juncture of (falsely) conflicting categories, such as race and gender, blackness and femininity, the human and the animal. The shifting position of these figures, which are unevenly placed, complicates and even violates categories that are supposed to be whole, pure, and inviolate. The book explores how "borders are cut and by whom,"[27] and provides new readings of canonical Victorian texts and the traditional classifications by which such texts are sustained. This book concerns itself, then, with intersecting constructions of race, class, gender, and sexuality in Victorian discourse.

In order to investigate the extent to which Victorian publics may have been familiar with representations of black caricature, we must shift our focus to popular performances, such as minstrelsy. This requires a move away from canonical texts, such as novels, to other cultural works. Those texts that are more ephemeral—such as theatrical performances, cartoons, and private papers—prove here to be valuable cultural sources. Attending to these other forms of textuality allows us to see how pervasive was the English interest in "black" Americana. The "evidence" for the argument that Englishmen were connected intimately to "black women" would be difficult to marshall if one were to rely solely on canonized Victorian literature. So too, a shift from a strictly literary focus to that of the "performative" (and to popular culture especially) allows one to track what might be the nineteenth century's metonymic miscegenated couple—namely, the repeated (and repeatedly elided) conjunction of race and gender signified by the alliances between white English men and black American women.

This work is indebted to Toni Morrison's book, *Playing in the Dark: Whiteness and the Literary Imagination,* which reads the influence of tropes of blackness in American literature. Morrison uses the term "Africanism" to describe,

the denotative and connotative blackness that African peoples have come to signify as well as the entire range of views, assumptions, readings, and misreadings that accompany Eurocentric learning about these people. As a trope, little restraint has been attached to its uses. As a disabling virus within . . . discourse, Africanism has become . . . both a way of talking about and policing matters of class, sexual license, and repression, formations and exercises of power, and meditations on ethics and accountability. Through the simple expedient of demonizing and reifying the range of color on a palette, American Africanism makes it possible to say and not say, to inscribe and erase, to escape and engage, to act out and act on, to historicize and render timeless. It provides a way of contemplating chaos and civilization, desire and fear.[28]

She goes on to explain that such figures of blackness are inextricably bound to corresponding images of whiteness. Morrison writes: "Through significant underscored omissions, startling contradictions . . . one can see that a real or fabricated Africanist presence was crucial to their sense of Americanness."[29]

A comparable "real or fabricated Africanist presence" played a role in the construction of Englishness.[30] The complex relationships between blackness and whiteness are illustrated linguistically by the etymology of the word *blac,* which in middle-English was easily confused if not equated with the term "blāc," which meant pale."[31] The *Oxford English Dictionary* (OED), 2d ed., which I rely on throughout this study as the definitive dictionary of the English language, includes the following meanings under the word *black:* "Black; . . . a word of difficult history. In OE. [Old English], found also . . . with long vowel blāce, blācan and thus confused with . . . blác shining, white . . . [the] two words are often distinguishable only by the context, and sometimes not by that."[32] The *OED* also notes that, in English, black has quite replaced the original color-word *swart,* which remains in other Teutonic languages. The archaic and confused etymology of the word *black* is cited here in an effort to point out the ways in which meaning is never stable but rather is constructed and reconstructed through repeated references.[33] *Impossible Purities* traces these convoluted constructions of pure whiteness and pure blackness in Victorian culture, pointing out that the words are themselves always already impure, hybrid terms.

Hybridity and purity are related terms that must be thought of as shifting and mutually constitutive representations.[34] This study argues that purity is impossible and, in fact, every mention of the related term, *hybrid,* only confirms a strategic taxonomy that constructs purity as a prior (fictive) ground. As we saw with Defoe's poem, "a true-born Englishman's a fiction," only an extracted, "second stage" cultural production. "Discrete" forms are indiscreet. Joseph Roach maintains that "the relentless search for purity of origins is a voyage not of discovery but of erasure. . . . Without failures of memory to obscure the mixtures, blends and provisional antitypes necessary to this production . . . 'whiteness' could not exist even as perjury, nor could there flourish more narrowly defined, subordinate designs such as 'Anglo-Saxon Liberty.' "[35] Forms of hybrid, black femininity might have been "invented" to differentiate between the *identical* production of so-called legitimate and illegitimate cultural categories. Ironically, hybrids produce "pure" forms and create culturally oppositional categories. Differences between blackness and Englishness may be manufactured and maintained in order to allay anxieties of sameness. The desire to see white as "white" and black as "black"—drives the division of the world according to absolute correspondences between colors, characters, and categories.[36]

When the products of mixed relations are classified as interstitial and hybrid, they confirm the culture's strategic taxonomy. Harryette Mullen explains that "racism reifies whiteness to the extent that it is known or presumed to be unmixed with blackness. 'Pure' whiteness is imagined as something that is both external and internal. While the white complexion of the mulatta, quadroon, or octoroon is imagined as something superficial, only skin-deep, the black blood passing onto the body an inherited impurity."[37] By naming the mixture as "mixed" and illegitimate, a fiction of prior purity and legitimacy is confirmed.[38] The implications for such a shift in our understanding of how purity has functioned historically are significant. An archaic, specifically Victorian meaning of the term *pure* is "excrement," which was used to purify leather. As Henry Mayhew discusses at some length, "pure-finders" were part of the London landscape throughout most of the nineteenth century.[39] This example illustrates the confused matter of purity.

In other words, the language of purity is imprecise and impossible, as are the lines that separate and distinguish (binary) categories. The endless creation of tentative taxonomies marks our desire to demarcate the relative differences between one thing and another—or as Michel

Foucault notes, to try to "tame the wild profusion of existing things [that] long afterwards disturb and threaten with collapse our age-old distinction between the Same and the Other."[40] This book discusses impossible attempts to fix pure forms of whiteness and white forms of purity in an effort to point out and play up the impossibility of producing fixed, pure, and stable identities of any sort. "Categorizing is not the sin; the problem is the lack of desire to examine how or where [and perhaps also why] we set our boundaries," asserts Patricia Williams.[41] It is this arbitrary, culturally determined desire to limit and delimit, to name and order, to distinguish and create identities that is examined in and performed by this study of complicating categories.

Chapter One

MISCEGENATING MULATTAROONS

Women of Colour

Olivia Fairfield to Mrs. Milbanke

At Sea, on board the ****

180—

Launched on a new world, what can have power to console me . . . leaving the scenes of my infancy, and the friend of my youth? Nothing but the consciousness of acting in obedience to the commands of my departed father. Oh, dearest Mrs. Milbanke! Your poor girl is every minute wishing for your friendly guidance, your maternal counsel. . . . Every day, as it takes me farther from Jamaica, as it brings me nearer to England, heightens my fears of the future. . . . I cannot help asking why . . . was it necessary for Olivia Fairfield to tempt the untried deep, and untried friends?—But I check these useless interrogatories, these vain regrets, by recollecting that it was the will of *him* who always studied the happiness of his child.

My dear father, doatingly fond as he was of his Olivia, saw her situation in a point of view which distressed his feeling heart. The illegitimate offspring of his *slave* could never be considered in the light of equality by the English planters. Such is their prejudice, such is the wretched state of degradation to which my unhappy fellow-creatures are sunk in the western hemisphere. We are considered . . . as an inferior race, but little removed from the brutes, because the Almighty Maker of all-created beings has tinged our skins with jet instead of ivory!—I say our, for though the jet has been faded to the olive in my own complexion, yet I am not ashamed to acknowledge my affinity with the swarthiest negro that was ever brought from Guinea's coast!—All are brethren, children of one common parent!

The soul of my mother, though shrouded in a sable covering, broke through the gloom of night, and shone celestial in her sparkling eyes!—Sprung from a race of native kings and heroes, with folded hands and tearful eyes, she saw herself torn from all the endearing ties to affinity. and relative intercourse! A gloomy, yet a proud sorrow, filled her indignant breast;

and when exhibited on the shores of my native island, the symmetry and
majesty of her form, the inflexible haughtiness of her manner, attracted the
attention of Mr. Fairfield. He purchased the youthful Marcia; his kindness,
his familiarity, his humanity, soon gained him an interest in her grateful
heart! She loved her master! (italics in original)

    This opening passage of the epistolary novel, *The Woman of Colour*,
appropriately begins in medias res with the woman of color, Olivia
Fairfield, "at sea"—spatiotemporally, emotionally, and geopolitically.[1]
Castaway from her Caribbean context, she sails toward England and
an uncertain future that is bound to be overdetermined by her past.[2]
Paradoxically, her journey "forward" is also a journey "back," since she
moves from a familiar *new* world to an unfamiliar *old* one. Printed for
the booksellers to the "honourable East India Company" in 1808, one
year after England ended the slave trade throughout its colonies, *The
Woman of Colour* stands as a record of the historic "interracial" relations and cultural commerce connected with the colonial enterprise.

    This first letter from Miss Fairfield to her nursemaid, Mrs. Milbanke,
mimics the former's transportation from the fair fields of a Jamaica
plantation to the more mundane "mill (and) bank" of England. Such a
journey replicates the exchange of material goods during the triangular
trade in which "raw" agrarian materials such as sugarcane, cotton, and
slaves were cultivated and then, in industrialized England, refined into
white sugar, shirts, and women of color. A direct product of overseas
venture-capital expeditions, which formed the basis of imperialism, the
text of *The Woman of Colour* serves as a material reminder (and re-
mainder) of such circum-Atlantic encounters.[3]

    These first three paragraphs provide a synopsis of the typical elements
expressed in early nineteenth-century narratives about Anglo-American
women of color. More often than not, these narratives brought otherwise disparate elements into proximity—sometimes blurring boundaries between binary oppositions such as colonizer/colonized, which
were represented, analogically, as a masculinized whiteness and femininized blackness. Olivia Fairfield is but one example of such women
of color who traveled across the Atlantic, from America to England, in
an order to be connected to their proper-tied *patria*.

    "The woman of color" (who can be designated also, if not always alternatively, as a mulatta, an octoroon, a quadroon, a mustee, mestico, griffe, or creole) is a highly ambiguous figure.[4] The (in)fractions of blood that govern her constitution occlude more than they reveal. For instance, this list of racialist labels tells us little or nothing about the so-called woman of color's status as either slave or free, nor do the labels easily correspond with "colors," which are figurative, subjective, imprecise, and culturally constructed (as we shall see later, being color-blind is both a social fact and, in some cases, a misguided political ideal). Because no word exists in the English language for this figure and because she functions as a figment of the concept of pigment, I have coined the word *mulattaroon* to suggest this figure's status as an unreal, impossible ideal whose corrupted and corrupting constitution inevitably causes conflicts in narratives that attempt to promote purity.

Between 1807, the end of the slave trade in England, and 1865, the end of the Civil War in America, such narratives of Anglo-American women of color were produced not only in literary fiction but also in the "parallel discourses" of science, law, and theater.[5] An American invention and New World product, the mulattaroon was a blood vessel who could be described as being neither black nor white, yet also as both white and black. Throughout most of the nineteenth century, the struggle to definitively define her unstable constitution (which, in the United States, included her constitutional instability) was a real concern. Although answers to the problem of her identity and, more crucially, her identifications varied, the mulattaroon usually served as an interstitial ideal whose complicated constitution both marked and masked the nineteenth century mésalliance known as *miscegenation.*[6]

Narratives of miscegenation are not monolithic.[7] Generally speaking, the sentimental and melodramatic narratives in which the mulattaroon appears represent her as a youthful, beautiful (because light-skinned), obliging, feminine figure of obscure, obscene (and therefore unseen) origins.[8] By contrast, some comic, gothic, and erotic narratives spectacularized the mulattaroon through overt visual representations of her as ludicrous, lurid, or alluring. Like other Anglo-American mulattaroons, Olivia Fairfield, the woman of color, both conceals and reveals conflicting ideas of difference. This chapter charts the complicated, circuitous course of several circum-Atlantic, Anglo-American mulattaroons in conjunction with various circumlocutions that obtain to their respective situations.

More specifically, it traces the roots/routes of three different Anglo-American mulattaroons: Olivia Fairfield, the central figure of the sentimental epistolary novel quoted above; the mulatta heiress, Rhoda Swartz, from William Makepeace Thackeray's dark comic novel, *Vanity Fair;* and the white-skinned octoroon, Zoe Peyton, from Dion Boucicault's melodrama, *The Octoroon.*[9] The differences among these representations of the mulattaroon occur as a result of changing conventions within specific genres (sentimental, comic, and melodramatic respectively) as well as the shifting sociopolitical, historical, and ideological forces associated with the times in which the narratives were initially published (1808, 1847–48, and in the case of *The Octoroon,* 1859 and 1861). That these feminine figures become purified, lightened, and whitened during repeated performances over the course of the century suggests that interest in the dark-skinned mulattaroon gradually fades, as does she.

In most English representations produced before the start of the American Civil War, however, even the "darker-skinned" mulattaroon was permitted to become a "proper" (and perhaps a propertied) *lady* provided that providence procured for her proximity to a white gentleman. Through controlled commerce with such a savior, she could be spared the sufferings of enslavement. She could secure a shift in her status only with the aid of an upstanding Englishman, typically her father or husband. Surprisingly, the mulattaroon's "singed" skin (or comparable dark mark) signifies not the sin of her white English father, but rather that of her black African mother. Although designated children of Ham, were slated to "follow in the condition of her Mother,"[10] Olivia Fairfield, Rhoda Swartz, and Zoe Peyton with varying degrees of success, follow their fathers. When the mulattaroon resurfaced after the Civil War as a stock character in African American fiction, she often performed as a ruined figure who could only be redeemed by a middle-class black gentleman, but more likely than not, was cast(e) aside and read as a traitor to the race. Thus, she must be either black or white— never a subject in between.

The mulattaroon has been marginalized in Victorian discourse, past and present, in part because her own overtly hybrid roots recall the miscegenated borders of the culture itself. Her appearance comments on the "illegitimate" sources of English wealth and the unseemly origins of English imperial power.[11] Bringing her formerly excluded narrative to the fore (centering her for a moment) re-members the always already hybrid origins of the English nation. The mulattaroon's shifting cultural placement is a symptom of the impossibility of purity understood as unmixed and immobile matter. The feminine mulattaroon functions as a floating signifier: torn asunder, she could still bring disparate discourses and differences into proximity. She is perpetually being erased or effaced in an effort to stabilize (reify) the tenuous, permeable boundaries between white and black, high and low, male and female, England and America, pure and impure (or passionate). The contested struggle to define "proper" boundaries—particularly the interdicted boundaries of gender, race, and sexual propriety—comes together in her peculiar person. She is pulled in one of two directions in this struggle: either "forward" (and up) to the homeland of her benevolent white father, or "backward" (and down) into the dark and circling waters of her black mother's womb.

This starkly drawn "choice" required that one move to the northern "free" states of America or to British soil (Canada or England, which welcomed so many slaves after the passage of the 1850 Fugitive Slave Law), or be sold down South, return to Africa (the choice suggested by *Uncle Tom's Cabin*), or be "saved" by the sea (as in the stones of the Ibo tribe, whose members walked on water—committed suicide)—thereby refusing to be enslaved. As Olivia Fairfield says of her mother, she "went down to that grave, where the captive is made free" (p. 7). These significations of whiteness and blackness are at work even in semiautobiographical slave narratives.[12]

Because England never had antimiscegenation laws, marrying the mulattaroon was not impossible, although it was viewed as both impolite and impolitic. Indeed, the subplot of the play *The Woman of Colour, or Slavery in Freedom* (which opened in London on October 22, 1853, at the Surrey Theatre) makes this point dramatically.[13] Its heroine, Florida Brandon, undergoes the experience of "slavery in freedom"—an oxymoronic phrase that confounds the concept of the culture's supposedly separate spheres. The playbill for this drama depicts the climactic "Res-

cue of Florida Brandon, the Woman of Colour, at the Grand Califor-
nian Assembly" (Figure 1). Lord Everton, Florida's devoted, regal lover,
rushes in as she is being arrested as the "stolen" property of Colonel
Brandon's estate. It is Everton's eloquent speech that saves his beloved
from being captured and enslaved.

Of the figures we study here, only Rhoda Swartz, who appears in a
comic play of morals, marries a Scottish gentleman.[14] Like Linda Brent's
Incidents in the Life of a Slave Girl (and unlike *Jane Eyre*), these narratives eschew the "standard" marriage plot developed in the English
novel. In England, such women are permitted to reproduce the nation
since they can be valued for their wealth and beauty; in America, however, where a more rigid binary system began to emerge, such unions
were discouraged. Thus, in the United States, black female subjects
rarely marry at the conclusion of their texts.[15]

A most precious if precarious bounty, the mulattaroon languished in
America until her luxuriousness (sometimes also her literal luxury in
dowry form) was recognized by an upstanding English gentleman and
she could be imported to England's welcoming, supposedly more democratic shores.[16] In the three paragraphs that open *The Woman of Colour*,
Olivia's own figure appears in the middle of the middle paragraph. Her
"identity" is positioned between the primary narrative of her father and
that of her mother, which in the order of the text, is secondary. She is
here "caught" between the two: unwilling to deny her mother and yet
willing to follow her father's orders. A product of the middle passage, she
is posited as a figure poised on the edge of New World territories. This
is another example of how such narratives privilege the white father.

In the nineteenth century, the emerging concept-metaphors of Europe, Africa, and the Americas, already catachrestically contained,
could be narrativized in *printed* text as a family romance. Indeed, *The
Woman of Colour* exemplifies this possibility. Visual iconography, however, represented Europe, Africa, and the Americas as *female* figures
resembling the three graces, such as the image produced by William
Blake for John Stedman's well-known history of Surinam. One of the
few, if only, "family" portraits in the nineteenth century of a white
father, a "black" slave mother, and a "mulattaroon" child is *Redenção
de Cam The Redemption of Ham*, an 1895 (postemancipation) grouping
painted by the Spanish-born Brazilian artist Modesto Brocos y Gomez

1. *The Woman of Colour, or Slavery in Freedom*, playbill, 1853. Courtesy of the Theatre Museum, Victoria and Albert, London.

(1852–1936).[17] The clandestine, illicit nature of such unions made their public exhibition virtually impossible. Family resemblance, inheritance, and constitution had to have an official, readable coherence. Such mésalliances could only be signaled covertly—behind closed doors; therefore, the mulattaroon performs as an iconic sign of miscegenation, whose signification summarizes otherwise unrepresentable, unspeakable acts. Her citation in any given text is a kind of circumlocution. She serves as the supreme signifier of and for miscegenating nations.

The encounter between the African "mother" and the European "father" that results in the birth of a new feminized American daughter has been seen as a spectacle in visual culture only rarely. This family "romance" was explored in slave narratives, which were sometimes called "printed sadism."[18] In Victorian illustrated serial novels, narrative paintings, and even stage productions, the story of miscegenation was told impossibly through absences and glaring gaps. Where indirection was deemed discrete, direct representations of desire were deflected. Thus, many of the narratives of miscegenation end abruptly before the birth of problematic progeny, and as we have seen with *The Woman of Colour*, begin in medias res. Such circular narratives may be an especially apt representation for the traffic of the triangular trade (in sugar, cotton, and slaves) and of the triangulated relationship between Europe, Africa, and the Americas.

Whether she will be feted or fettered on her arrival in the metropolitan center of London, the fate of the dark daughter is determined by the will (literal and figurative) of her enlightened white father. Obeying his laws, she obliges him by "acting in obedience to the commands of . . . [her] departed father." Thus is she willing and able to "check . . . [her] useless interrogatories, these vain regrets, by recollecting that it is the will of *him* who always studied the happiness of his child." Concomitant with the woman of color's transportation is her transformation from "colored" to "woman," from "black" to "white," as well as from Jamaica to England, country to city, poor to rich, slave to free. At the end of this first letter, cited above, she states that she would rather have remained on her "native" island and started a school or a philanthropic organization; but she is not free to choose her fate.

Although made in America, she is ensconced in England after surviving the journey across the Atlantic. On her dark body is carved the justification for English moral superiority. This aspect of her constitution consolidated the virility of the Englishmen who came to her rescue. If, as many commentators of Victorian culture have remarked, a revamped "medieval" chivalry hailed by Sir Walter Scott's *Ivanhoe* (1820) occurred, then the story of the maiden mulattaroon resembles the fairy tale of a dark daughter as damsel in distress who could be remade in marriage by the courtship of a chivalrous English gentleman. The woman of color's collusion with this rescue-fantasy scenario worked in concert with the "civilizing mission." Her degradation provided the Englishman with an object to lavish pity on, as well as to educate and enlighten. He comes to play the part of the white man burdened by the knowledge of the woman of color's background and, therefore, specially suited to alleviate her suffering.[19] The American mulattaroon's transportation and transplantation to English shores, shored up English moral superiority (as a similar importation would revive the cash-strapped aristocracy at the end of the century, when American heiresses such as Jennie Churchill and Henry James's *Wings of a Dove* were in vogue). Far from being seen as undesirable, the mulattaroon is portrayed over and over again in sentimental, melodramatic narratives as the most desirable woman imaginable.

Detailed descriptions in *The Woman of Colour* eroticize the black woman's body, whose difference is marked not only by "skin" but also by stylized gestures that feminize and idealize her otherwise fearsome form. Olivia's recounting of the "symmetry and majesty" of her mother Marcia's form, recalls the fearful symmetry of Blake's revolutionary poem, "The Tyger" (1789), that questions repeatedly:

Tyger, tyger, burning bright,
In the forests of the night:
What immortal hand or eye,
Could frame thy fearful symmetry?

In what distant deeps or skies
Burnt the fire of thine eyes?
On what wings dare he aspire?
What the hand dare seize the fire?

And what shoulder, & what art,
Could twist the sinews of thy heart?[20]

The "soul" of the African Marcia is privileged—indeed, it is the first word in the paragraph cataloging her distinguishing features and recalls the romantic notion realized by another Blake poem, "The Black Boy," in which the character's *soul* was "white." The inherited "nobility" and internal purity that asks the reader to look beyond the marred surface of this child of Ham is referenced here in the description of Marcia, Olivia's African mother.

As Olivia also notes, the body of her mother was "exhibited"—an allusion not only to the slave auctions and markets, but also to the carnivals where women of African descent were a popular sideshow attraction. Only in the space of the market, where buyer and seller are clearly delineated, can the interracial relationship occur. No pure parlor-love or naturalistic setting for their amorous attraction; these excluded "lovers" meet only on (un)fairgrounds, on commercial, colonial territory.

Olivia shares some minor qualities with her African mother. For example, the daughter's trip would seem to replicate her mother's journey in that each woman is forcibly removed, under radically different conditions (one above board, the other below), from native lands; however, the dark daughter's passage is procured by her paternal progenitor, an Englishman, who desires that this daughter be made over in his own image. Olivia reverses, replicates, and revises the journey of her father, who has crossed the Atlantic from England to Jamaica before her. In contrast to the marked bodies of Marcia and Olivia, the women of color recounted in the opening passage, the bodies of the white father and white nursemaid Mrs. Milbanke, remains unremarked. Indeed, olive-skinned Olivia omits any overt reference to her father's "physical" whiteness; rather, his "whiteness" is marked by his good and kind deeds. His position is that of the voyeur.

Mr. Fairfield is not the author of his attraction; rather, Marcia's formidable form, the "inflexible haughtiness of her manner," attract him. Although he has the power to purchase her, the scene is written so that he is passive. The black woman's body beckons him—entices and encourages him—to buy her. Mobilizing the melodramatic narrative

2. "Am I not a woman and a sister?" Courtesy of Swarthmore Library.

of noble suffering, the mother's African "majesty" and superior form
are posited as a natural phenomenon. Performing the feminine posture
"with folded hands and tearful eyes," she becomes a figure of repentance, acceptance, and duty. This gestural femininity, seen also in the
abolitionist logo so popular in this period, is meant to suggest the enslaved person's humanity, gentleness, and "Christian" spirit (figure 2).[21]
Displaying a body subdued and servile, she impersonates a supplicant
whose moral superiority is marked by her sense of shame. In this early,
sentimental narrative before the hardened advent of physiognomy as
destiny took hold and became hegemonic, the possibility of becoming
pious by converting to Christianity was prevalent. Again, with the help
of the (white) father, black children could be saved.

The logic here is that the mother was already noble and aristocrati-
cally classed (she is "sprung from a race of native kings and heroes,"
and therefore, possesses nobility naturally, even of the savage sort); she
learns to love the white man, who performs nobility not only in his
bearing (that is the job of the African Marcia, Olivia's mother), but also
in his actions. That the majestic Marcia responds to (her) Master Fair-

field's "kindness . . . familiarity . . . humanity," despite the fact that he owns her, body and soul, speaks to her native and natural (as in devoid of artifice) ability to benefit from a sentimental education. Indeed, she is "grateful" that her master is kind and humane. What we learn from this passage is that Marcia "loved her master!": we do not, however, learn in return, if her master loved her.

In fact, Mr. Fairfield's "love" is bestowed most generously on the delicate daughter of whom he is "doatingly fond." Here, the specter of "incest," which so often works in accord with "miscegenation," appears.[22] If the "departed father" is read also as the law or as laws of nature racially inflected, it is the fate of the woman of color to disappear in order to sustain the fiction of the pure, white family and the family of man, which functions as a homologue for the English nation. This figure's willingness to oblige the law of the absent father from a distant nation underscores the fact that "colonialism was both a paternal and a patriotic obligation."[23] Although the mulatta Olivia Fairfield expresses allegiance to a collective darker race (she replicates the dominant strategies of abolitionist discourse by stressing her "affinity" with the "swarthiest negro . . . brought from Guinea's coast," whom she considers her brethren), her primary allegiance takes the form of obedience to her benevolent white father. In expressing sympathy for her enslaved "brethren," Olivia espouses a monogenicist view of race. She proclaims that "all are brethren, children of one common parent!": of course, this common parent is a reference to an Anglican "God" who created "man" in his image. Thus, the analogy to the common parent—the one that mattered most—is the "holy" (white) father who was a good and kind master/father.[24]

The Woman of Colour concludes with the following "Dialogue between the Editor and a Friend" (p. 219).

Friend.—What do you propose from the publication of the foregoing tale? If your *Woman of Colour* be an imaginary character, I do not see the drift of your labours, as undoubtedly there is no moral to the work!
Editor.—How so?
Friend.—You have not rewarded Olivia even with the usual meed of virtue —*a husband!*
Editor.—Virtue, like Olivia Fairfield's, may truly be said to be its *own re-*

ward—the moral I would deduce from her story is, that there is no situation in which the mind . . . may not resist itself against misfortune, and become resigned to its fate. And *if* these pages should teach *one child of calamity* to seek *Him* in the hour of distress . . . if they teach one *skeptical European* to look with a compassionate eye towards the *despised native of Africa*— *then,* whether Olivia Fairfield be a *real* or *imaginary* character, I shall not regret that I have edited the Letters of a *Woman of Colour!* (p. 220, italics in original)

The final paragraph of this excerpt is notable for its lack of interest in the "truth" of her character and may be read as participating in "the unreal estate." Indeed, the phantasmagoric function is the fundamental feature of this figure—and necessarily so, since she is impossible. Well before the appearance of William Wells Brown's *Clotel, or the President's Daughter: A Narrative of Slave Life in the United States* (published in London in 1853), the African American mulatta in *The Woman of Colour* provides us with an idealized example of this important New World figure.

As the epilogue makes clear, *The Woman of Colour* may be understood as an abolitionist text. It is directed to a "skeptical European" audience in an era of increasing philanthropy for the enslaved African fostered by abolitionist activism, which was at its height in the first decades of the nineteenth century. This first-person account, like the slave narratives that were written as propaganda for the abolitionist cause, has been "edited" by a white person. After the slave trade had been abolished by an act of Parliament in 1807, the next demon to slay was the institution of slavery itself, which was abolished in Britain and its colonies in 1833. Following this success, an international cadre of black and white abolitionists fought to end slavery throughout the Americas. Abolitionist discourse, replete with racially motivated rescue mission zeal, was dedicated to liberating the Caliban-like "children of calamity." Numerous antislavery societies were established throughout the 1830s and 1840s. Such organizations were mocked in Dickens's *Bleak House,* where the infamous Mrs. Jellby neglects her own English children because she is concerned only with the infants in Bogglywolly. Similarly, in *Vanity Fair,* several characters donate regularly to the "Quashiamboo-Aid Society" (p. 100).

When the great satirist Thackeray came to write his masterful historical novel *Vanity Fair* in the 1840s, he no longer believed in the days of
"virtue rewarded" (a term related to the popular Puritan tome *Pilgrim's
Progress,* by John Bunyan, on which *Vanity Fair* is based). In the 1840s,
read as an age of doubt, such a sympathetic rendering of a virtuous,
husbandless woman of color was seen only rarely in Victorian England.
In an increasingly racist society, such sympathy was reserved only for
the *white*-appearing octoroon. This shift from a sympathetic rendering
of the mulattaroon toward a comic vision is marked by the contrast between Olivia Fairfield and Rhoda Swartz, the mulattaroon in *Vanity Fair.*

Putting up Miss Swartz

Like Olivia Fairfield, the "mulattaroon" heiress in Thackeray's first
novel, *Vanity Fair,* makes the journey from Caribbean America (the
island of St. Kitts) to metropolitan London after the death of her white
father.[25] The daughter of a German-Jewish "slave-holder . . . connected
with the Cannibal Islands in some way or other" (p. 246), Rhoda Swartz
is an orphan who has inherited her mother's color and her father's
money. Unlike Olivia, who is the central figure of her "first person"
account, Rhoda Swartz is a marginal character in *Vanity Fair;* and it
is precisely her marginality that makes her significant. In "putting up
Miss Swartz," this reading of her as a "socially marginal but symboli-
cally significant" character redresses readings of her as merely minor.[26]
    Indeed, Miss Swartz may be the most important of the many comic
characters in the text. Certainly, she is the most important of the several
black and mulatto/a characters in *Vanity Fair.*[27] She plays a decisive role
as the foil to the major female characters—the artless, angelic Amelia
Sedley and the artful, demonic Rebecca Sharp—whom the text follows
for more than 800 pages, from the eve of their departure from finishing
school, through their problematic marriages, the uneventful births of
their sons, and the deaths of their respective (but not respectful) husbands.
    Unlike the numerous "simple" and highly stereotyped black servants,
exemplified by Mr. Sambo, who populate *Vanity Fair* from the second
sentence to its close, Miss Swartz is represented as a dark, anomalous

creature who *ironically* sustains the dominant structures of the society that created her. Her role in Thackeray's canonical novel is, in part, to uncover the erased (im)purity of "Englishness." Miss Swartz's presence signals the colonial traces etched in the margins of Thackeray's "pen and pencil sketches of English society" (which was the original subtitle of the book).

Rhoda Swartz, long thought to be inessential to this quintessentially English novel, turns out to be a crucial character. Chapters 20 and 21 are devoted exclusively to discussing the merits (and possible demerits) of marrying Miss Swartz. There are even three illustrations of Rhoda (a full-size, captioned plate; a small chapter drawing; and a half-page sketch) done by Thackeray himself, who alone among Victorian novelists did his own drawings. This marks a significant change from the sentimental narratives exemplified by *The Woman of Colour*, where the mulattaroon serves as the main focus of the book and is offered the possibility of salvation.[28]

The title of this section, "Putting up Miss Swartz," puns on Rhoda's discarded and absurd position as the possible "heroine" of the narrative. Although *Vanity Fair* was subtitled "A Novel without a Hero" when it was published in 1848 as a single volume, the text does have two heroines.[29] The narrator even names Amelia as the "amiable heroine of this work . . . (whom we have selected for the very reason that she was the best-natured of all, otherwise what on earth was to have prevented us from putting up Miss Swartz . . . as heroine in her place?)" (p. 15). Here, the possibility of "putting up" Miss Swartz as the heroine is posed parenthetically, as if to marginalize her character even more. Such a prospect proves impossible; such a suggestion is merely a put on. Miss Swartz is held up (in both senses of the term) as an impossible alternative in the novel's romantic plot.

Vanity Fair is a self-consciously theatrical novel: it begins with a preface called "Before the Curtain." This preface was actually written after the novel had been published serially and, therefore, is technically an epilogue, whose construction mimics that of the retroactively produced narratives of nation. This theatrical frame sets the stage for the ensuing show by introducing its audience to several dramatis personae.[30] Chapter 1 formally introduces the audience to Rhoda Swartz and her school

chums, Amelia Sedley and Rebecca Sharp, on the eve of their gradua-
tion from Miss Pinkerton's Academy for Girls.

The first thing the audience learns is that "Miss Swartz, the rich
woolly-haired mulatto from St. Kitts . . . paid double" (p. 7) to attend
Miss Pinkerton's academy. Indeed, Rhoda must be doubly rich to be
desirable, as Rebecca must be doubly clever to succeed, in Vanity Fair.
The true-born, utterly English Amelia, however, has a singular character. Rhoda's character signifies both lack (she is "half" and also black)
and plentitude (she is excessively wealthy, both white and black).

Almost always described as the "woolly-haired mulatto heiress from
St. Kitts," this brief phrase denotes her race, class, and geographic/cul-
tural origins. Her stereotypical costume is an expensive yellow satin
ball gown, suggesting again her color, caste, and class, which according
to some African American cultures might be surmised as being "high
yellow." Her manner is summed up by another repeated action. "On
the day Amelia went away [Rhoda] was in such a passion of tears that
[Miss Pinkerton, the head of the finishing school, was] obliged to send
for Dr. Floss to half tipsify her with sal volatile" (p. 7). Miss Swartz's
"hysterical *yoops*. . . which no pen can depict and as the tender heart
[would] fain pass over" (p. 10), are too indelicate to render in the text.
Many readers, perhaps, have also followed the actor-manager's advice
and performed in accordance with the laws of propriety by passing over
the seemingly insignificant Miss Swartz.[31]

Critical accounts of *Vanity Fair* frequently overlook Miss Swartz in
favor of discussing Amelia Sedley and Becky Sharp. This attention given
to the contest of "heart over intellect which is the major theme of the
Becky-Amelia opposition"[32] misses the initial and important opposition
between Amelia and Miss Swartz, who throughout a substantial portion
of the novel vie for the affections of George Osborne. Before exploring how Miss Swartz comes to shadow and perform as a ghosted double
for Rebecca Sharp, I spell out the antagonistic relationship between
Amelia and Rhoda that is a major concern of the first part of the book.

Rhoda Swartz's connection to the main characters in the text is always
one of necessarily elided difference. Ultimately, she serves as a foil to
them; as an object that is more abject than their own corrupt values.
They may be immoral, but she is hopelessly and permanently hybrid.

She is the link between the heroines. Moreover, this link is literally unthinkable—it is the forgotten hyphen. On the scale that divides Rebecca's impure ambition from Amelia's pure submission, Rhoda ranks as the intermediate position.[33] She "whitens" Amelia and "blackens" Rebecca. Rhoda serves to underscore not only Rebecca's monstrous "brand" of femininity but also Amelia's disturbing purity.

Amelia—who is herself hypocritical, hypercritical, and vain—is an unheroic heroine, like so many of the other two-faced figures in the text. Her family has fallen on hard times and, in the Mammon-worshiping world of Vanity Fair, Amelia is therefore herself "discredited" as a result. The disgraced Amelia can only look good in comparison with the sheer hideousness of Miss Swartz. Miss Swartz (Miss "Black," according to the Teuton etymology that defines *swart* as black, as well as foreign and Jewish), in turn, is a parody of Amelia. Her English education does not take (she only knows two tunes and cannot spell, although she is nearly twenty-three when she finishes school).

Rhoda's "hysteria" and her honest hybridity underscore Amelia's desirability and her false purity; or rather, Amelia is only desirable when contrasted with the doubly debased Miss Swartz. As her suitor, George Osborne explains that "the contrast of her [Amelia's] manners and appearance with those of the heiress [Rhoda] made the idea of a union with the latter appear doubly ludicrous and odious" (p. 250). The narrative presents the ladylike Amelia Sedley and the unladylike Rhoda Swartz as binary opposites. Rhoda and Amelia are two sides of the same coin: they form the obverse/reverse, since one is "white" and pure and the other "black" and impure. The black woman serves as the basis of comparison that establishes and, in fact, embellishes the white woman; meanwhile, her own subjectivity remains both hypervisible and invisible.

George obsessively belittles Rhoda by referring to her as a "Hottentot Venus" or "a chimney-sweep"—references that show up the two distancing techniques (hypervisibility and invisibility) used by George to disassociate himself from the mulatta heiress. Such language denigrates her position in an effort to reveal how her wealth can be undercut by her racial status. She appears either as a staged spectacle captured in a cage for all the world to see (like the Hottentot Venus) or as a lowly chimney sweep confined to the literal interstices of middle-class domesticity (like the sweep hidden in the chimney). The reference to the "Hotten-tot Venus" alludes to the display of the now (as then) famous figure of Sarah Bartmann. This South African woman was exhibited in London in 1810.[34] In her best outfits, Rhoda appears to George "as elegantly decorated as a she chimney-sweep on May-Day" (p. 252). He exclaims: "Marry that mulatto woman? . . . I don't like her colour, sir. Ask the black that sweeps opposite Fleet Market, sir. *I'm* not going to marry a Hottentot Venus" (p. 259). George works very hard to make Miss Swartz more different, perhaps because "cultural difference becomes a prob-lem not when you can point to the Hottentot Venus . . . it does not have that kind of fixable visibility. It is as the strangeness of the familiar that it becomes more problematic . . . when the problem of cultural differ-ence is ourselves-as-others; others-as-ourselves—that borderline."[35]

Rhoda, therefore, must be distanced from the white characters: she cannot compare to Amelia; she must only always contrast. She is second best and, as George sees her, lacks the proper skills to replace Amelia in his eyes:

"Poor Swartz was seated in a place where Emmy had been accustomed to sit. Her bejewelled hands lay sprawling in her amber satin lap. Her tags and ear-rings twinkled and her big eyes rolled about. She was doing nothing with perfect contentment and thinking herself charming. . . . She looked like a China doll, which has nothing to do all day but to grin and wag its head" (p. 255).

This quotation demonstrates how she is employed in the text as an ex-aggerated half-wit who is excessively fond of her dear school friend, "Emmy," the true "heroine" of the text.

It is a toss-up as to whom the eligible if foppish George Osborne should marry—it will have to be one or the other. George's profound prejudices toward the wealthy mulatta are articulated at the end of chapter 20, where George and Amelia are courting surreptitiously. Of Miss Swartz, he says:

"My sisters say she has diamonds as big as pigeons eggs. . . . How they must set off her complexion! A perfect illumination it must be when her jewels are on her neck. Her jet-black hair is as curly as Sambo's. I dare say she wore a nose-ring when she went to Court; and a plume of feathers . . . a perfect *Belle Sauvage.*" (p. 245)

Recently arrived in Vanity Fair, Miss Swartz becomes the toast and the talk of the town. Even her banker, young Mr. Bullock, regrets that he is already engaged, wishing secretly for Rhoda's hand in marriage (or rather, to have his hand in her dowry).

As Amelia and George discuss Rhoda, she becomes the doubly inscribed object of their scorn and admiration. Rebecca expresses her envy of Miss Swartz by noting, "How [the other girls] cringe and bow to that Creole because of her hundred thousand pounds! I am a thousand times cleverer and more charming than that creature, for all her wealth . . . and yet every one passes me by here" (p. 19). Such a comment is not only an indictment of Rhoda but of Vanity Fair. It is Rhoda who most obviously embodies the values of Vanity Fair: she symbolizes the rampant, insatiable greed, since she is the object of desire for the money-worshiping inhabitants who value her as a vehicle for their own elevation in class terms. Rhoda

was reported to have I don't know how many plantations in the West Indies; a deal of money in the funds; and three stars to her name in the East India stockholders list. She had a mansion in Surrey, and a house in Portland Place. The name of the rich West India heiress had been mentioned with applause in the *Morning Post*. Mrs. Haggistroun, Colonel Haggistroun's widow, her relative, "chaperoned" her, and kept her house. She was just from school where she had completed her education, and George and his sisters had met her at an evening party at old Hulker's house. . . . (p. 245)

Rhoda's cultural capital is contingent on having a potential husband hungry for the power (perhaps a place in the Peerage?) that her pounds sterling can purchase. Thus, Amelia, "the bankrupt's daughter" (p. 279), is portrayed by many in Vanity Fair as an improper match when compared to the monied mulatta, Miss Swartz. Only George still thinks Amelia a desirable, if now destitute, mate.

Thackeray's desire to denounce the commercial, cash-nexus values of the nouveau riche in favor of "pure" family values devoid of gauche price tags coalesces when he makes Miss Swartz a good match in the high-stakes marriage *market* that is Vanity Fair. Her representation suggests all the ways in which the colonies threaten to overtake and consume, as well as stand beside and supplement, colonial centers. Like Dickens in *Our Mutual Friend*, with his description of the "Veneerings,"

Thackeray parodies people who value superficiality—the external trap-pings of wealth that are both a result and product of vanity. "Love may be felt for any young lady endowed with such qualities as Miss Swartz possessed" (p. 248).

One critic suggests that the many mulatto characters in Thackeray's fiction "were used as a permitted form of sexual humor and more seri-ously to emphasize one of the major contentions of the novels: English society is so money-centered that it will do anything, even marry into another race, to gain wealth" (p. 331).[36] This reading posits the other race as the limit-text of English society and, to an extent, concurs with this chapter's reading of Thackeray's work. Nonetheless, this descrip-tion of the characters' desire for commercial success neither critiques their use nor explains *why* these figures were seen as figures of *"per-mitted . . . sexual humor"* or as scapegoats of English mammonism. If, however, we examine Miss Swartz in the context of other mulatta char-acters in English culture, and within the system of purity and taboo being established by the desire for a pure English identity, the "theme" of miscegenation is seen as an "ornately . . . glaring absence" along the lines of Toni Morrison's reading of whiteness in literary culture, where she explains that even canonical novels without any explicitly black characters are marked by traces of an Africanist presence.[37]

Chapter 21 in *Vanity Fair*, entitled "A Quarrel about an Heiress," begins with a picture of a "white" woman holding up a black-faced doll. This illustration (see figure 3) shows Miss Swartz being toyed and played with. She is diminished as a rival for George Osborne's affection by the coy Amelia Sedley, who is in love with the "third-rate" hero. This prefatory illustration, according to one critic, "suggests that Miss Swartz is a puppet in the hands of the white characters and adds a sym-pathy which is largely lacking in the text."[38] The difficulty here is that *all* the characters in the book are "props" in an elaborate puppet show and, therefore, this fact alone does not "add sympathy" to her represen-tation. Although she is absolved from playing an active, self-conscious role in *Vanity Fair*—she is used by the other characters for their own purposes—she still belongs in Vanity Fair.

Throughout the text, moreover, the narrator carefully maintains a dis-tinction between dolls and puppets. Amelia is called a "doll" in the pref-ace and Miss Swartz is seen *as* a doll in the opening of chapter 21. Sig-

3. Illustration for Chapter 21, *Vanity Fair*, William Makepeace Thackeray, 1847–48. Courtesy of the Huntington Library.

nificantly, Becky is called a "puppet" in the prologue and, in chapter 2, she demonstrates her gifts for mimicry by playing with two dolls. This performance is pictured with a drawing in the text. The doll/puppet dichotomy suggests not only gendered differences, but also who can control the terms of representation versus those whose sad fate it is to merely act naturally—who have a "good" and honest, rather than a devious, nature. Since Rebecca has already been described as both a puppet and puppeteer, perhaps it is she, rather than Amelia, who tries to dangle Miss Swartz before George Osborne as a distraction. Whichever white-faced girl holds up the black-faced doll, the image once again proves the proximity between white and black that is one of the defining legacies of colonial commerce.

Perhaps the person who exemplifies this attitude and is most smitten with Miss Swartz's peculiar charms is Mr. Osborne, senior, George's father. He feels that his humble family would benefit from Rhoda's wealth and, not being "particular about a shade or two of tawny," gives

George an "imperative hint" (p. 250) that he should marry Miss Swartz. The suggestions of the senior Osborne drive George rebelliously into the arms of the forbidden Amelia, whom he secretly marries against his father's wishes. This battle of wills takes place over two central chapters in the text, for which Rhoda becomes the "dark object of the conspiracy into which the chiefs of the Osborne family had entered" (p. 251).

The elder Mr. Osborne puts Miss Swartz on a pedestal, drinking a champagne toast to her honor and extolling her virtues by pleading his own false modesty before her. On one of Rhoda's first visits to the Osborne home, the old man tells her:

You won't find . . . that splendour and rank to which you are accustomed at the West End, my dear miss, at our humble mansion in Russell Square. My daughters are plain, disinterested girls, but their hearts are in the right place and they've conceived an attachment for you which does them honour. . . . I'm a plain, humble British merchant—an honest one, as my respected friends . . . will vouch. . . . You'll find us a united, simple, happy and . . . respected family—a plain table, a plain people, but a warm welcome, my dear Miss Rhoda—Rhoda let me say, for my heart warms to you. . . . I'm a frank man and I like you. (p. 248)

In a discussion about his desire to have George marry Miss Swartz, he thinks about proposing to Rhoda himself; however, the "partisans of that lady [scornfully rejected his suit and] married her to a young sprig of Scotch nobility" (p. 535). Rhoda's marriage is again an ambiguous achievement, given that to enter into the ranks of Vanity Fair is no honor.

Like their father, George's "star-struck" sisters fawn over the heiress, whose funds quicken the sisters's fondness for their newfound, nouveau riche friend. The phrase, "An orphan in her position—with her money—so interesting!" (p. 245), sums up her "interests." In the eyes of the Misses Osborne, "Rhoda was everything they could wish—the frankest, kindest, most agreeable creature wanting a little polish . . . [with a] warm and impetuous nature . . . [and] tropical ardour" (p. 251). It is the smitten Misses Osborne who appear in the first full-plate illustration of Miss Swartz (figure 4).

The sisters kneel at Rhoda's side while helping the heiress with her elaborate dress. Rhoda's chaperon and a Miss Wirt "sat by and conned

4. Untitled illustration of Miss Swartz, *Vanity Fair*, William Makepeace
Thackeray, 1847–48. Courtesy of the Huntington Library.

over the *Peerage* and talked about nobility" (p. 252). Significantly, in
this first picture, Rhoda's face is "marred" by a number of lines that
shade her face. The cross-hatching on the top half of her face signals
her racial difference. Miss Swartz exemplifies the black caricatures in
circulation during this period.[39] The sisters see Rhoda as a noble and
romanticized savage; of course, Rhoda never describes her describers
in return. She has no agency of her own; rather, she is passive and
totally manipulated by the plot.

George enters the room straight from getting his allowance and visit-
ing "his dear little Amelia . . . to find his sisters spread in starched
muslin . . . the dowagers cackling in the background, and honest Miss
Swartz in her favourite amber-coloured satin, with turquoise-bracelets,

5. "Miss Swartz rehearsing for the Drawing Room," *Vanity Fair*, William Makepeace Thackeray, 1847–48. Courtesy of the Huntington Library.

countless rings, flowers, feathers, and all sorts of tags and gimcracks" (ibid.). This description clearly displays George's contempt for not only the heiress but also her American origins. The feathers and turquoise, moreover, may be meant to suggest the Carib "Indianness" of her West Indian heritage.

We see Miss Swartz "before" and "behind" the curtain, as it were, since this first image of her is "titled" "Miss Swartz *rehearsing* for the Drawing Room" (italics added), whereas in the second, untitled picture (figure 5), she is caught in media res, in the middle of a piano performance. As she is playing, she spies Amelia's name on the sheet music and, in her "impetuous" (p. 8) nature, blurts out, "Is that *my* Amelia from Miss P's?!" (p. 255). George's father has forbidden the mention of Amelia; however, this exclamation about her school friend provokes a positive reaction from George. Rhoda's doglike devotion to Amelia puts her in George Osborne's good graces. In reaction to hearing his intended's name, George lights up and, for a moment, becomes genuinely interested in his otherwise odious visitor, Miss Swartz. It is at this moment, in the middle of this passage, that Thackeray places a sketch of Miss Swartz sitting at a piano, her face directly confronting the viewer with its absurd gaze.[40]

This illustration of Miss Swartz is less indicting of her character than is the first, full-page plate described above. In figure 5, no lines color her complexion.[41] Here, illuminated by the reminder of Amelia, Rhoda is seen in a different light. She even appears (quite illogically) to have changed costumes. In this second picture, she no longer wears a gaudy, gargantuan feather on her head; deplumed of her "prodigious feathers" (p. 252) and no longer goggle-eyed, she appears more simply attired, with only a demure bow flowing from her corsetted waist. Even her shoulders slope in such a way that her body seems proportionate, as opposed to the deformed and masculine shape in the first formal portrait. Still, even this "sympathetic" rendering of Miss Swartz shows her slightly cross-eyed, mouth agape.

The narrator is only putting up Miss Swartz in order to substantiate Amelia. In this way, the "black" woman becomes an object that enables the "white" to perform femininity properly and with impunity. This strategy is repeated in the culture at large. In other words, pairing a black and a white woman rarely "works" to the advantage of the former. The subject who matters most is the white-skinned woman, of whatever racial background. Amelia is told by her suitor, George Osborne, "Dear little woman, you are the only person of our set who ever looked or thought or spoke like a lady: and you are so because you're an angel. . . . You *are* the only lady" (p. 247; italics in original). Still, Amelia "express[es] a great deal of pretty jealousy about Miss Swartz, and professes to be dreadfully frightened—like a hypocrite as she was—lest George should forget her for the heiress and her money and her estates in St. Kitts' (p. 247). The false modesty of such feelings proves unwarranted because immediately after chapter 21, "A Quarrel about an Heiress," is one called "A Marriage and Part of a Honeymoon," in which George and Amelia are married. Miss Swartz, then, plays a key role in the first half of *Vanity Fair*.

In the second of half, the focus shifts from an overt discussion of the rivalry between Amelia and Rhoda to the surreptitious articulation of suppressed similarities between Rebecca and Rhoda. The similarities

between the witty dissembling parvenue, Rebecca Sharp, and the un-
witting half-wit parvenue, Rhoda Swartz, are signified through subtle,
subtextual references to Rebecca's "blackness." Rather like a "black"
ghost, Rhoda Swartz, who has disappeared from the narrative, haunts
later representations of Rebecca Sharp.

Rebecca, the demonic heroine of the text, is opposed to Amelia's
sickly-sweet brand of angelic heroism. Described throughout the novel
as a "queer little wild vixen . . . who kept . . . all laughing with her
fun and mimicry" (p. 230), Rebecca, whose mother was a French rope-
dancer and whose father was English, crosses the nationally defined
boundaries between France and England. The clever daughter of "bo-
hemian" parents, she becomes closely allied with Rhoda (they share the
same initials, R. S.). Where Rhoda's "Jewishness" is explicit, Rebecca's
is implicit (for example, her name is from the Old Testament); where
Rhoda's father has something to do with the "cannibal" islands, Rebecca
takes shape as the mermaid whom the text describes as a "fiendish
marine cannibal" (p. 812).[42]

As the narrative progresses, Rebecca appears in blackface more frequently to signal that her moral character is blackened. Rebecca Sharp
is a kind of white-black actress, whose hybridity is hidden. If Rhoda is
the (black) monstrous and Amelia the (white) feminine, then Rebecca
is the black-white-monstrous-feminine. It is she who plays the part of
the dangerously dark "blackened" woman—the dissembling parvenue
who, with her green eyes, blond hair, and affecting, affective mask of
"whiteness," can act the innocent with great acumen because of her in-
nate mental acuity.

Becky begins with the taint of a French actress for a mother and
proceeds to be shaded literally in her second appearance as Clytemnes-
tra, illustrated in the text, where her face is marked with cross-hatched
lines to show the shadow of her concealing (and also revealing) curtain.
As discussed earlier, the "technique" of darkening a picture by putting
scratches on the face is employed in the first illustration of Rhoda,
where she appears to have on a mask. This trope surfaces again at the
end of the text, when Rebecca is seen actually wearing a black mask
that is also described as "foreign." When the narrator mentions that,
"The particulars of Becky's costume were in the newspapers—feathers,
lappets, superb diamonds, and that the rest" (p. 605), we are further

reminded of the numerous descriptions of Miss Swartz, which the narrator notes were published in the same "snobby" newspapers. Here we see how the "beautiful" savage, Miss Swartz, who also wore feathers and diamonds, transmogrifies into the savage beauty Rebecca in the second half of the book.

Indeed, tropes of blackness are ubiquitous in the novel—especially in connection with the upper-class English characters. Many of the supremely selfish members of Parliament are corrupt and, therefore, described as blackhearted. It makes sense, then, that Rebecca marries into the aristocratic family of Lord Crawley, who is repeatedly hailed as "black" and provides yet another example of the ways in which blackness permeates the text and Becky's character in particular. Throughout *Vanity Fair*, the aristocracy seems always already to have been "blackened." There are countless references to the "black horny hand" of Lord Crawley—indeed, almost all the aristocratic snobs in the book are described as "black."

The wealthy and odious Mr. and Mrs. Crawley, Rebecca's future in-laws who disinherit their son for marrying the governess, are characterized as black-faced. In a letter reprinted in the text, Rebecca herself calls Mrs. Bute Crawley "a little black-faced old woman in a turban rather crooked and with very twinkling eyes" (p. 122). Also, the eldest daughter of Mrs. Crawley "was a very swarthy short snub-nosed young lady . . . [although she] had some of the best blood in England in [her] veins" (p. 605). Mr. Crawley voices the chauvinistic view of "blood" when he tells Becky, "Blood is everything, after all" (p. 109). These discussions about "blood" and heritage are satirized in the novel since the "best" blood is itself ironically contaminated, tainted by the black deeds of imperialism.

Amelia's father, John Sedley, "Esquire of Russell Square and the Stock Exchange," remarks to his wife, "It's a mercy [our son Jos, newly returned from the colonies,] did not bring us over a black daughter-in-law, my dear. But mark my words, the first woman who fishes for him, hooks him. . . . The girl's a white face at any rate. *I* don't care who marries him. Let Joe please himself" (p. 36). Both Mr. and Mrs. Sedley feel that it would be better to have the "white-faced" Rebecca as a daughter-in-law, who is only a lowly governess, ". . . than a black Mrs. Sedley and a dozen mahogany grandchildren" (p. 62).[43] This is another reference to the inherent hybridity of English culture. So too, George Osborne, one of the best-natured and most gentlemanly men in the text, is described as having a "yellow" face—a mark of his possible "Creole" status. In a conversation, he exclaims: "Mine a yellow face? Stop till you see Dobbin. Why he had the yellow fever three times; twice in Nassau, and once at St. Kitts" (p. 57).

Here, too, we see the subtle, almost subtextual references to Miss Swartz, who emblematizes the seeping quality of the colonial enterprise that has "infected" the hearts and homes of England. Comparing the literally dark or shaded character of Rhoda Swartz with the comparable figuratively dark or shady Rebecca Sharp highlights the permeable link between these complexly commingled figures. The depictions of these different dark women in Thackeray's text reveal vital intersections that have been overlooked. This section emphasizes the often elided conjunction and the parallel representation of two types of "black" women in *Vanity Fair*.

Rhoda's origins derive from deviant or illicit racial relations. Rebecca, as an adulteress, participates in illicit sexual relations. These relationships are represented asymmetrically. In order to describe Rebecca's vices, the narrator of the text uses a strategy of displacement and indirection. Thus, Rebecca's evil deeds, whatever they may be (for we never know for sure exactly what she has done), are only spoken of indirectly.

The following, often-cited passage from the famous "Vagabond" chapter of *Vanity Fair* lets the "closet-skeletons" out and explains that what is "aboveboard" is a lie, whereas what is beneath the surface (like black blood under white skin and blue marks under mulattaroon fingernails requiring paint to hide the taint) is "true." As the narrator of *Vanity Fair* insists:

There are things we do know perfectly well in Vanity Fair, though we never speak of them. . . . It is only when their naughty names are called out that your modesty has any occasion to show alarm or sense of outrage and it has been the wish of the present writer, all through this story, deferentially to submit to the fashion at present prevailing and only to hint at the existence of wickedness in a light, easy . . . manner, so that nobody's fine feelings may be offended. I defy any one to say that our Becky, who has certainly some vices, has not been presented to the public in a perfectly genteel and in-offensive manner. In describing this siren, singing and smiling, coaxing and cajoling, the author, with modest pride, asks his readers all round, has he once forgotten the laws of politeness, and showed the monster's hideous tail above water? No! Those who like may peep down under waves that are pretty transparent, and see it writhing and twirling, diabolically hideous and slimy, flapping amongst bones, or curling round corpses but above the water line, I ask, has not everything been proper, agreeable, and decorous? (p. 812)

If Rhoda is the "Hottentot Venus," then similarly, Rebecca might resemble the stuffed mermaid brought to London in 1822 and exhibited at a local pub until she was purchased by the great American showman, P. T. Barnum. This particular specimen was examined by the head of the Royal Academy of Science before being declared a fake. A popular audience paid a shilling apiece to see the mermaid at the tavern where it was displayed. The mermaid was "constructed of the cobbled remains of an orangutan, a baboon, and a salmon."[44] Such a description suggests the hideous hybrid nature of Becky.

The quotation also points to the tension between the linguistic and visual registers in the text. Visual images of Becky portray her as a witch, a viper, and as other venal figures; these too, however, picture her at a remove—she is seen playing different roles, which suggests that she is dissembling. When the evil Sir Pitt proposes to Rebecca, she "went down on *her* knees in a most tragical way, and taking Sir Pitt's horny black hand between her own two (which were very pretty and white, and as soft as satin), looked up in his face with an expression of exquisite pathos and confidence" (p. 180). This is but one example of her ability to act: "The fair imposes a general linguistic principle which identifies the improper with the unspeakable, the unrepresentable [the (im)possible]. The ethical perspective binding narrative language has shifted from the transcendence of puritan allegory to mere principles of propriety. . . . though the indirectness of figurative language allows the unspeakable to be obscured, it is also a covert means of representation."[45]

We remember, too, that Miss Swartz's "hysterical *yoops*" cannot be depicted by the pen—they also are unrepresentable, beyond the pale, like Becky's hideous tale (which includes the suggestion that she has murdered her husband for his insurance money). This strategy of revealing through concealment is related to miscegenation, which is complicit with the tensions in the text between overt and covert forms of representation. Miscegenation as an act ironically endorses a culture of segregation, for to define the mulattaroon is to assume, after the fact, that her antecedents were racially pure, thereby justifying the contrast between white and black.

The (dark) difference of these figures stands inside and beside the norm, but it must be performed and narrativized as being somehow distinct from the normative. In short, the character's efficacy depends on elaboration—they must be explained, or written into existence and then, crucially, written out of existence in an effort to excise fears of their power. As hybrid beings, their definition is elaborate and not readily reduced to a single entity. This is true for Miss Swartz, who though dark and odious, is complicated by her oxymoronic heritage. She is black but wealthy; simultaneously devalued and overvalued. Or more accurately, in Thackeray's narrative, "blackness" is a mark of the grossest excess—black deeds that draw on the linguistic value of the term, which in Western culture has long been associated with depravity, baseness, and moral corruption.[46]

Rhoda is genetically black but metaphysically or morally fair, while the dissembling parvenue, Becky Sharp, is genetically fair but morally or metaphysically black. Rebecca and Rhoda rise—improve or maintain their ranks—through the marital relation; the former, however, is able to disguise her deviancy, whereas for the latter, erasing her malevolently marked materiality is an impossibility. Thus, the tales of these different figures reveal the instability of their identities as well as their differently represented duplicitous natures.

Their differences do enter the world in the (dis)guise of performance. Each proclaims her difference through her narrative, through her "lines" that lead back to her problematic history. White women who are sexually deviant are blackened; black women who are sexually virtuous are never really pure. There is a fundamental inequality in the perception of the performance. In short, the performance of propriety alone did not qualify certain subjects for inclusion in the realm of the proper.[47] The proximity of these different types of "black women" in Victorian narratives emphasizes the fact that each type emerges beside the other. They should be understood as twinned and entwined entities—as beings whose complex imbricated identities illustrate the categorical contradictions of the culture.

The shift in the narrative from a focus on Miss Swartz to one on Rebecca mimics the shift from a focus on "race" to "sexuality." In writing the white women's deviance, many Victorian authors, authorities, and discourses—medical and scientific—did so with the blackest of ink. Thus, these characters rely on the secreting (in both senses of this term) of sexual knowledge. Moreover, when the display of the black woman became indecorous, the decorative, less overtly sexual, white-appearing woman stepped in to fill the former's place. Where the sheer "fact of blackness,"[48] to quote Frantz Fanon, produced an aura of *extra*ordinary licentiousness, the face of whiteness became a purely ordinary occurrence. In short, a white-appearing body was inherently and mystically less vulgar than a black-appearing body.

Surprisingly, it is the angelic heroine Amelia whose sickly sweetness has the potential to cloy and destroy. George Osborne's description of his "sweet" Amelia uses the vocabulary of the purely passionate woman and hints at Amelia's slightly ominous compliance. Early in the text, George comments on Amelia's slavish nature: "This prostration and sweet unrepining obedience exquisitely touched and flattered George Osborne. He saw a slave before him in that simple yielding faithful creature, and his soul within him thrilled secretly somehow at the knowledge of his power" (p. 236).

Amelia's venal and vampiric nature is seen in her capitulation to William Dobbin, her second husband, whom she consents to marry after George has been killed in the battle at Waterloo. She "wished to give [Dobbin] nothing, but that he should give her all" (p. 853). Amelia is only slightly less selfish than Rebecca. This idea of the life-sucking, ultrafeminine parasite is elaborated in J. Hillis Miller's deconstructive discussion of the such figures. He writes:

"Parasitical"—the word suggests the image of "the obvious or univocal reading" as the mighty oak, rooted in solid ground, endangered by the insidious twining around it of deconstructive ivy. That ivy is somehow feminine, secondary, defective, or dependent. It is a clinging vine, able to live in no other way but by drawing the life sap of its host, cutting off its light and air. I think of Hardy's *The Ivy-Wife* or the end of Thackeray's *Vanity*

Fair: "God bless you, honest William!—Farewell, dear Amelia—Grow green again, tender little parasite, round the rugged old oak to which you cling!"[49]

Although Rebecca, as has been remarked, is a consummate actress whose powers of deception are legendary, we should not forget that Amelia is called a "hypocrite"—a Greek term for actor—throughout the book. She, too, has deceptive powers, which the narrator glosses as female. Despite the attention lavished on Miss Swartz's material possessions we must not think that George and Amelia have not been tainted by the values of "the fair." They are reluctant but willing participants in the play of vanity; in other words, they do not escape condemnation for what are often devious actions. The novel offers no salvation of the sentimental sort for when the drama dissolves the narrator exclaims, "*Vanitas Vanitatum!* Which of us is happy in the world? Which of us has his desire? or, having it is satisfied?—Come, children, let us shut up the box and the puppets, for our play is played out'" (p. 878). It is a dubious honor that each "Miss S." (Sedley, Sharpe, and Swartz) succeeds in securing a spot in Vanity Fair, which is "a very vain, wicked, foolish place, full of all sorts of humbugs, falseness and pretensions" (p. 95). Thus, Rhoda, a moral innocent without a will of her own, is granted a mediocre modicum of respect.

Rhoda's last appearance in the text is as the Honourable Mrs. McMull, wife of a wealthy Scotsman.[50] The final description of Rhoda reads: "Our old friend, Miss Swartz, and her husband [who] came thundering over from Hampton Court, with flaming yellow liveries, and was . . . impetuously fond of Amelia as ever. Swartz would have liked always if she could have seen her. One must do her that justice. But, *que voulez-vous?*—in this vast town one has not the time to go and seek one's friends; if they drop out of rank they disappear, and we march on without them. Who is ever missed in Vanity Fair?" (p. 781). The answer to this interrogatory is the hybridized Anglo-American mulattaroon, Rhoda Swartz, who is the missing integer in attempts to unify national narratives under a singular sign. Dropped out of rank and "disappeared," she has now been restored and re-membered, if only for a moment, as part of Victorian culture; rather than march on without her, we have in these pages put up (with) Miss Swartz.

Obliging Octoroons

The very name octoroon was an emotion. What word could
better hide a plot, a privy conspiracy of seduction and anarchy?
—Townsend Walsh, *The Career of Dion Boucicault*

Zoe, Zoe, witching and beautiful Zoe,
Thy charms unto my fancy seem,
a radiant impossible dream![51]
Reece and Farnie—*The Creole*

Zoe Peyton, the central character in Dion Boucicault's play, *The Octoroon, or Life in Louisiana,* which opened in New York in 1859, is the
supposedly freed "natural" daughter of a Judge Peyton, who owns the
Louisiana plantation, Terrebonne, where the drama takes place.[52] In
this melodrama, the heroic lovers, Zoe and the judge's prodigal nephew,
George, are thwarted in their quest for romantic love by the evil machi-
nations of a monied overseer named Jacob M'Closky. M'Closky cov-
ets Zoe and Terrebonne, and contrives a way to buy both; in the last
act, however, a "good" overseer, Scudder, a "Yankee and Photographic
Operator," provides evidence—in the form of a photograph of M'Closky
murdering a young slave—that hastens the play's denouement.[53]

   Zoe, like Rhoda Swartz, has "the education of a lady" (act 1); yet unlike Rhoda, Zoe's wild black roots have been trained and thoroughly
tamed so that she is virtually a white lady. Although the purely passionate Zoe, the tragic heroine, is the product of the judge's illicit adul-
terous affair with a quadroon slave, she is reared by the judge's white
widow.[54] While long-standing American antimiscegenation laws made
marriage between blacks and whites impossible, it did not expressly
forbid "merely" sexual relations between them. The exogamous arrangements represented in Boucicault's play were a normal part of the
"peculiar institution," if not their very raison d'être. Such forms of
amalgamation were seen as one of "the customs of Louisiana," where
in mid-nineteenth-century New Orleans, adultery with octoroon fancy
girls was the presumption (if not the requirement) of gentlemanly status.
Such *illegal* couplings undergird the belief that the octoroon's story was

inherently dramatic since it was ipso facto concerned with illicit desire, seduction, and anarchy.

Boucicault describes the origins and import of the octoroon's story as follows:

The word Octoroon signifies "one-eighth blood" or the child of a Quadroon by a white. The Octoroons have no apparent trace of the negro in their appearance but still are subject to the legal disabilities which attach them to the condition of blacks. The plot of this drama was suggested to the author by the following incident, which occurred in Louisiana and came under his notice during his residence in that State. The laws of Louisiana forbid the marriage of a white man with any woman having the smallest trace of black blood in her veins. The Quadroon and Octoroon girls, proud of their white blood, revolt from union with the black and are unable to form marriages with the white. They are thus driven into an equivocal position and form a section of New Orleans society, resembling the demi-monde of Paris. A young and wealthy planter of Louisiana fell deeply and sincerely in love with a Quadroon girl of great beauty and purity. The lovers found their union opposed by the law; but love knows no obstacles. The young man, in the presence of two friends, who served as witnesses, opened a vein in his arm and introduced into it a few drops of his mistress's blood; thus he was able to make oath that he had black blood in his veins, and being attested the marriage was performed. The great interest now so broadly felt in American affairs induces the author to present "The Octoroon" as the only American drama which has hitherto attempted to portray [sic] American homes, American scenery, and manners without either exaggeration or prejudice. The author has been informed of the strong objection to the scenes in this drama representing the slave sale at which Zoe is sold and to avoid her fate commits suicide. It has been stated that such circumstances are wholly improbable. In reply to these remarks he begs to quote from slave history the following episode: a young lady named Miss Winchester, the daughter of a wealthy planter in Kent had been educated in Boston where she was received in the best circles of society and universally admired for her great beauty and accomplishments. The news of her father's sudden death recalled her to Kentucky. Examination into the affairs of the deceased revealed the fact that Miss Winchester was the natural child of the planter by a quadroon slave; she was inventoried in chattels of the estate, and sold; the next day her body was found floating in the Ohio [River].[55]

Like Harriet Beecher Stowe's *Key to Uncle Tom's Cabin*,[56] Boucicault justifies his script by citing an episode from "slave history." This quotation is notable also for they way in which it explains the "equivocal position" of the white-appearing octoroons as a result of the pride in their white blood. Because of the octoroon's valued whiteness, they logically must "revolt from union with the black." Thus, the real problem is that these desirable (because white-appearing) young women are prevented from marrying white men. This aspect of Boucicault's drama signals a shift toward a marked concern with "white slaves"—not only to enslaved "white" octoroons such as Zoe, but also, and more important, to any "white-appearing" (and therefore presumed white) women who were mistreated. The horror of slavery, therefore, was increasingly emblematized by the degradation suffered by "white" women.[57]

There is no doubt that Zoe is a lady; and yet, because she is one-eighth black, she is seen as being luxurious. Zoe is the supreme object of desire. "Niggers [*sic*] get fresh at the sight of her . . . , the overseer M'Closky shivers to think of her," (p. 137) and George, the judge's nephew, is captivated instantly. She becomes the common denominator between these disparate men; yet only the southern hero, George—a perfect specimen of the aristocratic planter class—is deemed worthy of Zoe's love. In this way, Boucicault may have played to southern sentimental family values that worked to cover over the raw economics of slavery.

The New Orleans fancy girl auctions serve as the most blatant reminder that the nation's formation is inextricably bound up with (dark) female subjects. As Joseph Roach explains, the auctions, which took place in the rotunda at New Orleans's famous St. Louis Hotel, were staged as "competitions between men . . . [and] seethe[d] with the potential for homosocial violence. As theatrical spectacle, [the auctions] materialize the most intense of symbolic transactions in circum-Atlantic culture: money transforms flesh into property; property transforms flesh into money; flesh transforms money into property." [58] The first scene of the play allows, and even elicits, potential "buyers" in the form of the audiences who have paid money to see the white actress Agnes Robertson perform the part of Zoe and to look at her body. Moreover, we must remember that the audiences no doubt attempted to scrutinize her body for signs of her buried "black" life. As dramatic strategy, the signs of Zoe's blackness are staged in a way that—unlike a film, where the camera could zoom in for a close-up of the blue tinge of the actress's fingernails—the audience must imagine how her "deviant" difference might be written on her body.

Zoe changes her status in the play. In act 1, she believes that she is free and then finds out that she is a slave. The mixed-race heroine undergoes several transformations in which her contradictory body is pushed and pulled between its multiple significations. Zoe is free, then slave, then free again—the last time permanently in death. She "falls" in status. Ironically, Zoe's fall (her transformation from free woman to slave) is represented at the play's climax, in which she stands on top of a table—elevated above both the fleshmongers who bid on her body and the other black characters in the play. This staged inversion of the dominant codes reveals how value is inscribed on Zoe's body. She is, in fact, more valuable (as were the fancy girls) when the blackness of her body is performed in this manner. "The body of the white-appearing Octoroon . . . offers itself as the crucible in which a strange alchemy of cultural surrogation takes place. In the defining event of commercial exchange, from flesh to property, the object of desire mutates and transforms itself, from African to Woman." [59]

When the hero, George Peyton, declares his love to "African-derived" Zoe (and not to the white woman Dora Sunnyside), he says, "Love knows no prejudice" (p. 147),[60] and offers to marry Zoe, despite the fact that she is illegitimate. Zoe expects George's response to follow Shakespeare's lines: "My thoughts and my discourse as madmen's are, / At random from the truth vainly expressed: / For I have sworn thee fair, and thought thee bright, / Who are as black as hell, as dark as night."[61] George has been "educated in Europe and just returned home" (p. 100). No doubt his European education, if true to gentlemanly form, included trips to brothels, as was de rigueur for those taking the grand tour. Indeed, George's sojourn in Paris—the land of the sexually adventurous French—was meant to be an initiation into a man's world. We learn that "all the girls were in love with him in Paris (p. 140), and he even admits that he has been in love 249 times. Scudder alludes to this fact when he comments on George's admiration of Zoe's beauty. He states,

"Guess that you didn't leave anything female in Europe that can lift an eyelash beside that girl" (p. 137) or "who is more beautiful and polished in manners" (p. 138). Indeed, Zoe proves herself to be a lady not only in appearance, but also in fact, honorably informing George of her maternal heritage.

In a dramatic moment, Zoe declares herself "an unclean thing, forbidden by the laws" (p. 120), and asks for George's "pity." George, who is ignorant of American antimiscegenation legislation, is mortified to learn that the object of his desire cannot be recognized as his legal wife. Zoe points out the "bluish tinge under her nails and around her eyes as evidence of her Black" maternal roots, and states that "the dark fatal mark . . . is the ineffaceable curse of Cain."[62] Her solution to this dilemma is to commit suicide at the end of the play. Here, the disjunction between literal and figurative blackness is questioned by Zoe's peculiar person, underscoring the extent to which race must be understood as "performative." That is to say, the law that labels Zoe literally black, possessing black blood, is undercut by its clearly figurative use. In appearance, manner, and form, she is not "black"; her blackness must be written on her. It is her belabored confession that "delivers" her blackness.

The ontological assurance of what blackness "is" is never guaranteed in the play. Indeed, it is the purpose of the octoroon to pose (as) the problem of racial discernment. While her paradoxical social placement is clear from the beginning of the play, it is continually and more overtly confirmed during the play's performance. The inevitable drive toward Zoe's degradation (and increased gradation) is heightened by the presumption in the first act that she is free. In act 2, she learns that, in fact, she is enslaved. The massive contradictions that underwrite the play work to delegitimate certain societal values. The oppositions of slave and free, white and black are disrupted when figures such as Zoe enter the dominant national, familial structures. Read as disrupting forces, they must be destroyed.

In Boucicault's original version, performed in New York in 1859, Scudder's discovery comes too late to save Zoe from suicide; in another version of the drama, presented in London two years later, Zoe lives and, in the final tableau, is swept up in George's arms. In the English version of Boucicault's drama, Zoe ends up with her lover, an American man (merely of English descent), with whom it is declared "she will solemnize a lawful union in another [unspecified] land."[63]

In the American version, Zoe reacts to her fate by drinking a suicidal poison, like Shakespeare's Juliet. This action relieves her from becoming a slave and the property of the vile M'Closky, and is presented as the noble choice, since she lost her opportunity to become the wife and property of the aristocratic hero, George Peyton. She opts to go to the "free" land so often celebrated in "Negro" spirituals. She is purified in death. Zoe's ingestion of the poison is an attempt to solidify her body formally—to make her taint more permanent. If she has been "poisoned" with the blood of her African American mother, then she replicates this "original sin" for George. At the end of the play, however, the script says that she turns "white"—again following the typical trajectory of the octoroon.

The difference between the two versions points to the very different politics of race in the two nations. English audiences, who were at a remove from the direct, systematic, and legal divisions of racial conflict, could radically rewrite the octoroon's narrative. As Boucicault reported in a London playbill from 1861: "Mr. B. begs to acknowledge the hourly receipt of so many letters entreating that the termination of the Octoroon should be modified and the slave heroine saved from an unhappy end. He cannot resist the kind feeling expressed throughout this correspondence nor refuse compliance with the request so easily granted. A new last act of the drama composed by the public and edited by the author will be represented on Monday night."[64] In the first version of the play, Zoe enacts her understanding of cultural binaries and her low other position vis-à-vis such boundaries. Furthermore, she decides to maintain and not transgress such boundaries. In the English version, however, she allows George to follow his heart, even at the expense of breaking the law. That true love triumphs is the stock-in-trade of melodrama; but even here, the implied blissful future of the lovers is not guaranteed.

Their reconsolidation is also undercut by the fact that in all versions of the drama, Agnes Robertson, a white woman and Boucicault's wife, played the part of Zoe, ensuring that an "actual" interracial kiss did not occur—only an apparent (or a white-parented) woman can portray purity properly as a property only of "whites." Boucicault's decision to cast his wife in the lead role of the octoroon resonates with Robertson's repertoire. Before this part, she had a reputation for playing breeches roles (in which female actresses wore trousers for part of the production) with great panache. Known also for the acumen with which she performed multiple parts in a single drama, Robertson seemed to be the perfect figure to dramatize the destabilized body of Zoe. In this regard, she epitomized Victorian actresses, who used disguises to change themselves and to emphasize the fact that women's bodies, like viscous material, can be malleable and cannot be contained.

So too, more than her impersonation, her performances remind us of Becky Sharp's acting the part of the perfect innocent ingenue though her roots were dirty, dark, and dangerous. Such representations may be said to be both represented and "erased" in performances by Agnes Robertson. Although "tawny" stage makeup was manufactured in the 1800s, it is unlikely that Robertson would have "blacked up" for her performances. Indeed, that was the beauty of her performance of this role; it required only the "natural" skills of melodramatic femininity. In an edition of the drama printed for Dicks's plays, the cover shows Zoe with M'Closky and Scudder. Interestingly, Zoe wears a white dress, has a white face, and long straight dark hair, whereas her white male companions are drawn with dark faces and clothes (figure 6). Again, we come to see how white and black signified as morally coded terms in melodrama could be (mis)applied to racially white or black figures.

This problem of mismatching signifiers and signified was examined in nineteenth-century U.S. legal cases. For instance, in America, the courts attempted to define "whiteness" and "blackness" even before the famous 1896 case of *Plessy v. Ferguson*. In her analysis of the genre of legal miscegenation Eva Saks reveals how "courts, looking for external objective referents for blood (brown skin) were also implicitly attempting to forge a way of representing race that was referential, to invent mimetic terms that referred to something beyond figures of speech. However, the ironic result of this double search—for referents and for *referentiality*—was that courts often found only other legal texts, prior legal inscriptions."[65] "Race" must always be understood to be performative and without a fixed, essential origin or sign.

Technically, the octoroon is not obliged to perform in concert with

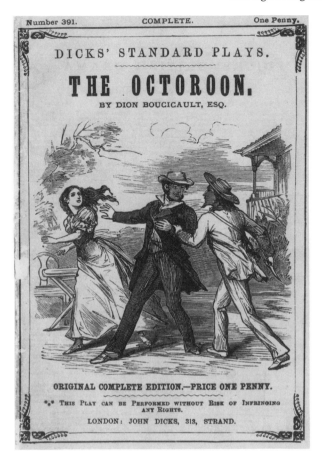

Number 391.   COMPLETE.   One Penny.

DICKS' STANDARD PLAYS.

THE OCTOROON.

BY DION BOUCICAULT, ESQ.

ORIGINAL COMPLETE EDITION.—PRICE ONE PENNY.

₊ THIS PLAY CAN BE PERFORMED WITHOUT RISK OF INFRINGING ANY RIGHTS.

LONDON: JOHN DICKS, 313, STRAND.

6. *The Octoroon,* Dick's Plays, 1859. Courtesy of the Theatre Museum, Victoria and Albert, London.

the law that both denies and creates her; yet she plays out this specifically gendered tragic role, one that marks her, over and over again, as an obliging octoroon. The exemplary instance occurs in Boucicault's drama when Zoe decries her "tainted" maternal lineage by stating, "I am an unclean thing forbidden by the laws!" Because the octoroon's origins almost always are obscured, audiences must succumb to the pleasure of reading an "open secret" and connecting the lines of descent torn asunder under the aegis of miscegenation laws.[66] A harsher view of this situation is expressed in another 1861 play, *Cora, the Octoroon Slave of Louisiana,* where the character Marbee exclaims, "paternal love is a wealth a slave ought not possess."[67] By possessing legitimate paternal love, the slave can shift from being property to having property. As we saw earlier, the "wealth" of the benevolent white father could uplift his daughter; bestowing property becomes a gift of paternal love. Indeed, most nineteenth-century Anglo-American narratives present the mulattaroon as the twice-owned property of a white patriarch.

The aptly named Amanda America Dickson (1849–93) was a real-life example of one such "woman of color and daughter of privilege," born in pre–Civil War Georgia. Her birth was the result of a planter's rape of a female slave belonging to his mother. This incident in the life of the slave girl who was Amanda America's mother has been narrated by a recent biographer as follows: "One day in the middle of February 1849, [wealthy, white] David Dickson rode across his fallow fields . . . [and] he spotted a young female slave playing. . . . Deliberately, he rode up beside the slave child and reached down and swung her up behind him on his saddle. . . . The slave's childhood ended as Amanda America Dickson's life began, on that day when her father raped her mother."[68]

Both despite and because of her specific entrance into the world, Amanda's fate, which might have been fatal, turned fortunate owing to the fact that she had a kind and doting father. Amanda grew up "in her white father's household, inside the boundary of his family, as his daughter. She married a white Civil War veteran and had children of her own. She inherited her father's enormous estate . . . [and] died amid luxury and comfort" (p. 2). The question of her personal identity reveals that "her class solidarity with her father, that is, her socialization as his daughter, and her gender role as lady" (ibid.), complicated her racial demarcation.

The scientist Josiah Nott believed similarly that "when a *Negro* man married a white woman, the offspring partook more largely of the Negro type than when the reverse [between white male and black female] connection had effect."[69] The dark daughter, obliquely placed, nevertheless could be cast as the closest comfort to the white father.[70] Her story provides the occasion for speculation about his own difference, identity, and desire. Because white men controlled miscegenation, they were the ones who made black women and women black.

In many fictional accounts, the closeness between the white father and the black daughter was expressed as having an incestuous character. As Henry Hughes, a nineteenth-century theorist, even claimed: "Hybridism is heinous. Impurity of races is against the law of nature. Mulattoes are monsters. The law of nature is the law of God. The same law which forbids consanguineous amalgamation forbids ethnical amalgamation. Both are incestuous. Amalgamation is incest.[71] An example of this illicit desire between father and daughter is hinted at in Boucicault's *The Octoroon*. The dialogue in the drama makes continual references to the young Peyton's striking similarity to his dead uncle, the judge, who is Zoe's father, therefore making the nephew Zoe's cousin. This family resemblance provides evidence of the "incest" that is read as being coterminous with "miscegenation" and other forms of illicit amalgamation.

Some nineteenth-century thinkers elided the differences between incest, miscegenation, and adultery, and placed these phenomena in the common category of the illegitimate or culturally anomalous. These confused and confusing categories are consistently juxtaposed with a pure and proper one, namely, the nuclear family epitomized by white Christian marriage. If the proper family is the building block of a strong nation, then incest, miscegenation, and hybridity threaten the family (of man), and by extension, the nation (of proper gentlemen). The precarious sexual nature of women who are not wives and mothers, like Zoe, complicates the pure and proper perpetuation of this national family. Victorian conventions (predominantly promoted by middle-class men) about female sexual transgression impose borders by systematically classifying and differentiating between pure women and passionate women, between licit and illicit sex.

The Octoroon is continually concerned with the maintenance and production of civilized subjects, and ultimately, the Christian characters prevail. As the overseer Scudder notes:

Natur' has said that where the white man sets his foot the red man and the black man shall up sticks and stan'round [they will salute him and make him the center]. Now, what do we pay for that possession? In cash? No—in kind—that is, in protection . . . in gentleness [gentlemanliness?] and in all them goods that show the critturs the difference between the Christian and the Savage. Now what have you done to show 'em the distinction? (p. 189)

Scudder's speech to the Western white men who are *behaving* like savages affirms the divide between these two groups at the same time that it reveals one can become the other—that the tame and the wild are only *relative* positions (in both senses of the italicized word). Here again, good characters are seen as white, while bad ones are seen as black.

Boucicault's drama provides us with a parable, "The Yankee Hugging the Creole" (act 1), told by Scudder, the northern overseer who is "here somewhere interferin" (and is indeed the voice of God-fearing, Christian right reason in the text), to M'Closky. The parable presents a model of white northern appropriation. He says:

D'ye see that tree? It's a live oak, and is a native here; beside it grows a creeper; year after year that creeper twines its long arms round . . . the tree—sucking the earth dry all about its roots—living on its life—overrunning its branches until at last the live oak withers and dies out. Do you know what the niggers [*sic*] call that sight? They call it the Yankee hugging the Creole. (p. 142)

Not only is this a metaphor for miscegenation, but also for nation formation in the shape of appropriative violence—what has been described as the rape of the land under colonialism. This tale, told from the "native" perspective, casts the Yankee as the vampiric, parasitic substance that creeps and kills (Creole) life. The Yankee sees to it that the native dies out. Here, "forgetting, like miscegenation, [proves to be] an opportunistic tactic of whiteness."[72] The patriarchal bias of some forms of miscegenation does privilege whiteness. "Bred (retrospectively) to be pure, the national-family tree is miscegenated at its roots."[73] That is to say, the production of whiteness depends on "miscegenation" and is therefore not "pure." It, too, is "divided." As J. Hillis Miller explains:

The uncanny antithetical relation exists not only between pairs of words in the system, host and parasite . . . but within each word itself. . . . Each word in itself becomes divided by the strange logic of the "para" [hyphen/hybrid] membrane which divides inside from outside and yet joins them in a hymeneal bond, or which allows an osmotic mixing, making the stranger friend, the distant near, the *Unheimlich heimlich* . . . without for all its closeness and similarity, ceasing to be strange, distant, dissimilar.[74]

The references here signify in another way, since the Yankee himself was already a Creole according to the definition of the term. A "Creole" is one born in the Americas whose parents, of whatever race, were born elsewhere. So too, one could become a Creole based on how long one stayed in the colonies. As we saw in *Vanity Fair*, the slippage between race and national origin, of living at home and abroad, made purity impossible. The Yankee is only a Yankee because he has remembered to forget that he was a Creole. The category "whiteness" is an identity to be performed, preserved, restored, retained, contained, and "achieved" through repetition. Anxiety about the destruction of one's whiteness as a legacy is expressed through references to the figure of the blackened woman.

J. Hillis Miller defines the most dangerous parasite as "the virus, the uneasy border between life and death . . . that does not eat but only reproduces" (ibid.). This is an excellent description of the simultaneous contamination of the figures discussed in this chapter. Moreover, Miller continues, "the genetic pattern of the virus is so coded that it can enter a host cell and violently reprogram all the genetic material in that cell, turning the cell into a little factory for manufacturing copies of itself, so destroying it" (p. 222). This is the process of vampirism practiced not only by fictitious characters, or infecting black figures, but from another perspective, by real-life white figures as well. Indeed, this is the ideology of whiteness that without a body of its own is unmarked. It appropriates, needs, and wants to co-opt technology to reproduce itself—all the while denying the utility of native power for the fulfillment of such a project.

As several historians of blacks in England have also noted, the black population was absorbed into the general population.[75] This idea of absorption, the ultimate assimilation, problematizes notions of "whiteness" and purity by alluding to the fundamental hybridity of nations. This re-membering of the artificial construction of historical "development" dismembers "naturalized" teleological notions of the progress and unity deployed in most narratives of national history. Thus, "nation-time" works by a future-anterior logic of identity that claims "we will be what we have been." Such false homologies connect the past, unknown origins that, once selected, can be revised and endlessly (if not effortlessly) performed in the present.

Zoe ultimately serves to establish the establishment. *The Octoroon* performs the otherwise hidden and private artificial construction of national identity that is naturalized as unmediated inheritance. For ex-

ample, in the English version of Boucicault's play, Zoe's suicide frees
George from entering a tainted affair. The elimination or sublimation
of the disturbing dark lady results in the reconsolidation of discrete and
dominant forms.

The dominant codes presumed that good women passively existed in
the world, like Mrs. Peyton, while good men actively asserted themselves on the world, like Judge Peyton. Good women were to be pure
and good men were to have passion (for work, class, and nation).[76] The
feminized ideal that Zoe both embodied and challenged required that
there be strict divisions not only between the sexes, but within "the
sex." Racial and sexual acts were linked. This movement that links the
stain or *taint* of "blackness" to the formerly "white" woman is represented by these vernacular phrases: "To wash a negro, to attempt an
impossible task" (*OED*); and "When a woman falls from purity there is
no return for her—as well one may attempt to wash the stain from the
sullied snow. Men sin and are forgiven; but the memory of a woman's
guilt cannot be removed on earth."[77] Black deeds became determining
forces of identity.

The sex instinct is simultaneously conflated with and divorced from
the fraught issue of race preservation. This is another great paradox in
which the figure of the mulattaroon plays a key role. On the one hand,
such figures were seen as preservers of the patriarchal family—an out-
let for the father who would not contest his legitimate reproduction—
and on the other, as a threat to the "legitimate" family because she was
a source of potential confusion between the illicit and licit. "Beyond the
sphere of domesticity, the sexual . . . effects synonymity with the illicit,
the wild, the mysterious, . . . [Moreover] one of its signs is the mulatta,
who has no personhood, but locates in the flesh a site of cultural and
political maneuver."[78] If Zoe could be classed as outside of and different from the "true white" family, if her whiteness could be suppressed,
then order would be preserved. Reading the fallen mulattaroon as a
sign of either distilled or still(ed) life shows how her reproduction of
blackened femininity was limited and stalled.

Chapter Two
CASTING THE DYE

It sometimes happens that one may learn something useful about works of art from translation into another medium, especially when these appear to be vulgarizations.—Martin Meisel

The title of this chapter, "Casting the Dye," refers to the idea of hardening racial and sexual categories—so that what are, in fact, permeable differences between "black" and "white," female and male, appear to be both sutured and separated in Victorian discourse.[1] Indeed, the title's pun foregrounds the suppressed relation between the seemingly unrelated discourses of necrophilia and negrophilia. These "disorders" are emblematized in British culture by the popular, often imitated figures of the hyperembodied, overly animated, "live" black Topsy and the angelic, disembodied, "dead" white Little Eva from the best-selling Victorian novel, *Uncle Tom's Cabin.* In reading diverse instances of the desire for purity, this chapter reveals how similar differences are made absolute (and absolutely different) through the process of purification. In an effort to emphasize the extremely exaggerated effects that made identities appear as opposites, the text that follows is relentlessly black and white.

Blacking Out and Whiting Up

Alexandre Dumas père's novel *The Black Tulip* chronicles the quest of a seventeenth-century Dutch tulip grower and hybridizer named Cornelius Van Bearle to create a black tulip.[2] The novel tells of Van Bearle's attempt to produce "the impossible"—a black tulip without a spot of color—a thing "as chimerical as the black swan of Horace or the white blackbird of French Tradition" (p. 57). These chimerical, oxymoronic figures—the "black swan" and the "white blackbird"—correspond to the figures of the black tulip and the white slave. Each is presented as an aberrant curiosity that fascinates spectators who read these figures as spectacular fantasies—as impossible purities.

The black tulip is a conundrum whose impossible purity is the result of man's triumphant manipulation of an otherwise unruly female nature. Van Bearle, whom Dumas represents as being benevolent, is a true and just patriarchal creator who deals in the refined realm of horticulture. Van Bearle's complete possession of the pure black tulip contrasts with H. G. Wells's impure (incomplete) black puma in *The Island of Dr. Moreau,* discussed in chapter 4.[3] The black tulip is appealingly delicate; that is, it is stereotypically exotic, feminine, "beautiful, smooth, well-formed [with] the air of melancholy about [her] which promises to produce a flower the color of ebony. On the skin one cannot even distinguish the veins with the naked eye" (p. 45). Like the mulattaroons discussed previously, the black tulip is a quintessentially feminine object created by a white male who falls in love with his perfect design. Indeed, *The Black Tulip* might be read as a modern Pygmalion story.

There is overwhelming evidence to suggest that nineteenth-century artists had an obsession with this story.[4] The myth of the Greek sculptor Pygmalion and his statue (identified as Galatea in Jean-Jacques Rousseau's eighteenth-century version) was ubiquitous in Victorian art. The story begins with the artist working on a beautiful statue that he wishes to "bring to life" (perhaps literally, perhaps metaphorically). He prays for assistance and, when the female nude comes to life, Pygmalion instantly falls in love with her. There were many variations of this story (it was reworked most famously by George Bernard Shaw in his play of the same name).[5] The Pygmalion myth is reminiscent of our earlier discussions of the binding together of the father/creator with his creation. The fantasy woman—an impossible dream come true—is always troubled by unnatural origins that are "naturalized" by the intervention (if not the invention) of white male authority.

The Dutch hybridizer, Van Bearle, makes purity from hybridity with his proven technological mastery of a black, feminine nature. The crossbreeder spends hours trying to create the fascinating flower. He is seen in his laboratory

. . . heating certain grains, then moistening them, then combining them with others by a sort of grafting,—a minute and marvelously delicate manipulation,— . . . he shut up in darkness those which were expected to furnish the black colour, exposed to sun or to lamp those which were to produce red, and to the endless reflection of two water-mirrors those intended to be white, and to represent the liquid element in all its purity. (p. 58)

This description makes clear that Van Bearle grafts other elements on to the segregated "black" grain in order to produce an even purer form of blackness. Purity, then, is the product of amalgamation. The technique of grafting, which is aligned more with cloning than the reproduction of new organisms, requires only one parent. The "minute and marvelously delicate manipulation" managed by the hybridizer, who becomes father to his creation, is the key ingredient in the perpetuation of purity.[6] The offspring that most closely resembles the father, the one whom he designates as the inheritor of genetic and/or material possessions, is precious and powerful. Although the line of succession should ideally result in a male heir, female children could inherit. Indeed, the phenomenon of Queen Victoria herself proved this point. She was only the second female leader of Great Britain, and her rarity justifies the decision to allow lines of descent to extend to decent daughters.

The black tulip is a hybrid; paradoxically, it is also perfectly pure. When produced by the father figure, its purity can be worshiped and is apparent to all who gaze on its perfection. "The public display of the tulip was an act of homage rendered by a whole nation" (p. 234). It is placed on a pedestal as the "Queen of excellence and purity" (p. 243). It is "a consummate masterpiece of art and nature in collaboration" (p. 241). Art here is synonymous with man's ability to civilize feminine nature, for only his influence can purify and make ideal feminine nature. The consummation is less a collaboration than the strange fruit of the laboratory labor of the hybridizer, who ultimately claims complete ownership of his creation.

The tulip, however, is stolen by Van Bearle's evil neighbor, Boxtel. Both men have been engaged in a race to produce the black tulip in order to win a contest. The theft ignites a rivalry between Van Bearle and Boxtel, pointing to the problem of patriarchal possession. The flower, like a daughter, is a prize that is literally worth several thousand florins. By falsely asserting his ownership, Boxtel usurps Van Bearle's— the true father's—authority. Moreover, both Van Bearle and Boxtel are rivals for the affection of a beautiful maiden named Rosa. As her name suggests, she too is seen as an idealized feminine figure. Indeed, Van

Bearle's love for his flower is similar to his love for the maiden Rosa, whom he cultivates as he does his tulip. Van Bearle, who is significantly older than Rosa, who is a blooming youth, admires her from afar. In the beginning of the novel, he seems to offer her "fatherly" advice; he does not admit that he desires her until later in the text. This mirrors the way in which he views the black tulip: he awaits the flowering of both objects of his affection.

In the chapter "The Blooming of the Flower," Van Bearle imagines: "Rosa is holding the stem of the tulip in her soft warm fingers. Touch the stem gently, Rosa! Perhaps she is touching the half-opened calyx with her lips. Breathe carefully upon it, Rosa. . . . Perhaps at this instant my two loves are kissing each other, with only God to see" (p. 173). This fantasy scene is one of classic voyeurism and fetishization. Van Bearle looks on at this creation from a godlike vantage point, and directs the action of Rosa and the flower, creating a pornographic spectacle of feminine eroticism. The "lesbian" spectacle imagined by its male creator draws on a tradition of representing two women—one dark, one light—as lovers. The erotic and exotic portrayal conflates blackness and sexualized femininity.

At the climax of the novel, Van Bearle adopts the same position as voyeur when he glimpses his stolen prize from a carriage window. He exclaims: "What! the thing I see down there, the black tulip,—quite black? . . . Is it possible? . . . It must have some spots; it must be imperfect, perhaps it has only been dyed black. Oh, if only I were closer I could tell!" (p. 335). This quotation emphasizes the problem of perspective. Van Bearle again looks on from a distance as he tries to determine if the flower is perfect, natural or imperfect, "dyed" black. "If only he were closer he could tell." Although dealing with a black flower, Van Bearle desires a *pure* one. Even if this ideal emerges from hybrid roots, it has been produced (and purified) by a proper man's power. As the text says, a man's "instrumentality has forced Nature to produce a black flower . . . tulipa nigra" (p. 237). Again, only man's power over nature can (re)produce purity. *The Black Tulip* ends with the restoration of Van Bearle's precious creations, which both become his property when he marries Rosa and gets credit for producing the tulip.

If *The Black Tulip* is the story of a hybrid that becomes perfectly black, a scene from Harriet Beecher Stowe's novel, *Uncle Tom's Cabin*,[7] may be read as the narrative of a hybrid who becomes perfectly white. Both narratives record the desire for absolute purity. Like *The Black Tulip*, Stowe's novel erases the hybrid roots of the mulattaroon, Eliza Harris, in order to represent her as an idealized "white" woman. This transformation works because Stowe's novel depends on a moral economy in which maternal femininity is valued most of all. That is, Stowe believed that mothers were the moral center of society. This is important to note as the crux of Eliza's story is told in chapter 2, entitled "The Mother." Indeed, Angela Davis claims that "Eliza is white motherhood incarnate, but in blackface — or rather, because she is a 'quadroon,' in just-a-little-less-than-whiteface."[8]

The chapter begins with a lengthy discussion of Eliza, who is described as possessing "a peculiar air of refinement, which seems in many cases to be the particular gift to the quadroon and mulatto women. These natural graces in the quadroon are often united with beauty of the most dazzling kind, and in almost every case with a personal appearance prepossessing and agreeable" (p. 54). We learn that Eliza, "safe under the protection of her mistress" (ibid.), reached maturity without being raped. Indeed, she is married to the militant mulatto hero of the story, George Harris. A morally pure character, Eliza is represented as the perfect(ed) vision of whiteness.

When Eliza finds out that she is being sold to a slave trader, she decides to escape with her son, Harry. She plans to cross the Ohio River from Kentucky. In a dramatic scene from the novel, Eliza crosses the river over floes of ice, thereby escaping her pursuers and passing from slavery to freedom. In this moment on the ice, Eliza is suspended between hybridity and purity, slavery and freedom, and is therefore a floating signifier.

In the novel, Eliza makes her escape "in the dusk of twilight [over the river] ". . . swollen with great cakes of floating ice swinging heavily to and fro in the turbid waters . . . form[ing] a temporary barrier" (p. 121). Prevented from crossing, she finds shelter for the evening; yet when detected by her pursuers, Eliza is forced to brave the river.

[W]ith one wild cry and flying leap, she vaulted sheer over the turbid current by the shore, onto the raft of ice beyond. . . . [T]he huge green fragment of ice on which she alighted pitched and creaked as her weight came on it. . . . [S]he leaped to another and still another cake; stumbling—leaping—slipping—springing upwards again! Her shoes are gone—her stockings cut from her feet—while blood marked every step; but she saw nothing, felt nothing, till dimly, as in a dream, she saw the Ohio side, and a man helping her up the bank. (pp. 117–18)

This melodramatic description, with its list of active verbs punctuated by dashes, was an ideal scene for translation to the stage and, indeed, it was presented often in the hundreds of staged versions of the novel in England and America. Also depicted in lithographs, on porcelain figurines, and on film, this scene is one of the most reproduced iconographic moments associated with the narrative not only for its inherent drama but also for its overt production of purified whiteness.

In a well-known staged version adapted by George Aiken and performed in Troy, New York in 1852, Eliza makes her great escape in scene 5, which opens with a "Snow Landscape—Music," and Eliza entering with Harry hurriedly.[9] Eliza, speaking to the audience and her son, says:

They press upon my footsteps—the river is my only hope. Heaven grant me strength to reach it, ere they overtake me! Courage, my child!—we will be free—or perish! (Rushes off, R. H.—Music continued.)

[There is a short interlude during which her pursuers discuss the chase, followed by] Scene 6.—The entire depth of stage, representing the Ohio River filled with Floating Ice.— . . . ELIZA appears, with Harry, R. H., on a cake of ice, and floats slowly across to L. H.—[as her pursuers look on].

Scene 6 closes act I with a strong curtain ending.

Typically, the scene was staged as a dazzling spectacle of whiteness. Although Eliza is already pure in the reader's eyes, the scene plays upon viewers' desire to see her escape the threat of blackness (which is sexual because, if caught, she will be sold down south and sexually exploited). Her own purity is highlighted in her successful "crossing" that keeps the base forces of blackness at bay. Surrounded by the brilliant glare of the white stage, lit brightly, according to early films, stage directions, and lithographs, she appeared in a white dress with her dark hair streaming behind her (figure 7). Given the association between whiteness and purity, it makes sense that the "mulattaroon" dresses in

7. Eliza crossing the ice, *Uncle Tom's Cabin*, woodcut, undated. Courtesy of the Huntington Library.

white without wearing any blackface (or even tawny makeup). As we have seen, this image, realized so often on Victorian stages, represents the possibility of purifying an enslaved figure.

Unlike the novel—which mentions other colors, such as the green tint of the ice and the red blood of Eliza's cut feet—the staged versions, more like the lithographs that depicted the scene, highlight the stark contrast between black and white. Martin Meisel uses the term *realization* to describe the nineteenth-century convention of *tableaux vivants* (living pictures). He makes the point that there was a close relationship between two- and three-dimensional arts, where the "same" images could be seen on stage and in prints and paintings. Most Victorian melodramas included several "realizations" in which the actors would adopt a frozen pose, many of which would have been familiar to theater audiences from pictorial representations. Thus, translations from one genre to another provided literate audiences with the pleasure of recognition and created a kind of fluidity between staged and etched or painted representations. The widely distributed promotional lithograph for an early American production of *Uncle Tom's Cabin* is therefore closely related to the staged versions of the novel. That the *tableau vivant* of "Eliza's perils on the ice" was selected so frequently for reproduction may have been connected to the desire to see purity in absolute terms—as the whiteness of white and the blackness of black.

The belief that black and white are binary oppositions, or exact opposites, is a long-standing cultural fiction. In his philosophical inquiry on the sublime and the beautiful, Edmund Burke asserts: "Black and white may soften, may blend, but they are not therefore the same. Nor when they are so softened and blended with each other or with different colors, is the power of black as black or white as white so strong as when each stands uniform and distinguished."[10] The appeal and the power, then, of this tableau and lithograph may derive from the desire to purify Eliza—to make her whiter than white.

The production of purity (for example, wholesomeness) depends on the erasure of hybridity. Ironically, purity requires hybridity understood as unstable intermixture. The pure includes the erasure of the impure other. Both the black tulip and Eliza Harris are hybrids; they appear, however, as "pure" figures. The desire for permanent, perfect purity is preferable to the permeable imperfect impurity—whether "white" or "black." The visibility of perfect whiteness (or blackness) may be merely the suppression and denial of blackness (or whiteness).

The definition of purity makes clear that it is a chimerical concept. The *Oxford English Dictionary* defines purity as

I. a. not mixed with anything else; free from admixture or adulteration; unmixed, unalloyed, often qualifying names of colours. b. not mixed with or not having in or upon it anything that defiles, corrupts, or impairs; unsullied untainted, clean. c. visibly or optically clear, spotless, stainless, clear transparent. d. intact, unbroken, perfect, entire. (There is a wide range of sense here but *lines of division cannot well be drawn among quotations, many of which unite more than one shade of meaning*). (italics added)

This definition underscores that purity as a concept-metaphor is not pure. It is defined always through negation. Moreover, the invocation of any of the terms, as seen above and in our earlier examples, denotes more than one register of meaning. Words such as "spotless," "unsul-lied," and "unbroken" can be both literal and figurative. So too, the feminization is inherent in the very terms used to define purity itself, since many of these words correspond to aspects of feminine sexuality related to virginity. The use of "shades of meaning" quoted in the dictio-nary definition refers to the multiple registers connoted by the phrase. Thus, an object or a person can be "unsullied." Also, the words taint, adulterate, alloyed, mixed, and broken inform purity, pointing to the way in which the definitions themselves are impure.

Paradoxically, purity has its roots in hybridity. In a discussion of Vic-torian culture, Robert Young asserts:

Hybridity makes difference into sameness, and sameness into difference, but in a way that makes the same no longer the same and the different no longer simply different. In that sense, it operates according to the form of logic that Derrida isolates in the term "brisure," a breaking and a joining at the same time, in the same place: difference and sameness in an appar-ently impossible simultaneity.[11]

Purity and hybridity are therefore mutually constitutive rather than mutually exclusive. Pure purity is an impossibility.

Petrifying Purity

When shown in London at the Great Exhibition of 1851, the sculpture of *The Greek Slave* by the American Hiram Powers generated unequivo-cal praise. Observers hailed the idealized figure of the female slave as the pinnacle of female purity (figure 8). Displayed on a pedestal in the main court pavilion, the statue received as much adulation as it had previously when, in the 1840s, it had been exhibited in twelve cities throughout America.[12]

Powers wrote a narrative to accompany the statue that stressed how the Greek slave, depicted in a moment of contemplation as she is about to be sold to a Turkish harem, is the essence of demure femininity. The sculptor intended his nude to represent a chaste Christian girl, awaiting her fate with dignity. She was meant to portray the triumph of purity over adversity. In Powers' words, the statue was "a pure abstract human

8. *The Greek Slave,* Hiram Powers, 1847. Courtesy of the New York Public Library.

form tempered with chaste expression and attitude . . . calculated to awaken the highest emotions of the soul for the pure and beautiful."[13]

Numerous critics testified to the success of Powers's "intentions." Exhibited *un*painted, the sculpture was revered and described by Elizabeth Barrett Browning as "passionless perfection . . . [that would strike the viewer with] thunders of white silence."[14] Suturing, reifying, setting in stone the analogies between whiteness and perfect hardness, critics in and of Victorian culture commented on the connections between whiteness, beauty, and purity.

In the nineteenth century, marblish parian (imitation marble) casts appeared in numerous middle-class homes. Reproductions (of reproductions, it turns out) of Greek sculpture abounded in museums, public parks, and even on stage. More important, the values attributed to sculpture, and the way in which the debate about its inherent properties was cast, tell us much about pure forms and their link to moral and ethical issues about purity. So too, the color white was related to the "material" in an equation that reads as follows: White = pure = solid = cold = complete = perfect. These concept-metaphors were equated and understood as being not only analogous, but synonymous. In Victorian discourse, almost invariably, one term connotes and signifies the others. Thus, when most Victorians—such as Dickens, George Eliot, and anonymous journalists (with the notable exception of John Ruskin)—spoke about the beauty of sculpture—of its pure white forms, smooth unblemished surfaces, and unchanging solid structure—they spoke simultaneously of an idealized form of white beauty that complimented their racialized nationalistic ethos. Henry James described Powers's marmorean figure, as "so undressed, yet so refined, even so pensive, in sugarwhite alabaster, exposed under little glass covers in such American homes as could bring themselves to think such things right."[15]

An exception to the overwhelming reverence the statue evoked in both America and England was made by an anonymous illustrator for *Punch* magazine. A satirical engraving of Powers's masterpiece appeared with the following title: "The Virginian Slave, Intended as a Companion to Powers' 'Greek Slave'" (figure 9). In contrast to the idealized classical perfection noted so often by viewers of Powers's sculpture, the *Punch* cartoon transforms the pure Greek slave into a debased Virginia slave. This vulgar translation drew on several different kinds of unstable tensions inherent in the "original" version (original appears in quotations because Powers sculpted six versions of the piece).

The sculpture depicts the slave with her eyes cast down demurely. In the etching, her eyes confront the viewer; her wide-eyed, almost caricatured gaze suggests the stereotyped image deployed by minstrel performers. Indeed, the latter is a minstrelized version of the former. Moreover, the explicit references to an American state—the phrase "e pluribus unum" and an American flag accompany the *Punch* version—debase and defile because these details make the image geo-

9. "The Virginian Slave," *Punch*, 1851. Courtesy of the Huntington Library.

graphically specific, contemporary rather than universal and transcendent. The translation of the Greek (English) slave into the Virginian (American) slave exemplifies how some English viewers were able to identify themselves as English and white in contrast to the Americans, who were "black."

Whereas the Greek slave was intended to and indeed did appear as the essence of purity, the Virginia slave lampooned such high cultural sentiment by disrobing its allegory to reveal its mundane references. Where one is white, the other is black; where one is three-dimensional, the other is two-dimensional; one exalted, the other debased; one emblematic of England (by virtue of being Greek), the other emblematic of America (by being black); one redolent of the past, the other rooted in the present; one marmoreal, the other ephemeral; one nude, the other naked; one ideal, the other real; one pure, the other impure.

These representations demonstrate the difficulty of stabilizing what turn out to be unstable forms. In looking carefully at the language used to describe this figure, there is an almost blind praise for pure, *white* figures. The discussion of the pure and perfect whiteness of the Greek slave was, to judge by contemporary *reviews*, one of the artwork's salient features. This is notable because, in a broader context, we see the development of a discourse that exalted not only purity, but "white" purity in particular. The evangelical Christian call for the "white life for two" (as in chastity for men and women, man and wife) exemplifies the blurring of these ideas.

Despite Powers's efforts to transform the impure situation into a pure one, he was not successful, as the *Punch* cartoon illustrates. Some viewers minstrelized his text by filling in the blank with what they imagined were erased aspects of the slave's story. In their eyes, she was salacious. They may have been aware of the fact that the invocation of a slave could never distance itself from its illicit thematics or its black, sexually licentious trace. These readers defiled Powers's pure figure with prurient gazes.

The firm conviction that led many Victorian viewers to associate whiteness with purity is demonstrated in the reception of another sculpture, John Gibson's *Tinted Venus* (figure 10), which was also shown at the Great Exhibition. Like actual Greek sculpture, Gibson's statue was painted and, thus, appeared as the color of "flesh." Many read the authentic painted surface of the sculpture as vulgar and vile. The sculpture invoked invective. Its flesh tones intoned indecent sexuality. Its color conveyed concupiscence. This is ironic because if purity and authenticity are related, many Victorian viewers, in their reverence for Greece, selected to worship a "false" representation of the antique. In a letter dated January 15, 1874, playwright Henrik Ibsen wrote to British writer Edmund Gosse, "We are no longer living in the age of Shakespeare. Among sculptors there is already talk of painting statues in the natural colors. Much can be said both for and against this. I have no desire to see the Venus of Milo painted, but I would rather see the head

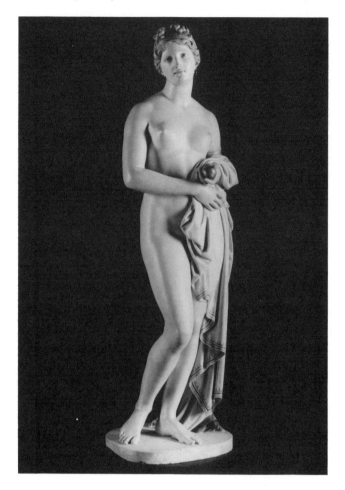

10. *Tinted Venus*, John Gibson, 1851. Courtesy of the National Museums and Galleries on Merseyside, Walker Art Gallery, Liverpool.

of a Negro executed in black than in white marble. Speaking gener-ally, the style must conform to the degree of ideality which pervades the representation."[16] This statement concurs with my own reading of the desire to see "blacks" as black, and "whites" as white. Like English-ness itself, the tradition of all-white (unpainted) Greek sculpture was a modern British invention.

The debate about an original versus copies, rooted in Platonic dialogues, is related to this discussion. In an age already replete with reproductions of ruined pasts (epitomized by the eighteenth-century construction of ancient ruins) and with advanced technology capable of mass-producing copies of antique statuary, the Victorian conception of the classical past was compromised. The concern generated by the difficulty of recovering a pure past is expressed in Walter Benjamin's essay, "The Work of Art in the Age of Mechanical Reproduction," where he notes: "Even the most perfect reproduction of a work of art is lacking in one element: its presence in time and space, its unique existence at the place where it happens to be. This unique existence of the work of art determined the history to which it was subject throughout the time of its existence. . . . The presence of the original is the prerequisite to the concept of authenticity."[17]

Powers's use of marble sculpture, along with the cleansing trope of classicism as a way of effacing the material history of his subject, reflects the impossibility of creating absolute purity. As Benjamin's essay makes clear, a pure recovery of the past is impossible. Even the so-called original Greek statues were often copies of either other Greek statues or Roman reproductions of Greek statues. The ersatz is the only possible authentic form because a pure past is impossible. Thus, as Richard Jenkyns explains:

The experience of seeing the Elgin Marbles and other authentic Greek statuary—the Venus de Milo, the Winged Victory of Samothrace, the sculptures of the Delphi and Olympia were all 19th century discoveries—gradually taught the world that the antique statues which it had most revered were reproductions, and sometimes not very good reproductions. Moreover, most people's knowledge of art before the 19th century had been a knowledge not of originals but of casts, copies, and engravings. The camera and the railway changed all this . . . bringing more accurate reproductions into their drawing rooms . . . [and creating] a cult of the original.[18]

Dying the Cast

Faced with anything foreign, the Established Order knows only two types of behaviour, which are both mutilating: either to acknowledge it as a Punch and Judy show, or to defuse it as a pure reflection of the West.
—Roland Barthes

On Thursday, May 12, 1853, the *Lucas Guardian and Hitchin Advertiser*, a local paper published in the county of Hertford, England, reviewed a production of *Uncle Tom's Cabin*.[19] This minstrel version of the narrative, produced in the provinces of England one year after the book's publication, reflects what was, in fact, a well-established theatrical tradition. In the early 1820s, the English actor Charles Matthews may have been the first white man to portray an American black. Matthews's one-man show, in which he blacked up and played characters such as a New York black sailor, preceded the large-scale blackface extravaganzas associated with this unique American art form whose origins were nevertheless tied to English blackface minstrelsy. English novelists Dickens and Thackeray observed early minstrel performers in America (indeed, their eyewitness accounts serve as authoritative claims in virtually every recent study of minstrelsy), and the most famous troupes toured both countries.[20] Townsend Walsh, Boucicault's biographer, asserted that "although of American origin the minstrel business was brought to its highest state of perfection in this country [England]."[21] Blackface minstrelsy is, then, another exemplary instance of circum-Atlantic traffic.[22]

The entertainment at Hitchin's town hall received a review testifying to the popularity of these shows. The review states:

Everybody who has nothing to do, or can speak in public or sing a little is now trading upon Mrs. Stowe's capital and travelling about the country with some Uncle Tom entertainment prostituting Mrs. Stowe's great work to the purposes of the dissolving view, the song and the dialogue. We are not exempt here since Crummell the black we have had last Monday Mr. Grant (?) who had been in America and gave an account of the horrors of slavery with the additional horrors of bad dissolving views. He kept open two nights and had very few spectators and very few of them respectable. This last Monday and Tuesday we have had the J. E. Carpenter with

a grand musico, dramatico entertainment, also with the worst possible dissolving views. We had been given to expect that the singing would repay
us for going. Mr. Carpenter having some reputation as a composer and the
name of Miss Jolly being promising but at half past eight we found ourselves in the large room with about 40 other dupes listening to a kind of
synopsis of Mrs. Stowe's great book given in a vulgar familiar tune inter-
spersed with songs by the too Miss Jolly to whom ("none but themselves
can be their parallel") their singing was very loud and jarring and their
appearance most masculine. The piano was played with very little taste or
judgement and in so loud a key as completely to destroy the effect of the
singing. We left long before the entertainment terminated more prejudice
than ever against the Uncle Tom pirates.[23]

The language used to describe this "vulgar" translation of Stowe's
moral narrative is reminiscent of our earlier discussion of debased
copies. The reviewer, expecting a high-toned production befitting
Stowe's "great work," shudders at the tasteless "musico, dramatico entertainment" that "prostitutes" Uncle Tom's Cabin. Feeling that he has
been cheated, he leaves the performance before its conclusion, noting
that such "Uncle Tom pirates" did more harm than good for the noble
cause of abolition. This reviewer, like Stowe herself, objected to staged
versions of the novel that vulgarized what were meant to be high-
minded, sentimental portrayals.[24] In contrast, the majority of the British
play-going population must have been enchanted with the "Tomitudes,"
given that there were numerous theatrical productions of Uncle Tom's
Cabin in England.

In the six-month period between September 1852 and February 1853,
the Lord Chamberlain, who censored plays, approved more than fifteen
productions based on the novel.[25] One of the first productions took
place on September 8, 1852, at the Standard Theatre. Called Uncle Tom's
Cabin or the Negro Slave: A Drama in Two Acts,[26] it was a highbrow version in which "black" Tom was portrayed sympathetically (although he
spoke lower-class cockney English) and the actors who played "white"
Eliza and George spoke upper-class "Oxford" English. This respectful
version was relatively faithful to the novel, especially when compared
to a minstrel version of the play called Uncle Tom's Cabin: A Nigger
Drama in Two Acts,[27] presented at the Royal Pavilion Theatre just one

month later. This latter version, penned by George Pitt, began like the novel, with Eliza being offered for sale. In act I, however, the minstrel version took liberties with the text by introducing a new, specifically English character named Billy Bombast.

In act I, scene 1, Billy Bombast is brought on stage by Sam, a slave on the Shelley plantation. In the scene, Sam exclaims:

Mafaa somesing so berry funny here is a white man turned into a nigger come to beg some yams and bread . . .

Mr. Shelley: Do you call it funny when a man is in distress? Bring him in so that I may see if he is an imposter.

[Sam brings in Billy Bombast]

Billy: I'm Billy Bombast from Whitechapel London costermonger and hearing you was by birth an Englishman I just called in for grub . . .

Mr. Shelley: Are you not sorry for having come on such a wild goose chase?

Billy: Had I stayed in the old country I should have starved there in another month.

[Mr. Shelley agrees to find him a post on the plantation]

Then Sam asks Billy "Is that the natural colour of your cheeks, Massa?" to which Billy replies: "No, not exactly, my wife was a black nigger taken away by the chickchaws.

Sam: She was a blackbird taken by Jack Daws?

Billy: She didn't like my color so she rubbed my face over with charcoal and grease and then scrubbed me til at last I [blackened?]

[He sings an ad lib]

This excerpt is typical of English minstrels in that it makes use of a white English character who is blackened, puns excessively, and portrays miscegenation in a comic light. Billy functions most obviously as a figure of identification for British audiences, who were often working-class men from neighborhoods such as Whitechapel.[28] The script (however it may have been performed on stage) connects Billy with both Sam, the black American slave, and, more importantly with his white American master, Mr. Shelley, suggesting the formation of an international, cross-class, white brotherhood.

Billy's status shifts throughout the scene. He is introduced as "a white man turned into a nigger." The fact that Sam utters this line at all reminds the audience that this is an inauthentic production in which white people are playing black people. The visual ambiguity that, like a palimpsest, reads blackness onto whiteness, is duplicated in the performance itself. Sam is unsure as to the reception Billy will receive from Master Shelley. Interestingly, Shelley responds to Billy in a most humane fashion, calling him a man "in distress," recognizing his Englishness, and welcoming him onto the plantation (perhaps he smells the blood of a fellow Englishman beneath the mask of blackness). Noting the affinity between his master and Billy, Sam is quick to address the former "nigger" as "Massa." Still, there is confusion about Billy's character. When questioned about why his skin is black, Billy responds ambiguously by explaining that he has been blackened by his wife with "charcoal and grease." Moreover, by using the phrase "not exactly," he leaves his exact coloring open to revision.

The reference to his black skin is also linked to the fact that he has a black American wife. As we have seen, color is relative—often related to one's proximity to difference. Where the mulattaroons were whitened by the blood of their fathers, Billy is blackened by the hand of his wife. The direct expression of the desire to turn white men into black men (almost always voiced by a black female character) is a typical ploy of British minstrelsy.

Perhaps one motivation for white men's blackface performances was the desire to defuse the presumed sexual prowess of black men, whom the black female characters purportedly wished them to become. Such portrayals also imply that miscegenation was undesirable: the shows invariably pair "black" women with "black" men (although both were white men). Other minstrel shows had the performer remove his black mask in order to win a white woman—thus aligning white with white. This latter move is suggested at the end of Billy Bombast's introduction: since his wife has been taken away by the Chickchaws—a Native American tribe—he may now be free to become white when he assumes his position on the plantation. The mask of blackness, then, allows Billy to reproduce himself as white. Indeed, this is one of the main uses of blackface minstrelsy.

Blackface minstrelsy supported Anglo-American white supremacy. The suturing of whiteness and Englishness through minstrel performance sought to achieve the effect of difference between what might have been the potential sameness of black and white. Becoming English required one to be white and one is white if one is not black. This kind of commonsense logic defines whiteness as not-blackness through exaggerated, elaborate investments—of dress, time, and money. Such performances are motivated by both dread of and desire for a paradoxically material and immaterial blackness that would somehow ground whiteness.

Another minstrel version of Stowe's book, titled "Uncle Tom's Crib, or Nigger Life in London," produced in October 1852 at the Strand Theatre, has the black female character Dinah tell her suitor Jim that she prefers blackness.[29] When Dinah asks Jim to declare his love, he answers: "I swear by the moon that I lub you," to which Dinah retorts: "Don't swear by the moon—de white faced moon dat changes ebery month! I hate white faces dey're always wanting washing dey change color so. . . . Don't swear at all [but if you must at least] swear by your own full face dat's warranted fast color good deep black neber turns pale and doesn't show dirt." Thus, Jim swears to love her, "the fairest and blackest of her sex." This scene idealizes "fast, good, unchanging blackness"—or pure blackness. It seems to argue against impure situations of layered complexity, of depth and interiority. As such, it serves Michael Pickering's reading of the practice in which he notes that

the pejorative senses of deceit and falseness which usually colour attitudes to masks and masking are not generally applicable to minstrelsy, and this may be explained by the fact that the blackface persona encouraged an emotional response to stereotyped characteristics rather than to psychologically rounded characters, and did not require a consistently upheld suspension of disbelief in the activity of impersonation."[30]

Thus did white men control blacks by playing them, miming difference in order to make it their own. As Roland Barthes theorizes,

"unable to imagine the Other . . . he comes face to face with him, he blinds himself, ignores or denies him, or else transforms him into himself . . . [A]ny otherness is reduced to sameness. The spectacle . . . where the other threatens to appear in full view, become[s] a mirror. This is because the Other is a scandal which threatens his essence. . . . Sometimes—rarely—the Other is revealed as irreducible: not because of a sudden scruple, but because *common sense* rebels: a man does not have a white skin, but a black one. . . . How can one assimilate the Negro . . . ? There is here a figure for emergencies: exoticism. The Other becomes a pure object, a spectacle, a clown. (p. 152)[31]

Barthes's suggestive reading relates to minstrelsy. The first strategy he describes for diffusing the threat of difference requires the white man to self-reflexively "blind himself" to blackness. The second strategy, perhaps the essence of minstrelsy, is to erase the distance by pretending to become the other. A third strategy, reserved for "emergencies," allows one to recognize forms of black power—"a man has a black skin"— if only to make this difference into a "pure object." With this strategy, the other is stereotyped safely as an exotic primitive whom the civilized man may take delight in denigrating.

In the relentlessly classed society of England, wealth could at times "cancel" racial subjugation, especially for the non-Irish. The depiction of elite black figures was put up in order to reaffirm lower-class white figures. As we saw with Miss Swartz, upper-class blacks turn out to be less valuable than those with white skin, even if lower-class. From Dickens's biting critique of Mrs. Jellby—who cared more for the poor blacks in Africa than for her own family at home—to the lower-middle-class whites—who resented upper-class English sympathy for and involvement in abolitionism—English men of means who spared charity for "those dear bracks" [sic] (a play by minstrel writer William Brough) were castigated by the lower-class English poor, who resented having to compete with "foreign" causes. In bids to help "little England," blackface minstrelsy was used to consolidate alliances that privileged white racial features over class differences. In a strategy not unlike the turmoil that erupted in the United States over the relationship between white feminists' bid for suffrage and the granting of the vote first to black men, poor whites and those who argued their cause, such as Thomas Carlyle and even Dickens, attempted to "use" racial tropes as a means to consolidate a racialized idea of class power.

A cartoon from the weekly journal, The Lantern Weekly, illustrates this idea. It shows a poor London family "blacking up" (figure 11) in order to simulate the numerous roving "negro" street minstrels, few of whom were actually black, who begged with greater success than did those with white faces. The caption for the image has the "Head of the Family" state: "THAT'S RIGHT, POLLY! GIVE HIM A LICK OF PAINT

11. "The Black Dodge," *The Lantern Weekly*, circa 1853.

—THERE AIN'T NO COLOR GOES DOWN NOW BUT UNCLE TOM'S. NIGGERS [*sic*] IS UP — WHITES IS DOWN!" Beyond the convoluted inversions of up and down as signs of value, such tensions between class and race are apparent even in abolitionist discourse, which often analogized class and race, and therefore, made "blacks" stand-ins for the more pressing national concern of *white* slavery. Drawing on the tradition established in the slave narratives, the scene compares the status of working-class whites in England with black slaves in the Americas. White authors, such as Thomas Carlyle, in his racist tract, *Occasional Discourse on the Nigger Question*, argued that the "white slaves" of England lived in worse conditions than the "Black[s] rich in pumpkin, imbibing saccharine juices, and much at ease."[32] By contrast, black authors, such as Mary Prince and Harriet Jacobs, tended to note the freedoms accorded British workers in the same period. Such comparisons of "white" and "black" slavery, common to both British minstrels and slave narratives, served very different, indeed opposing, causes, yet used the same discourse.

In other words, this desire to read black as white was an impulse not only in the minstrel tradition but also in abolitionist discourse. Although minstrel performers and abolitionists had different goals, at times they employed the same language to describe blacks. Indeed, "without minstrelsy, *Uncle Tom's Cabin* would not have existed,"[33] and without *Uncle Tom's Cabin*, minstrelsy in Britain would not have flourished. The ability to erase the black slave features present in Stowe's narrative is mentioned explicitly in the following article about the effect of *Uncle Tom's Cabin* in Europe.

The color of the heroes of the tale was soon lost sight of by the European reader. His passions are stirred by the wrongs of injured individuals—men like himself. . . . All he notes is the oppression they are painted as suffering. Without any extraordinary effort of imagination he draws a plausible analogy between the conditions of his own fellow-countrymen and that of the Uncle Toms of romance.[34]

Here we see the strategy outlined by Barthes, in which blackness becomes white in order to be palatable.

Similarly, in 1852, the anonymous author of *Uncle Tom in England; or, A Proof That Black's White,* a novel that "may be looked upon as an Echo, or Sequel to 'Uncle Tom,'" elects to extend the abandoned or abbreviated story of Susan, Emmeline, and Cassy, who are each light-skinned mulattaroon characters.[35] This demonstrates that the greatest sympathy was reserved for the whitest characters in the book. As the preface explains, "After Emmeline's escape with Cassy, Mrs. Stowe dismisses her with a few words, in which she is stated to have become the wife of a mate of a vessel. The Author of *Uncle Tom in England* could not help feeling that something more was needed, from the interest centered in her character, than that she should be *mated* off in this way" (p. iii; italics in original).

An abolitionist tract par excellence, this novel—which in true social protest form, concludes with "actual" documents, speeches, and testaments to the horrors of slavery—also suggests a rationale for the English entanglement with America. The special "relationship" is articulated in racialist terms, and sets up the dynamic referenced earlier of paternalism, Anglo-American racial nationalism, and the moral superiority of the English. In one speech printed at the end of the volume, a passionate abolitionist intones:

If the good works of Englishmen may excite emulation in the breast of their brethren of France, Germany, and Spain, how much greater will be their influence upon a people speaking the same tongue, having the same common origin, and united to each other by the links of the most inseparable kind? . . . England, perhaps, more than any other nation owes a duty to America and certainly no other people can perform such a duty so effectively as the English. We owe it, then, as a duty to God and to man, and to the Americans especially, to speak out against the dreadful oppression of which the black slave is a victim. (p. 210)

The "white man's burden" expressed so clearly in this quotation also signals the boundaries of whiteness that stretch across the Atlantic to form the roots of an international white brotherhood.

The obsession with class and race in British minstrel shows traded on the well-known melodramatic convention of the marriage plot. Where some of the earlier narratives dealt with the difficulties of marrying the black daughter, exemplified by Miss Swartz and Zoe Peyton, minstrels increasingly concerned themselves with the problems of marrying white daughters across race and class. This is the central point of the 1883 production of a minstrel play called, *Flip, Flap, Flop.*[36] Like numerous blackface shows, the piece presents black swells, fops, and dandies attempting to woo white English daughters, often at their cash-strapped father's request (as we saw in *Vanity Fair*). This pub drama reveals how complicated issues of race and class result in the valorization of whiteness as a racial identity that can have primacy over class differences.

Flip, Flap, Flop tells the story of a white pub owner who wishes to marry his niece and surrogate daughter, Susie, who is also white, to a wealthy black man. Susie is already in love with a boy of her own class standing and race, a strapping young white man, ironically named Tom.

In an effort to win Susie's hand, Tom devises a plan to appear as the black suitor preferred by Susie's uncle. Through a madcap comedy of errors (in fact, the byzantine plot is nearly identical to Oscar Wilde's *The Importance of Being Earnest*), Tom's impersonation succeeds, and he is granted permission to marry Susie. Indeed, when his ruse is revealed, the uncle exclaims, "Thank heaven he is White!" This final statement confirms the way in which whiteness is valued over class mobility and, thus, underscores the reaffirmation of whiteness that not only characterized British blackface minstrelsy but also was its raison d'être.

Of course, as I have argued throughout this book, the performance of "race" is also always a *gendered* performance. The practice of blackface cross-dressing—white males impersonating black women—in minstrel shows may also be read as a form of miscegenation. Taking on the body of a "black" woman," the white man unites with or perhaps expresses his own repression of blackened femininity.[37] So too, like the Pygmalion story, such representations reveal the latent desire to create and control differences. Such impersonations are complex: they expose the multiple and contradictory readings of blackness and femininity that circulated in Victorian culture.

Blackface cross-dressing brings into play a multiplicity of illicit crossings. The account of the black female slave, Ellen Craft, who actually escaped dressed as a white master, has been discussed in William Craft's narrative, *Running a Thousand Miles for Freedom*, as well as in William Wells Brown's fictional *Clotel, or the President's Daughter*.[38] While Craft literally gained her freedom through white male impersonation, white male minstrels gained a figurative freedom through their impersonations of black women. The practice of white men pretending to be black women on stage served complicated desires for misogyny, sexual freedom, and racist ridicule. Such performances, in a sense, related the supposedly distant categories of the white man and the black woman. Indeed, this close proximity, even though it was the very vehicle to produce distance and difference, created the possibility of their approximating one another.

In an effort to control black women, and the threat of both sameness and difference, the performances of some white men as black women distanced through proximity. So too, in a homoerotic context, such performances may have made another white male body "safe" for sexual play, as Eric Lott has discussed. When representations of blackness, femininity, whiteness, and masculinity collide, the white man playing the part of the black woman comes face-to-face with the forbidden. The evocation of one category, in other words, carries with it the other, because blackness, femininity, and illicit sexuality are related in this imaginary schema.

While there is certainly a pleasure in disguise and disidentification apparent in these cross-dressed, cross-racial performances, there may also be a more fundamental motive for this phenomenon. Indeed, it can be argued that these performances served to define and produce white masculinity. Consider, for instance, Paul de Man's discussion of Ferdinand de Saussure's analysis of the *hypogram*, a Greek term meaning, "to underscore by means of makeup the features of the face" (*souligner au moyen du fard les traits du visage*). De Man writes:

This usage is not incompatible with his own adoption of the term which by analogy underscores a name, a word, by trying to repeat its syllables and thus giving it another artificial mode of being added . . . to the original mode of the word. Hypographein is close in this meaning to prosopon, mask or face. Hypogram is close to prosopopeia, the trope of apostrophe . . . provided one assumes . . . the stable existence of an original face that can be embellished or supplemented by the hypogram. But prosopon-poeine means to give a face and therefore implies that the original face can be missing or nonexistent. The trope which coins a name for a still unnamed entity which gives face to the faceless is . . . catachresis.[39]

This idea is expressed in the black vernacular phrase, "giving face," which means to cast one's face as a mask.

The disruptive relationship between blackness and whiteness enacted in minstrelsy subjects the white and the black in different ways. The white man becomes a subject through the subjection (as in ridicule and subjugation) of the black. By giving a face to what is an abstracted, objectified, and actually absent black female, the white male creates and expropriates the black other, thereby reproducing and supplementing white male identity. Where neither existed previously, the performance creates both figures in an asymmetrical play of power. Whereas black women are absent presences (they are seen, but never present), white men are present absences (they are present, but not seen as themselves).

In the minstrel show, white men "make up" (invent) black women by putting them on and, simultaneously, white men make up the category white men by putting black women on. This performance works in two directions at once. By putting on and making up, creatively deforming the differences between black and white, the source of the categories of pure white and pure black is revealed to be the same: a projection of white male desire. The process of differentiation is everywhere displayed in the performative practice of minstrelsy.

By imitating black people, pretending to copy black forms, "white" practitioners mixed up the difference between imitation and original and invented the blackness they copied. For their intents and purposes, the blacks they performed were the (un)real thing.[40] Indeed, the entire practice of blackface minstrelsy as it was performed in England had everything to do with the construction of Englishness as white. Taking on the guise of another was a sure way to discover oneself or at least to attempt to define through negation what one might be if not who one was.

As a means of distancing and controlling, "white" men became "black" women, white played black, and white played white in a triple play whose sameness of "before and after," within and without, in front of and behind the mask was, in fact, mediated by the show of blackness. The exaggerated difference of the temporary turn might have been a primary pleasure of blackface shows. In order to "become white," one consciously became black in a gesture of becoming, so that retroactively, one will have been what one was or should be. It is, then, the ritual of blackening up and whiting out that becomes the arbitrary arbiter of difference. The performance of black femininity momentarily fills in the nothing that was the before of white masculinity. As Barbara Johnson notes, "Difference is not engendered in the space between identities; it is what makes all totalization of the identity of a self or the meaning of a text impossible."[41] Pretending, putting on, and producing/performing the play of differences acknowledges and recognizes the power of pretense (pre-tense). After the fun has been displayed, the natural returns with a greater force as *naturalized* whiteness, which is contrasted to the now unnatural performance of blackness.

The tradition of masking one's face was transformed when British performers actually began putting on "white" face. Female performers went beyond the use of face makeup and began to dye their hair blond. "Ada with the Golden Hair," a popular, exclusively English minstrel song from 1868, recorded this practice.

Oh! Ada, do you love me?
Tell me if you love me.
She said, I love you;
Which made me feel so queer,
As we walked in Brompton Square.
Her eyes so blue, her feet so small,
I thought I should die right there.
She took my arm—oh, yes she did,
Ada with the golden hair.

One day I called on Ada,
My sweet little Ada,
Dear little Ada.
Her Mamma told me she was dying;
I thought I should drop right there.
I rushed up-stairs—Ada screamed out,
"Just come in if you dare."
"Are you dying, my dear?"
"Why you silly," she said,
"I'm only *dye*—ing my hair![42]

This explicitly British minstrel song by G. W. Moore of Moore and Burgess, minstrels who performed for Queen Victoria, furthers our discussion of the problematics of the impossible appearance of pure blackness and pure whiteness. Beginning in the 1860s, several white men played black women as "beautiful" blond women. In America, after the Civil War, the performer known as the "Only Leon" was said to set the fashion for New York society matrons with his consummate style. Playing one of the increasingly ubiquitous "yella gal" parts, Leon set a precedent for rarified forms of beauty. In Britain, however, in the early part of the century, the ideal Victorian heroine often had dark hair, as did Jeanie Deans in Sir Walter Scott's novel *The Heart of Midlothian*.[43] Minstrelsy helped to usher in the cult of the blond, which explains some of the significance of Ada dying her hair.

12. *Mr. G.W. Moore to Mr. F. Burgess:* "I dare say they understand most things in France, Fred, but I'm blowed if nigger minstrelsy is one of 'em!", Alfred Bryan, *Punch*, circa 1896.

Hair has long been considered a signifier of race, class, and gender, as well as a marker of sexuality. In European culture, blond hair in particular came to be associated with forms of idealized femininity. The so-called "style/politics" of hair, to quote Kobena Mercer, makes it an important marker of cultural differences. Nineteenth-century commentary about "the blond," the fair, and the golden haired tended to associate blondness with both purity and power. According to James Snead, "The Blonde Venus has . . . usurped not merely black vigor, but male privilege. [Her] mythification elevates [her] over white men as well as black women, while borrowing crucial characteristics of each. Female blondness integrates categories of blackness and maleness."[44] Snead's provocative reading of Marlene Dietrich's performance in Josef Von Sternberg's film, *Blonde Venus,* as the apotheosis of the blond seems to have a precedent, if not a corollary, in the performances of the minstrel troupe known as the British Blondes.

The roots of the clichéd concept of the blond, an Anglo-American invention, reach back to the nineteenth century into the circum-Atlantic vortex in which whiteness covers over blackness.[45] It is a truism that the best blondes were "originally" brunettes.[46] Like the Victorian fashion of whitening one's skin—an effect achieved by the ingestion of arsenic and/or the application of powder—blond beauty was made-up—a fabrication of British culture. The use of the blond wigs, and the dying of one's hair, expresses a need to artificially construct whiteness in an effort to emphasize difference—to make the whiteness of whiteness hypervisible.[47]

Lydia Thompson, the founder of the burlesque troupe known as the British Blondes, had each of the shapely performers in her company peroxide her hair.[48] The old association of blondness with innocence now became both a way of legitimizing the new sensuality and of heightening it by combining both purity and voluptuousness . . . [indeed, the British Blondes's hair was described as] golden clouds which envelop all imperfections" (p. 124). This reading resonates with a comment made in 1899 by German gynecologist Carl Heinrich Stratz, in which he elaborated the aesthetic appeal of light hair: it compliments the soft contours of a woman's body.[49]

The erotic charge of the British Blondes derived from the traces of blackness in their hair, the vestiges of the minstrel show in their burlesque, and their assumption of masculine power. "To justify wearing tights, the women all played male roles [often they were kings, vagabonds, soldiers, pirates] . . . [and] they spoke with impeccable upper-class British accents."[50] At once hyper-feminine and erotic in their attempts to play with modes of masculinity, the astounding success of the British Blondes suggests the ironic purification and idealization of exaggerated whiteness; however, such displays of hyper-white femininity were simultaneously impure because they were also "black" and "masculine." Paradoxically, their effort to perform paradigmatic whiteness failed: to William Dean Howells and others the Blondes were "creatures of an alien sex."[51] They, too, evoked comparison with grisettes, soubrettes, and other figures of the demimonde.[52] In short, they were read as exotic, erotic, and "black."

Liquifying Impurities

Alexandre Dumas fils's novel *La Dame aux Camellias* was written in France, performed as a melodrama in England and France (with a blond actress in the lead), and minstrelized in America.[53] The mixed-race author—the son of Dumas père, who wrote *The Black Tulip*—also wrote the play based on the novel, called *Camille*.[54] *La Dame aux Camellias* is the story of a prostitute, Marguerite Gauthier, who falls in love with one of her patrons, Armand Duval, who loves her in return. When Armand proposes to Marguerite, she rejects him because Armand's father objects to their union. In sacrificing herself for Armand, Marguerite becomes a tragic heroine. Adding to the pathos of this tale is the fact that Marguerite is dying of consumption. Her body is diseased. Marguerite represents the legions of fallen women whose tainted moral character is redeemed through death. So too, the story dramatizes the idea that the state of one's body bespeaks one's actions. The descriptions of her physiognomy paint her as an unstable, hybrid figure.

Dumas's novel, *La Dame aux Camellias*, discusses the danger of the hybrid woman. She is hybridized because she is simultaneously pure (she shares a pure love with Armand) and debased (she is a prostitute). The descriptions of Marguerite in the text are contradictory— she is elegant and diseased (as well as deceased), in a state of dying throughout. Indeed, in an 1897 edition of the novel, the first illustration is of a collapsing Marguerite, followed by a written description of her great beauty and, finally, an etching of her being exhumed.[55] Dumas describes this scene with sensuous detail, noting that as the coffin was opened, "a tainted odor exhaled from it, notwithstanding the aromatic herbs with which it was spread."[56] Camellias, of course, were used to mask the scent of death and decay. Thus, Marguerite's connection to the flower, referenced in the title, signifies not only her fleeting beauty, but also her dying. The associations between femininity, sex, and death in Western culture are long-standing.

Marguerite's "rose and white complexion" is visible even in death. She carries white or red camellias to the opera to signify when she is menstruating (and perhaps available). This iconography of the fallen woman is ubiquitous. She is a tainted thing to be discarded; and yet, she is also a thing of beauty to be gazed on. Marguerite is aware of the fact that women such as herself stand first in [men's] self-esteem and last in their esteem. Thus, when she tells Armand, "I feel that you love me for myself and not for yourself while all the others have only loved me for themselves" (p. 113), she questions the relationship between possessor and possession. She is a character who demands "recognition."

An early description of Marguerite confounds the evidence of the art/nature dichotomy. "It was impossible to behold beauty more captivating than Marguerite's. . . . Her face, a marvel, was the object of most fastidious attentions. . . . [Her] mother has surely made it so" (p. 8). The choice of the word "made" here resonates with our earlier discussion of giving face. The narrator asks the reader to "place two dark eyes beneath her brows so cleanly arched that they might have been painted on" (p. 16). Dumas commands the reader to *create* and to actively envision Marguerite, "her jet-black hair, naturally or artfully waved . . . her ears hung with diamonds worth four or five thousand francs" (p. 16).[57] The descriptions of her hair are ambiguous: is it naturally or artfully waved? So too, is her beauty "natural" or the result of artifice? Etymologically, to *prostitute* means to put forth in public; as such, Marguerite's ostentatious display of her wealth adds to and expresses her own expensive charms.

The first scene describes the manner in which potential "buyers" of Marguerite's estate, who file into her apartment after her funeral, "look for traces of the courtesan's life. Unfortunately the mystery had vanished with the goddess" (p. 3). Her well-stocked vanity is a major focus of the public sale taking place in her apartment. The viewers in the scene attempt to read Marguerite's deviant lifestyle from her "things." Marguerite's absence from the text is actually a present absence. Her actual body is missing (until it is described in the second chapter), but her things are present. And what is Marguerite (a prostitute) but a thing? The text states, in fact, that "nothing was lacking" in her apartment. Among the buyers are several "virtuous wives," ladies who are permitted to "penetrate even into the bedchamber of the courtesan [because] . . . death had purified the air of this splendid cloaca" (p. 5).[58] Although technically, Marguerite has died, the order of the text has the odd effect of "bringing her back to life." The first description of

Marguerite appears in the form of a blazon, in which she is complimented for her ability to cover up nature's flaws with her clothes. In
this regard, she resembles the Victorian actresses who used disguises to
change themselves and to stress the fact that women's bodies are like
malleable viscous material that cannot be completely immobilized.

The emphasis on a viewing public described in the sale scene contributed to the success of the stage version, *Camille*, produced in 1848.
One key difference between these versions of the story is the representation of Marguerite's body. In the drama, she does not die until the
final Pietà-like tableau; thus, the picture we see of her throughout is
relatively constant when compared to the novel, in which her visage
varies. Had the play been more "experimental" or metatheatrical in its
presentation, it might have been more disturbing. The Marguerite of
the novel is more difficult to control because she is more amorphous.

In a sense, Marguerite is vampiric—she is undead—a hybridized
being who exists in liminal territory. This notion is borne out in the
version of *Camille* performed by Christy's minstrels in New York. In
this minstrel version, entitled *Camille, an Ethiopian Interlude*, the famous minstrel team of G. W. H. Griffin and George performs Dumas's
melodrama as a "hospital tragedy"[59] starring two performers named
Sam and Julius. The opening puns, like the opening of the novel, stress
sickness and death. In a very clever, if subtle reversal, Julius calls attention to the dupe that he is about to pull on the audience (the minstrel
shows were about putting on, mis-recognition, and slippery speech). He
translates Sam's order for him to "address the audience, to employ their
attention, and take up time" (p. 4). As Sam leaves to transform himself
into Camille, Julius says to the audience, "I am to dress you all, find out
your intentions, and take up the dimes" (p. 4). The word substitutions
in these lines that change address for dress, attention for intention, and
time for dimes, highlight the spectators' complicity in the drama—they,
too, are reminded of their crucial participation in the co-creation of the
performance.

Marguerite, here called "Camille," literally falls down during the
final part of the skit. The parody concludes as she rises to bash "Army"
(Armand) in the head with a slapstick, a convention derived from the
British Punch and Judy shows, which often also featured a "Jim Crow"
minstrel character.[60] The finale of the minstrel sketch reads:

Camille [Marguerite] falls on stage and dies. **Army** gets up, looks affectionately at her—takes out his handkerchief and wipes his eyes. "She am dead! She am defunct!" Goes over to lounge; leans with his face in his hands. . . . **Camille** gets up slyly, goes off and gets stuffed club, goes over to him, while he is weeping, and giving him a tremendous blow behind, says: "She am dead, am she?"[61]

As in the novel, Marguerite (Camille) does not simply die; rather, her vampiric rise rehearses the endless representations of her story, ensuring her triumph and her revenge.[62]

The association of flowers with femininity is a cliché—almost a dead metaphor. Imbued with beauty, fragility, and delicacy, flowers are represented as emblems of perfect beauty. Nevertheless, they may also symbolize blackened femininity: they can be Venus flytraps, poisonous vines produced in hothouses, and figures such as Marguerite—all dangerous growths that convey decidedly different meanings. Charles Baudelaire's infamous collection of poems, *Flowers of Evil* (*Fleurs du Mal*), published in 1857, seven years after Dumas's *The Black Tulip*, deals with such deadly flowers.[63] Baudelaire's final title for his collection, *Flowers of Evil*, thematizes the problematic of "black femininity." Devoted to various topics, the poems (more than 125 in all) have titles such as "The Vampires," "The Metamorphoses of the Vampire," "The Dancing Serpent," "A Phantom," "Condemned Women" (*Femmes Damnees*), "Lesbos," and "For a Creole Lady."[64] Baudelaire's volume, among the most influential of modern poetry, reveals a profound fascination with forms of black femininity.

Almost all of the poems are both inspired by and dedicated to Baudelaire's mistresses, many of whom were also actresses. One woman in particular, known as Jeanne Duval (or Jeanne Prosper), and described by Jerome McGann as a mulatto actress and prostitute, is the purported subject of several poems, sometimes called the cycle of the "Black Venus." A famous image of Duval was painted by Edouard Manet, who also combined the related tropes of blackness, femininity, and flowers in his painting, *Olympia* (figure 13). One of the nineteenth century's most famous representations of a white and a black woman, *Olympia* stages the complex commodification of blackened femininities.[65]

Manet's *Olympia* depicts a white prostitute and her black maid, who

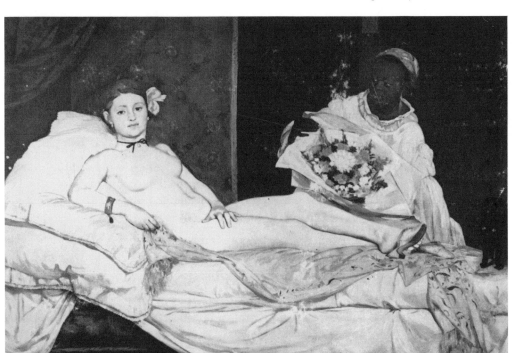

13. *Olympia*, Manet, 1863. Courtesy of the Musée d'Orsay, Paris.

presents a bouquet of flowers to her mistress. The backgrounded body of the black servant in a white dress contrasts with the foregrounded body of the white woman. The two figures function as projections of each other, perhaps representing a Western white fantasy that always reads these figures in relation to each other. Rather than seeing the black woman as the literal re-presentation of the white woman with a black heart (interior)—that is, with a white veneer and dark interior— we might read these figures as inversions of each other. They share a debased social status. They are understood as figures *in relation* to culturally volatile terms of black and white. Linda Nochlin comments on Manet's untraditional odalisque by noting that,

she embodies a timely idea of elegant artificiality and, with her mules, her velvet ribbon, her black cat, and Negro servant carrying a token of admiration up to her boudoir is very different . . . from . . . idealized nudes.

Manet transform[s] the orchid, flower of lasciviousness, and the black cat, promiscuous beast, from *hidden symbols* into *natural accessories* of the mid-nineteenth century demi-mondaine, although the chilly aura of luxurious perversity may . . . take us back . . . to a work like Girodet's crystalline *Danae* or forward to the femmes fatales of the fin de siècle.[66]

The black woman belongs to the white woman; at the same time, the black woman's presence and assumed hypersexuality possesses the white woman, stains her black in nearly every reading, as the cartoon by Cham depicts. Olympia, the "white" woman, is thus re-possessed and re-constituted as a white (black) prostitute or, to use the dominant concern in the comments is not with the black background but with the white fore-figure. Nineteenth-century audiences who viewed Manet's *Olympia* did not desire the black woman in the background; rather, they seemed to displace her presumed lasciviousness onto the "obvious" object—namely, Olympia herself.[67]

Lorraine O'Grady argues this point in her piece, "Olympia's Maid: Reclaiming Black Female Subjectivity":

[The non-white woman is] castrata and whore. . . . [Her] place is outside what can be conceived of as woman. She is the chaos that must be excised, and it is her excision that stabilizes the West's construct of the female body, for the "femininity" of the white female body is insured by assigning the non-white to a chaos safely removed from sight. Thus, only the white body remains as the object of a voyeuristic, fetishizing male gaze. The non-white body has been made opaque by a blank stare.[68]

This construction assumes that the black subject is not sexualized, or rather is so sexualized that she must *only* represent the "black" sexuality of the white woman with whom she appears. Readings of her body show how white woman are blackened.

Baudelaire's *Flowers of Evil* and Manet's *Olympia* bring together some of the concerns of this chapter. Their complicated conception of the powers of the white-femme-black-fatale speaks directly to the related issues of blackness and femininity that are compounded (literally) in the signification of the "black woman" understood as both a visually and morally compromised woman. The allure of the blackened feminine can be excised through killing the black object of one's affection; as we have seen, however, blackened femininity as an unstable sub-

14. *Manet, La Naissance du petit ébéniste*, Cham, *Le Charivari*, wood engraving, 14 May 1865.

stance resists complete erasure. The troubling substance, like the return of the repressed, requires the subject that it haunts to be ever vigilant. A resolution to this dilemma is to "stop" the wild and wily black feminine substance by limiting its power—by destroying it.

Creators, according to Charles Bernheimer,

seem to relish their reduction of the fallen woman to a dead and decomposing body, a painted corpse. Their rhetoric may be sensationalistic and hyperbolic, but its emphasis on absence, negativity, lack, and decay reveals deep-seated anxiety that is at once expressed and controlled through this morbid imagery.[69]

The female figure, then, offers a tantalizing hybrid mixture of resistance and compliance. In other words, the female figure whose dark interior makes her other is marked as both possession and possessor.

Given the tendency in such narratives of tainted women to fall and reveal their dark otherness, many (male-authored) fantasies attempted to
alleviate the danger of such women by destroying them. Women's passion could be purified only when petrified. This belief is manifested by
and in the numerous portrayals of dead fallen woman, and in the atten-
dant necrophilia of such portraits. Thomas Hood's poem, "The Bridge
of Sighs," epitomizes this attitude toward an idealized version of the
fallen woman.

Touch her not scornfully;
Think of her mournfully,
Gently and humanly;
Not of the stains of her,
All that remains of her
Now is pure womanly.[70]

In the nineteenth century, when the category *chattel personal* made
people into property, Jean-Paul Sartre's description of the slimy helps
to explain the dynamics between a class of white men and their black
female possessions. According to Sartre, the slimy is

degraded . . . it is a trap. The sliding is *sucked* in by the sliding substance,
and it leaves its traces on me. The slime is like a liquid seen in a nightmare, where all its properties are animated by a sort of life and turn back
against me. A sickly-sweet feminine revenge . . . but at the same time, the
slimy is myself, by the very fact that I outline an appropriation of the slimy
substance. . . . If I sink in the slimy I feel that I am going to be lost in
it . . . because the slimy is in the process of solidification. . . . [It is like] the
haunting memory of a metamorphosis.[71]

The nightmarish and feminine aspects of such viscous material threaten
to subsume supposedly solid (male) subjects that invade its malleable
parameters.

Sartre's slip in revealing his own bias (why label this dangerous material feminine?) is useful to this discussion. His description engenders
the female body with qualities of the unstable. These fallen, liminal,
displaced women are always on the brink (of conflicting categories),
leaping into turbulent serpentine waters (or emerging from them).[72] In-

deed, the phrase "on the brink" is repeated consistently by Victorian authors to describe the fallen women's liminal status.[73]

The extreme oscillations of such characterizations are both a cause and result of their hybrid backgrounds; yet the sweet beauty of these possessed (in both senses of the word) rare beauties is deceptive. It is precisely their sweetness that cloys and destroys those who attempt to seduce them. One might describe them as "slithy," Lewis Carroll's marvelous portmanteau word that combines "lithe and slimy."[74] This is a perfect description of the "dark" ladies, who are represented as lithe and viscous beings on the territorial edge.[75] While the movements required to enact this repossession of the dispossessed are executed with difficulty, they do temporarily "still" or "fix" the problematic other.

For example, such women are controlled through the assertion that both the prostitute and the mulattaroon, should they live, prove to be *barren*. In this sense, they are stereotypical hybrids incapable of proper or substantial reproduction. Identifying and isolating these figures proved difficult since, as social critic William Acton recognized, "the corruptible are wedged in with corruption; and youth and virtue are with difficulty extricated from the *mélee*."[76]

This formula returns us to the "extraction" of the pure from the throngs of the mixed multitudes, which is also similar to the position of the flaneur associated with Baudelaire. By looking at the reproduction of black tulips, white sculptures, British Blondes, and colored creole camellias, we have seen how forms and figures of "black" femininity functioned in relation to the reproduction of whiteness and masculinity. So too, we have seen how anomalous females were integral to and integrated within discourses that struggled to define proper boundaries — particularly the shifting, interdicted boundaries of gender, class, race, and sexual propriety.

Chapter Three

MASKING FACES

A mask tells us more than a face—Oscar Wilde

Although Victorian novelist and playwright Charles Reade (1814–84) is best known for his novel, *The Cloister and the Hearth*,[1] this chapter discusses his play, *Masks and Faces: or, Before and Behind the Curtain* (written in collaboration with Tom Taylor), in which he dramatized the life of the famous eighteenth-century actress Margaret Woffington (circa 1718–60); his first novel, the eponymously titled *Peg Woffington*, which also chronicled the actress's life "on and off the boards"; and finally, Reade's posthumously published article, "Androgynism; or Woman Playing at Man," a fictional account of a cross-dressing woman based on newspaper articles.[2] In each of these works, Reade reveals his fascination with ambiguous female figures whose protean performances complicate conventional scripts. So too, each of these works theorizes about the instability of gender categories in Victorian culture. Thus, what is at stake in this chapter is the idea that gender, no less than race, is *performative*.

Reade's interest in the mundane aspects of his time compelled him to cull newspapers and magazines for pictures, articles, and advertisements that would aid him in his writing. Cutting and pasting ephemera into more than seventy separate notebooks, he collated a valuable cache of materials that confirmed his fascination with mass culture.[3] For example, a notebook labeled "Authors" contains a newsprint engraving of the famous writer Alexandre Dumas père—whose image was among the most widely distributed of any nineteenth-century author.[4] Reade penciled the phrase, "Dumas with Negro hair," in the margins of the notebook in which he had pasted the picture. This annotation indicates Reade's racialized response and confirms the extent to which ideas of "race" permeated daily discourse.

Reade, as well as numerous other Victorian playwrights, reworked French material for English consumption; however, he also valued

American sources. Like his colleague and onetime cocollaborator Dion Boucicault, who also wrote a play about Peg Woffington, Reade embraced the political "social problem" novel so closely associated with American literature. The following quotation from Reade's notebooks illustrates his ideas about the value of uniquely American subjects:

What new material has the English artist compared with that gold mine of nature, incident, passion, and character—life in the vast American Republic? Here you may run on one rail from the highest civilization to the lowest, and inspect the intervening phases, and write the scale of man. You may gather in a month amidst the noblest scenes of nature the history of the human mind and note its progress. Here are red man, black man, and white man. With us man is all of a colour, and nearly all of a piece; there contrasts more piquant than we ever see spring thick as weeds.[5]

Despite detailing such differences between English and American subjects, Reade still wrote in a notebook that "an American is only an Englishman carried to excess." Reade's enthusiasm for such idealized American subjects merits attention because it, too, is part of the nineteenth-century Anglo-American traffic.[6]

In the summer of 1852, as Stowe's novel, *Uncle Tom's Cabin* became the runaway best-seller of the nineteenth century, Charles Reade wrote in his "Americana" notebook, "The book *Uncle Tom* [*sic*] is a story which discusses the largest human topic that can ever arise; for the human race is bisected into black and white."[7] As this line suggests, some fifty years before W. E. B. DuBois determined that the "problem of the twentieth century is the problem of the color-line," Reade observed that it was a defining problem for the nineteenth as well.[8] Reade's use of the active verb, "bisected," captures the agency involved in racial division and divisiveness. Moreover, his statement testifies to the British public's familiarity with Stowe's text, which expanded English audiences' knowledge of "black" female characters such as Topsy as well as the mulattaroons Eliza and Cassy. The following fragments in the "Americana" notebook even suggest that he planned to write a piece engaging similar issues:

Mulatto girl . . . —mulattoes delicate.
Religious mistress. frailty, order

her 190 lashes and then sent to the plantation
on a horse—corpse arrived on the horse
tantum religio potuit.

Mrs. Merryweather at the ball
beautiful. softened light in her once.
Messenger sent to arrest her: how they managed.

The second half of the fragment is reminiscent of *The Woman of Colour,* discussed in chapter 1. Perhaps Reade decided against developing this schema into a full-fledged drama because the popularity of mulattaroon figures was waning, as the changes made to Boucicault's London production suggest. In the late 1860s, after the American Civil War and the emancipation of the slaves, interest in abolitionist topics declined. As England's empire expanded, there was a shift in focus away from America's racial others to those in India, Australia, the Caribbean, Ireland, and Africa. During this period, Reade wrote a play, entitled *It's Never Too Late to Mend,* about the colony of Australia. The drama featured a black-faced Aboriginal character named "Jacky."[9]

Reade's notebooks attest to his interest in a host of issues related to questions of blackness, femininity, and androgyny: they contain entries on "negrocide," slavery, *feomina vera,* and *nigri loci.*[10] Reade had an obsession with "unnatural" pairings and chiasmatic figures—in short, with key concepts such as miscegenation and homoeroticism. He wrote about twins, mistaken identities, rivalrous relationships between suitors, and women who played men.[11] His fascination with the eighteenth-century actress Peg Woffington derived, in part, from her success as one of the first women to perform male roles.[12] Peg's image was familiar to the privileged male actors and playwrights (including Reade) who belonged to the Garrick Club. Reade claims that it was William Hogarth's famous portrait of Peg playing the part of Sir Harry Wildair that sparked his interest in the actress. In his novel *Peg Woffington,* he describes one of her cross-dressed performances as Sir Wildair.

. . . an old woman in [Peg's] hands was a thorough woman, thoroughly old, not a cackling young person of epicene gender. She played Sir Harry Wildair like a man which is how he ought to be played (or which is better still not at all), so that Garrick acknowledged her as a rival and abandoned the part he no longer monopolized. It has been my misfortune to see . . . [no name given] play the man. Nature forgive them . . . for art never will; they never reached any idea more manly than a steady resolve to exhibit the points of a woman with greater ferocity than they could in a gown. . . . But, in Margaret Woffington's Sir Harry Wildair she parted with a woman's mincing foot and tongue and played the man in a style large, spirited and élancé.[13]

What Reade values in this passage is Peg's consummate performance: she becomes her part completely. Peg's performance in the lead role of this William Congreve drama differed from the more usual "temporary" breeches roles, in which the audience was aware of the impersonation. In most breeches roles, a woman disguised herself as a man in a comic ploy that resulted in the consummation of a heterosexual union between either the main characters or another couple. Breeches roles (including Peg's) were notable also for their display of the female form, since the costumes revealed women's legs. The emphasis in Reade's quotation makes clear, however, that he valued Peg's ability to transform her persona. He notes that the verisimilitude of her staged masculinity rivaled that of actor David Garrick (who was her lover). In commenting on the phenomenon of women's ability to assume male roles, Reade wrote: "There is no limit to illusion."[14] The title of his play about Peg, *Masks and Faces: or, Before and Behind the Curtain*, testifies to his interest in the performativity of gender.

Masks and Faces, written in 1851, opened at London's Haymarket Theater on November 20, 1852, nine days before his coauthor Tom Taylor had a hit at the Aldephi with his *Uncle Tom's Cabin*. At this point, Reade had not met with success as a playwright, having only adapted two French plays for the English stage. *Masks and Faces* was his first original piece, and it was he who chose the subject matter and sketched several scenes, which Taylor (the more experienced playwright) readily rejected. The process of revision continued until Reade claimed that "the thing got so mixed that hang me if I couldn't tell which was [Taylor's] and which was mine."[15] Neither writer was satisfied with the final result, least of all Reade, who went on to write a separate novel about *his* beloved actress. Although Reade dedicated his novel to Taylor, the latter was upset that Reade had reproduced Taylor's witty dialogue in the novel almost verbatim.

The play's plot hinges on the exposure of Ernest Vane, a lecherous husband who divides himself between Mabel, his innocent wife in the country, and Peg, his worldly London mistress. Act 1 takes place backstage in the greenroom, where the actors and critics cavort. The subplot involves the adoration of Peg by another character, the aristocrat Sir Charles Pomander, as well as by a starving master of three arts—painting, playwriting, and poetry—named, appropriately enough, Mr. Triplet.

Triplet pursues Peg not for her beauty but, rather, for the power and influence her beauty has helped her to attain. He writes tragedies for Peg to perform and has been at work on a portrait of her for a number of years. Triplet's attempts to portray Peg are ultimately unsuccessful. Aspects of the actress remain beyond the boundary of the texts that try to bind her. In other words, the actual Peg Woffington has been reduced to parts (a set of lines in plays) and pieces that are (and were) never whole. Unlike stock characters in melodrama, the actress as actress is never defined by a stable role.

Although Peg is a professional actress, the play concerns itself with her "triumphs outside the theater," since it is her purportedly "private" life that is performed publicly in the stage play. In the process of collapsing the distance between the greenroom (the private space of public performers and a place of transformation) and the private drawing room, the play performs the fear of collapsing social, economic, and cultural categories. Placing Peg between several competing admirers— including Pomander and Vane—the first line of the play, "His inamorata, Mrs. Woffington, of this theater," frames her as a possession both of these men and the theater itself. This, in turn, adds to the force of the climax of the play when Peg decides to frame herself, literally transforming herself into art and becoming the author of her own representation.

Masks and Faces is metatheatrical: it reminds its audience of its own artifice and yet, paradoxically, wants to claim that artifice is sincere, or perhaps, more precisely, that artifice has a "real" referent beyond the production. This is seen most clearly in the focus on Peg's offstage persona. In other words, the play's realism (it is based on a historical figure, and its costumes, stage sets, and dialogue are "realistic") exposes its own impure and unnatural roots by focusing on the slippage between seemingly sound classifications. The piece plays with drama "on both sides of the curtain" and seeks to obliterate the lines that supposedly separate classes, genders, races, not to mention earnestness, from play.

The mixing of binaries, from public to private, to pure and impure, is problematic in Victorian texts, as Judith Halberstam and others have agreed.[16] Reade uses Peg's character and the play about her to explore the configurations of this hybrid problematic. The articulation of both "men-women" and "public women" exposes one of the sources for the extreme anxieties about women's roles that surfaced at mid-century. In general, the overwhelmingly negative responses to women's increased public visibility in different representations were grounded in the fear of the fragmentation of a civilized English identity, as well as in the instability of rapidly changing moral and socioeconomic boundaries. In a popular play like *Masks and Faces*, the recognition of dangerous "public" women had to be followed by the heroine's subsequent surrender to the proper patriarchal principles (and principals), reconsolidating a threatened Englishness.

Appearances are important in the work. Peg plays the leading lady who is always aware of how she is seen. In this sense, she embodies the drama's desire to play with notions of appearance and reality, image and action. The drama is a comment on actresses acting both on and offstage. *Masks and Faces* persistently asks, as in act 2, "who ever saw Peggy's real face?" This query is never answered definitively, although the play suggests that Mabel Vane, the pure wife, has identified the real Peggy's sacrificing "nature" by impossibly seeing *through* her performance. As Wilde wrote in his play *An Ideal Husband*, "It is only the shallow people who do not judge by appearances."[17]

The proliferation of Peg's character(s) is the result of props (a mirror, her portrait) and dialogue. Oral descriptions are supplemented when Triplet enters carrying an "unframed portrait" of "La Woffington," as Peg is called (the definite article marks an attempt to see her definitively), wrapped in baize. Peg's image is quite literally in the hands of others. At the same time, the concealment of Peg's portrait, and the fact that it is unfinished, suggest that her character is similarly opaque, concealed, unframed (perhaps uncontainable), and in process.

Peg enters acting and we see her reenacting several other parts, such as Lady Betty Modish and a Dublin orange girl (an earlier self complete with its own alias).[18] She is not merely Janus; she represents a conglomerate of beings. Peg's performance mutates and produces multiple selves. The last line of the drama claims that "there is more than one Peg to hang your applause on" and, therefore, emphasizes the protean character of the protagonist. When, on several occasions, she takes control of the stage and literally directs the action of the play, she becomes allied most closely with her artist friend, Mr. Triplet. In actually assuming (as opposed to merely adapting the costuming of) male authority, Peg proves herself to be a powerful if temporary threat to the male artist in the play.

At one point in her conversation with Triplet in act I, as she removes the baize on her portrait, Peg exclaims, "My own portrait as I live! And a good likeness too or my glass flatters me like the rest of them." This quotation brings together the various aspects of Peg's character: her corporeal self, her image in art, and her image in the mirror. Triplet tells Peg, "I have carried your face home with me every night, forgive my presumption, and tried to *fix* in the studio the impression of the stage." (italics added)

The tension among Peg's representations becomes overt in act 2, when she literally becomes her picture and then turns art into "life." In this key scene, Triplet defaces Peg's painted face while calling his portrait "a vile caricature of life and beauty." Triplet stabs his painting because he fears that it is "stony and detestable . . . [and unable] to capture the continual play of light that graces [Peg's] mobile face." This destructive gesture occurs moments before a group of critics is to arrive for a viewing of the portrait. Peg acts by cutting away the rest of her "painted" face and placing her "real" face in the picture. The critics reject Peg's "true" face, denouncing it by stating, "Your Woffington is not a woman sir, nor nature!" Woffington then reveals her trick: "Woman! For she has tricked four men. Nature! For a fluent dunce does not know her when he sees her." This act is an attempt to divorce her connection as an actress with other "painted ladies" (i.e., prostitutes) and to show her "respectable" face to her public. Of course, since stage makeup was called "paint," and the actress actually acting Peg's part would have been "painted" or made-up for the stage, this scene consists of layers of complexity that are intimately linked to Peg's contradictory construction. Several decades before the publication of Wilde's *The Picture of Dorian Gray*, Reade's drama plays with "living portraits" and "Vane" characters; in the latter narrative, however, it is the immobile face that is destroyed, rather than the transmogrifying one.

At the climax of act 1, Mable Vane unexpectedly arrives in her husband's London home. She asks to be introduced to the company that is gathered in the drawing room. Her husband tries to rebuff his wife's request by saying that it is not fashionable to be introduced when in the city; yet Peg contradicts him and takes control of the scene. As Mrs. Vane enters the room, the stage directions read, "Peg rises." This seemingly insignificant detail is symbolic, for Peg literally rises to the occasion by assuming the identity of Lady Betty Modish. She acts to such effect that she ultimately fools her lover's wife. Peg survives this potentially devastating and humiliating experience by transforming herself. It is this ability that allows her to control her emotions—to juggle and juxtapose masks that make her both artificial and sincere.

She is quick to contrive a plot to resolve all. She delights in duping her audiences and in defying those who seek to possess her image. Although this comedy, like most comedies, returns to the status quo—the actors return to the greenroom, the Vanes's marriage is preserved—a disruption has occurred.[19] Peg redeems herself at the end of the play by renouncing Vane, rejecting Pomander, and securing a regular salary for the previously starving Triplet from Pomander.

Masks and Faces retained many of the conventions found in Restoration comedies. One example is the inclusion of an epilogue. Here, the epilogue is less bawdy than its Restoration predecessors and spoken by the entire cast rather than a young woman, but it is present nonetheless. In combining aspects of Restoration comedy with the domestic realism that came to characterize popular Victorian pieces, the play holds a unique position in theater history. Despite specific gestures toward a more playful play, the final statement in Reade's work confirms conventional Victorian values: Peg gives up her false mask for an honest face.[20]

The comic ending of this production of *Masks and Faces* contrasts greatly with the tragic ending of an 1875 revival, which concludes with the actress's demise. The later versions of this dramatic story culminate with Peg's denunciation of her former life as an actress. The conservative alterations to the play may have been a product of the changing times. Beginning in the 1870s, the theater became the site of family entertainment and bourgeois edification. The illicit aspects of the theater were erased in concurrence with the infamous nineteenth-century bowdlerization of Shakespeare and the "domestication" of the theater itself by managers such as Squire and Marie Bancroft, who restaged *Masks and Faces* in 1875. In *Realizations*, Martin Meisel discusses the transforming moment when the Bancrofts actually enclosed the stage with a gilded frame—thus making clearer the connection between plays and other professional arts (painting, in particular).[21] The London drama moved closer, conceptually, to those other popular "galleries" where narrative paintings were the privileged genre. Reformers like Tom Robertson and the Bancrofts succeeded in their crusade to make the theater more respectable and, therefore, more "domestic"— to bring it closer to the middle-class ideal of the English Home.[22]

This "taming" of the theater was achieved by increasing the price of tickets, placing antimacassars on the seats, and using actual doorknobs to suggest the realism of the bourgeois home on stage, as well as by reducing the number of plays seen each evening. Unlike the eighteenth-century theater, which was characterized by its notoriously chaotic atmosphere and multiple spectacular events, many actor-managers courted respectability by producing realistic domestic melodramas that were meant to be appealing to the audience. Thus, the theater became "respectable" through concerted efforts to sanitize it and make it safe (literally and figuratively) for the Victorian family. These changes may have influenced the Bancrofts' decision to delete the comic epilogue from *Masks and Faces*. Certainly, this reading concurs with the characterization of them as "reformers" of the theater who focused on the elimination of impure practices, such as having young actresses speak risqué if not actually raunchy epilogues.

Contemporary reviewers of the 1875 production at the Prince of Wales Theater elaborated the differences from its 1852 predecessor. Many Victorian critics preferred Peg's honesty to her subversive comedy. One notice described the revival of *Masks and Faces* as follows: "Mrs. Bancroft's Peg was a charming conception, natural in its joy, heartfelt in its grief. It contained no artifice or trick. It was the work of an artist in every phase."[23] This quotation illustrates the change that was taking place in the theater as the century came to a close. Here, Clement Scott, the Victorian theater's most conservative critic, privileges the "natural," "heartfelt," and "artistic" performance of Mrs. Bancroft. These qualities, moreover, lift her performance to the realm of art as opposed to mere "artifice or trick."

A later review compared Mrs. Stirling's debut in 1852 (the actress who originated the part) with that of her successor. The comparison reads: "Mrs. Bancroft's Peg Woffington differs from that of Mrs. Stirling. . . . With Mrs. Stirling, the triumph of goodness . . . seemed due to a rich and ripe nature and an overflow of animal spirits."[24] The Bancrofts' revival of the play was changed after a bitter fight with Reade. Bancroft claims that "our great fight was over the ending and only after many struggles did Reade allow us to cut out the old, stagey, rhyming tag [the epilogue that foregrounded the pretense of the play] and agree to the pathetic ending we proposed."[25] Thus, the last stage appearance of Peg converts her into a pious, penitent, and therefore, popular Victorian heroine.

Like the 1875 script, Reade's novel from 1852, *Peg Woffington*, focuses on Peg's transgressive parts and Reade's increasingly negative reactions to them. The novel is not strictly a melodrama or situation comedy, in which the plot is the driving force of "stock" characters; rather, it attempts to bridge the gap between history, biography, and fiction. The difference in the titles is telling: *Masks and Faces* is an ensemble piece, whereas *Peg Woffington* centers more narrowly on its heroine. Also, *Masks and Faces* does not present the gender crossings that appear in *Peg Woffington*.[26]

Reade gives the following explanation of why he chose to publish his novel: ". . . first I was unwilling to lose altogether some matter which we [he and his collaborator, Tom Taylor] had condemned as unfit for our dramatic purpose; secondly, the exigencies of the stage had, in my opinion, somewhat disturbed the natural current of our story; thirdly, it is my fate to love this dead heroine and I wished to make her known in literature."[27] This last statement recalls Baudelaire's belief that "art is prostitution," by which he meant that according to the etymology of the word ("to put forth in public"), art may be seen as "the making public of private fantasies."[28] John Coleman quotes Reade as saying, "I was enraged beyond endurance with the barbarous treatment accorded to my play (for it was *mine*). I determined to write a novel on the subject determined . . . that they shouldn't lay violent hands on that as well!" (italics in original)[29] This is the most explicit example of Reade's desire to tell his own version of Peg's story.

The successful market for novels must also have influenced Reade's decision to shape his Peg Woffington material into a book. Moreover, in the 1850s, a novel was a more private form than a play, for the former was not subject to the stricter legal licensing of the lord chamberlain's office. Of course, informal censorship did exist in Mudie's Circulating Library, which did not stock *Peg Woffington*. Finally, as the sole author, Reade had more command of his subject matter in the novel than he had as a collaborator on a script for the theater.

In the first chapter, the reader sees Peg as several characters described by the narrator. In most novels, one blazon suffices to fix the features of the heroine; in Reade's novel, however, there are numerous accounts of the actress from different perspectives. Peg's multiplicity was performed on the stage; Reade's novel affords her different and more disturbing personae. In the novel, Reade associates Peg with other "low" creatures, such as rats, monkeys, and her black servant, Pompey, who has a bit part in the play (in blackface).

The end of chapter 3 introduces the reader to Pompey and explains his place in Peg's household.[30] Pompey plays a traitor to Peg and a pawn to Sir Charles Pomander, who purchased him as a gift for his lover. We are told that Peg pleases herself by whipping Pompey periodically.[31] On one level, Peg's abuse of Pompey connects her with him in that she is also abused and "owned" by Pomander. So too, in describing Pompey as the "pawn" that is passed between two owners, the black servant occupies the traditional place of the Western woman who is traded "between men."[32] When not sadistically beating the boy, Peg treats him "as a lapdog . . . and nurses him herself,"[33] as if she were a wicked hag coddling her familiar like the witches in *Macbeth*. The main passage that summarizes Peg's relationship to Pompey reads:

. . . he was fed like a game-cock, and dressed like a Barbaric prince; and once, when he was sick his mistress . . . nursed him, and tended to him with the same white hand that plied the obnoxious whip; . . . but when Sir Charles's agent proposed to him certain silver coins, the ebony ape grinned till he turned half ivory, and became a spy in the house of his mistress. (p. 46)

The image of the black servant, so common in English art, is a sign of both wealth and moral corruption. Peg is blackened by her association with him in a manner analogous to the blackening of Becky by Rhoda in *Vanity Fair*. In addition, the scene draws on the numerous descriptions in slave narratives of white women sadistically whipping their slave servants.[34]

In the novel, Pomander, an aristocrat, hopes to control and woo Peg with jewels and other items (like Pompey), but she refuses most of his material gifts in favor of the middle-class Vane's adoration. In order for Peg to be a sympathetic (or pathetic) character, she must affirm the genteel love professed by Vane and reject Pomander's "gross" gifts. This sadistic side of Peg's character would have been difficult to present on stage (even though nearly every production of *Uncle Tom's Cabin* contained both an auction block and a whipping scene). Perhaps it was permitted in the novel because the written text was, at least formally, addressed to an exclusively male audience (even if his novel was read by women): Reade calls his readers "Gentlemen." The novel comes close to replicating scenes in erotic works. The inclusion of whipping scenes on stage was part of the new tradition of sensation that, in fact, competed with novels at the time. Reade was captivated by such scenes of sadism and transgressive sexuality throughout his career, as evidenced by the culturally marginal topics included in his personal notebooks.[35]

The following quotation is similar to stories found in Reade's "Calibani" notebook, although it is from *Peg Woffington*: "Women will more readily forgive disgusting physical deformity.... Women would embrace with more rapture a famous ourang-outang, than we [men] would an illustrious chimpanzee."[36] The entangled stereotypes that trouble Peg's characterization proliferate in Reade's narrative. Moreover, Reade's work obsessively delineates the essentialized "separateness" of male identity from that of the female. This difference testifies to the import of biological selection and raises the question of women's propensity for primates as opposed to proper mates. The unsettling implications of this conflict are confirmed in a subsequent scene where Peg cavorts with an Irishman.

Peg herself is Irish and, thus, in the world of Victorian stereotypes, related to the simian stereotype, "Irish Paddy," who with his prognathous jaw appeared so often in the pages of *Punch*.[37] At this critical juncture in the novel, Pomander (like Iago) determines to reveal Peg's degenerate nature to the smitten Mr. Vane.[38] The two men follow her and hear, signs of an Irish orgie [*sic*]—rattling jig played and danced with the in-spiriting interjections of that frolicsome nature. Pomander says, "I prepare you for what you are sure to see. [Peg] was an Irish bricklayer's daughter, and what is bred in bone never comes out in flesh; you will find her sitting on some Irishman's knee, whose limbs are stouter than yours. . . . [T]hese things would be monstrous if they were not common; incredible if we did not see them everyday."[39]

That Pomander needs to imagine Peg's rejection of him as the result of her "inbred" preference for her own race is evident in this imagined episode. This characterization also provides the comforting knowledge that everything remains in its proper place after all. Reade uses and perpetuates racial or national identities, while equating reviled figures and showing that they are hybrid and disturbing. It seems to exemplify the dictum that "the world being a great theater of evil . . . laughter and merriment make a human being no better than a baboon."[40]

The angelic middle-class wife in the story, Mabel Vane, who is shocked to hear that her husband has been keeping company with an actress, admires Peg when she confronts the odious woman in the flesh. As described earlier, when Mabel is first introduced to Peg, the latter is playing the role of Lady Betty Modish. Mabel, thoroughly ignorant of the stage persona (Lady Betty is a character from Colly Cibber's drama), assumes that Peg really is a lady. Mabel shows that it was the name of the actress and not the thing itself that she feared. It is the signifier that shocks, not the signified.

In act 2, Peg's mutability is set off against Mabel's "diamond-like, unchanging love." Peg, in being neither art nor nature, is paradoxical and punished. And yet, an interesting exchange occurs between Peg and Mabel. In his desire to expose Pomander's and even Vane's dan-gerous duplicity, Reade sets up a dichotomy between the sexes. The women (even Peg) are more moral than the upper-middle-class men. Thus, Peg can claim that she can love Mabel "as no man ever could." The scene that makes Peg and Mabel "sisters" prefigures the recogni-tion scene in Wilde's *Lady Windermere's Fan* (1893), in which the fallen mother, Mrs. Erlynne, sacrifices herself for her pure daughter, as well as the many other meetings of pure and passionate women who exchange identities.[41]

The innocent Mabel, who is "a reader of faces, as was her aunt before her,"[42] kneels down before the portrait of the "beautiful, terrible woman." Significantly, this scene is the frontispiece illustration in each of the nineteenth-century editions of the novel. Following this exchange, Peg assumes Mabel Vane's identity. Sir Charles is given his due and is duped by Peg's "pure white hand," which he believes to be Mabel's. Like her other fallen sisters, Peg has little difficulty feigning purity and mocking male prerogative. We see here Reade's preoccupation with the excesses of female power and the desire to define its limits.

Peg consents to play to the stereotype of the fallen woman who must degrade herself and become the shamed Magdalene. The difference here, however, is that Peg makes her pact not with a patriarch but a *sister*. The erotic scene in which the two women pledge their love for one another is the true climax of the tale. Peg tells Mabel, "If you are happy, remember you owe something to me. If you are unhappy, come to me and I will love you as men cannot love" (p. 133). This statement occurs just before the last paragraph of the novel proper (as in George Eliot's *Middlemarch* and many other novels, there is an epilogue that contains synopses of the protagonists' final years). This novel, like most others in the English tradition, ends with a marriage: but the marriage here is a spiritual one between two women. Peg's conversion to Christianity saves her soul and allows her to reach Heaven—where she is purified and able to join the ranks of other earnest angels, like Mabel Vane.

At the end of her life, Peg works only "to efface the memory of her former self and to give as many years to purity and piety as she had to folly and frailty" (p. 142). This desire recurs in many late Victorian images of "fallen" heroes and heroines. Pinero's married ex-prostitute, the second Mrs. Tanqueray from the smash drama of the same name, exemplifies those figures who, like Dorian Gray, try to "kill the past."[43] Finally, Peg succumbs to a painful illness and is buried under a headstone marked, "Peg Woffington, Spinster." In this instant, she is reduced to a single entity, bereft of her constantly changing, man-made masks and wearing a singular, unmoving face. Her death ultimately allows her to be reborn and made immortal in the works (including this one) that revive her partial presence. Death fixes her momentarily (as in the frame) and tries to remove or peg, Peg's restless incarnations.[44]

Shortly after completing his works about Peg Woffington, Reade became interested in newspaper reports about women who cross-dressed. He claimed that "between 1858 and 1862 the years [he] began to collect material from the real life for [his] dramas, many instances of androgynism occurred or were brought to light with unusual frequency. [He] devoted a folio of 250 leaves to tabulating them."[45] From this material, Reade wrote a lengthy fictional account of a cross-dressing woman whom he named Kate Tozer. Published posthumously in 1911 under the title "Androgynism; or, Woman Playing at Man,"[46] Reade's pseudodocumentary account of Kate Tozer's male impersonation relies on metaphors of race to mark what becomes Kate's sexually indecent exposure. For example, he quotes Becky Sharp as saying that women "can make [men] believe that black is white!" (p. 10). The essay struggles with the terms (literal and figurative) of Kate's actions and the reactions to her performance, which is distinguished from "naturally masculine, sexual mistakes, physiological freaks . . . [whose] manliness . . . was most virile" (p. 11). The narrative follows the young wife, Kate Tozer, as she impersonates a journeyman painter with her husband for economic gain, through Kate's love affair with Nelly, a naive country girl who is ignorant, supposedly, of Kate's "true" sex, to the court-trial conclusion, where Kate's crime of impersonation results in her being forced by the court to appear exclusively in female garb from that date forward.

Reade's article unmasks, through an exposition on the masked, the essentially performative nature of gender and exposes the sex/gender system as a regulatory practice that, in some exceptional cases, circumscribed individual lives.[47] Reade's representation of the case of the cross-dressing Kate Tozer (alias Fred) may be read as an example of an ambiguous body that appears in "the margins of hegemonic discourses, social spaces carved in the interstices of institutions . . . [where] the terms of a different construction of gender can be posed."[48] Reade's reading of Kate's titillating travesty that turns into a threatening vested interest when Kate falls in love with Nelly, provides us with insights into the productive formation of Victorian gender and sexuality.[49]

Reade claims that he selected Kate's tale for its dramatic potential, its "piquancy, pathos, and colour."[50] He reconstructs Kate Tozer's escapade, in which she "passed" as her husband's son and worked with him as a journeyman painter, by combining dialogue with the presentation of letters and his own commentary. As such, his essay is itself performative—and may be read as an amalgam of artifacts—rather like Kate herself.

Reade asks, "Is the congenital *role* of women to play a false part?" (p. 10), and then answers his question by declaring that: "I do believe that some women have an overpowering itch for simulating. Among actresses, the androgyne, or woman-man has figured not quite ingloriously in the pages of history" (p. 10). It should be noted that such waffling typifies Reade's eccentric prose; nonetheless, this statement does allow him to critique and differentiate among images of women. By stating that only *some* women have this itch for simulating, Reade deconstructs the stereotype of a unified idea of *the* Victorian woman. This is not to say, however, that Reade *embraces* the subversiveness of Kate's mode of dress; rather, it suggests that he was aware of the power of appearances and of women's particular penchant for female impersonation, implicit in idealized performances of femininity.

As evidence for his belief that a disproportionate number of women do indeed play a false part, Reade provides his readers with a litany of androgynes (a term he uses for female transvestites). His collection of famous impostors includes Becky Sharp, Chevalier D'Eon de Beaumont, Pope Joan, Joan of Arc, Lady Hester Stanhope, and several "nuns who passed their lives as monks" (p. 11).[51] Reade's discussion recalls the section in *Vanity Fair* in which the author notes:

> . . . a polite public will no more bear to read an authentic description of vice than a truly-refined English or American female will permit the word "breeches" to be pronounced in her chaste hearing. And yet . . . both are walking the world before our faces everyday, without much shocking us. If you were to blush every time they went by, what complexions you would have![52]

This description not only marks the wearing of breeches by women as an everyday occurrence, but it also suggests the unspeakable nature of such acts that, in fact, have the potential to reveal the shame of the viewer in the form of a blush.[53]

Reade uses the line, "When hollow hearts shall wear a mask," by an unidentified Irish poet as a means of explaining the conundrum that the androgynous actress represents. The mixed metaphor serves as an excellent emblem of the "ourself behind ourselves concealed" that Emily

Dickinson assures us, "Should startle most."[54] In other words, where Reade once claimed that beneath the superficial mask of the actress was an "honest face," he now claims that the honest heart no longer holds the "truth": rather, the heart is hollow. The appeal to and of "sentiment" served as a safeguard to the theatrical practice of women playing men. Jean Howard explains, "While cross-dressing can cause semiotic and sexual confusion, and therefore is to be shunned, it is not truly a problem for the social order if the heart [of the heroine] is untouched."[55] In short, according to Tracy Davis, "the point of the practice was to please, not deceive . . . the raison d'être of women's cross-dressing was allure."[56] Ultimately, the narrative "redeems" Kate by claiming that her heart remained whole if hollow.

When an androgyne acts as or plays the role of a "woman-man," she comes dangerously close to becoming a public woman who perpetually plays false parts. Reade's treatment of Kate allows her, in the words of Ann Rosiland Jones and Peter Stallybrass, to "articulate gender itself as a fetish."[57] She is doubly false and, therefore, doubly dangerous. Reade asserts, "In Kate you may recognise a consummate hypocrite, Greek for actress, which again is latin for player."[58] Although Reade would have been familiar with the male impersonators found in music halls and pantomime, he chooses, as do so many other Victorian writers, to discuss only the "female" male impersonators. Again, his focus on the female body allows him to speculate about an-other body that is seen as being distinct and distant from his own bodily configuration.

Reade's attitude toward androgynous actors is summarized by the character Coleman in the novel *Peg Woffington:* "Call that epicene creature with the parrot's nose and the peacock's voice—that featherbed tied in the middle . . . that Punch-like thing the genial, jovial manly— No! No!—these things must not be thought . . . it will drive us mad."[59] Reade seems to express greater contempt for epicene men than he does for epicene women, perhaps because the "us" that they deconstruct resides too closely to Reade's own gender identity.

His representation and translation of Kate's case (significantly, it is not yet a medicalized/pathologized *case*) may be read as "*using* the whole world as theater in an . . . instrumental fashion . . . [so that] the very subjects which [he] politically excludes become exotic costumes which [he] assumes in order to play out the disorders of [his] own identity," according to Peter Stallybrass and Allon White.[60] But this definition of the construction of bourgeois identity that illuminates part of Reade's recurrent desire to see the androgynous actress act his own (male) role is, at the same time, an expression of larger cultural values. In other words, the question of how (as opposed to why) Reade envisions Kate as an "odd, unnatural but not uninteresting" cultural figure provides us with clues to his complex imagining of Victorian sexualities.[61]

For example, after telling Kate's tale "simply, as a slender illustration of the aphorism, 'truth is stranger than fiction'" (p. 12), Reade concedes that the value of her story may be in presenting "one of those things . . . not heretofore dreamt of, an ethical solecism" (p. 11). Reade's choice of the term *solecism* to describe Kate's transgression, along with his description of her as a "violatrix," reveals that her actions violate quite explicitly "the rules of grammar," as well as impropriety. If, as Teresa deLauretis has pointed out, "gender represents a grammatical relation,"[62] then we can see how Reade's reading of Kate's androgynous figure is an incongruity and a challenge to binary oppositions. Indeed, she occupies, quite precariously, several positions among a set of contrary categories.

Also complicating this relation is the fact that the narrative collapses the distinction between actresses "on and off the boards" (a technique also used in *Peg Woffington* and *Masks and Faces*). By conflating the three terms, *actress, androgyne,* and *woman-man,* Reade questions the relation between representation and the real—a question that can never be resolved. The terms are interchangeable—as are the "gendered parts" from which they are constructed. As Reade writes, "Try to grasp the transformation. . . . She stands before her appalled spouse no longer to outward view feminine, but androgynous, sartorially epicene" (p. 17). Kate's husband, Tom, remarks, "I saw a kiddy of the same cut at the theayter once," to which Reade adds, "Good criticism, that for *Mister* Kate had overdone it. Her get-up was of the stage, stagey" (p. 18). The generic "kiddy"—the boy-woman of pantomime who disturbs not only gender boundaries, but age and other national (class, family) boundaries—was a ubiquitous figure in Victorian theaters. So too, the excessive marks of the overdone appearance of Kate signify the imagined "difference" between the made-up impersonator and the elusive "real thing."

Reade notes that in her new garb, Kate was the "image of a very pretty fellow" (p. 17).[63] He seems to delight in the perverse inversion of a woman in man's clothes and, throughout his career, continued to record such phenomena. Reade claims that it is better to play like a man than a "person of epicene gender." Charles Dickens makes the same claim about the actress Marie Wilton when he says, she was "so stupendously like a boy and unlike a woman, that it [her performance] is perfectly free from offence."[64] Why would Reade and Dickens prefer to see these women, or rather not to see them, "acting" as boys?

The answer to this dilemma might lie in Jean Baudrillard's distinction between "dissembling" or "feigning" and "simulation."[65] In the former, one "can simply . . . make believe . . . [whereas in the latter] . . . one must produce . . . symptoms. Thus, feigning or dissimulating leaves the reality principle intact: the difference is always clear, only masked; whereas simulation threatens the difference between true and false, between real and imaginary" (p. 5). It would appear that men like Reade and Dickens enjoyed knowing that the "men" they watched were merely masked and could not be "mistaken" as men. In such cases, women in breeches parts were recuperated by Victorian culture: they were only somewhat subversive.

In Reade's reading, Kate is the third term, androgyne—a member of the third sex.[66] Actually, as a woman-man, Kate embodies the unstable hyphenated identity that is destined to evolve (or devolve) into a unified whole. Because the normative rules of the culture favor stability, one cannot exist indefinitely in space and time as a hyphenated/hybrid being. The hyphenated man-woman must embrace one gender or the other: it cannot be both and survive. Nonetheless, Reade permits and even encourages Kate to maintain her equivocal nature, precisely because it *is* her nature. He mixes the sentimental and the theatrical to the extent that the former is revealed to be empty (false) and the latter excessive (doubly false). The first important premise posed in the article is that there is no reality—only theatricality, or to put it differently, reality is always already theatricality.

This notion has important consequences for Victorian culture. Matthew Arnold's declaration, "True piety is in acting what one knows," is anything but a simple or straightforward moral maxim in light of this assertion. Indeed, this statement is susceptible to the subversive theatricality it seems to allay. It is another example, asserts Nina Auerbach, of "Victorian [humanism that] conveys a covert fear that any activity is destructive of character because all activity smacks of acting."[67] Reade alludes to this great paradox of his age (and ours) when he uses the term "locomutation" as a replacement for "locomotion."[68] His neologism, "locomutation," foregrounds the fact that all motion (formation) is also mutation and transformation. Reade exposes the hidden elision between these terms, and in a sense, prefigures the monstrous mutations and tumultuous transformations (the "sexual anarchy," to borrow Elaine Showalter's title) of fin de siècle culture. While Reade makes consistent references to Kate's simulating nature, he also periodically asserts that she is not immoral. His commentary cuts both ways, as does the chiasmic figure of Kate.

When Kate goes to work with her husband, she is named "his 'prentice" (p. 18). The abbreviated form signifies both their dialect/class positionality and Kate's abbreviated (and deviated) gender. The mark stands in for missing parts: she is not a full apprentice, but rather a " 'prentice." This is another way in which Reade subtly marks her difference. Perhaps more appallingly, Tom, Kate's husband and cousin, plays her father and, as a sham father, mocks patriarchal prerogative. When Kate becomes Tom's son, she also becomes an adult-child.

There is an interesting resonance to this restructuring of gender and the family in a remark from Reade's notebooks. A character states, "Well, I've seen it. I declare I took him for Desdemona's little black boy." Reade's remarks about the construction of the ideal family place Tom and Kate already outside of the patriarchal family structure. By playing false parts, they resemble the figure of the deconstructor as described by Hillis Miller: "It suggests the image of a child taking apart his father's watch, reducing it back to useless parts, beyond any reconstitution. A deconstructionist is not a parasite but a parricide. He [sic] is a bad son demolishing beyond hope of repair the machine of Western metaphysics."[69] Indeed, this couple demolishes the machine of Western metaphysics by unmasking its oxymoronic performative nature.

This is particularly true of Kate, who even before designing her ingenious scam of passing as her husband's son for pecuniary gain, is marked as an odd woman: a woman at odds with the system. Reade characterizes her as being:

. . . excluded from the category of those wives who love their lords, failed to fulfill the primary object, *teste* the Church of England, for which matrimony was instituted. She was . . . childless. On the other hand, the defaulting spouse indirectly atoned for her neglect of Tom by corresponding indifference to the entire male sex. . . . Not caring . . . for her husband, Kate nevertheless exhibited a paradoxical fidelity.[70]

This reading of Kate allows us to see her sartorial transformation and transmutation as an ironical realization of her "true" character. Already *excluded* from the defined category of woman, she is then an other.

Her refusal to have sexual relations with her husband makes her an anomaly.

Marriage for her had proved a fatal blunder. . . . Since then, life had sludged on somehow, with a husband for a friend and protector but not a lover. Overpowering instincts . . . repelled her from the male sex; though she had voluntarily taken a working place among those from whose very touch she revolted. Such a being—in whom it is not easy to recognise either womanhood or manhood—occupied a quasi-neutral position; nevertheless, experience goes to demonstrate the absolute impossibility of the heart, even in the case of the congenitally epicene, being utterly impervious. (p. 21)

Neutered and neutralized, Kate is spared because even she has a heart. She remains, in essence, a woman in Reade's eyes. Or almost so.

Kate's case is complicated. As she stands in her masculine attire, she proclaims: "The things will soon fit me, and I the things" (p. 23). Indeed, Kate seems to become her things. Impersonation produces the effect of her "true" character, an idea implicit in Oscar Wilde's phrase, "being natural is . . . a pose."[71] Kate's "temperament assimilated easily with the adjuncts of the male."[72] In other words, Kate's "unnatural" garb reveals her natural form. Kate's simulation proclaims her clothes to be the arbiter of her "true" nature. This is the crux of Reade's investigation: he presents a figure who, in Baudrillard's terms, produces symptoms, a woman who subversively simulates by producing the symptom of "real" desire for another woman. As Francette Pacteau explains, "Fantasy does away with distance; the androgyne is situated at the locus of desire, but never itself desires."[73]

Reade's androgyne does the impossible by being not only the product of desire, but also the producer of desire. While posing as "Fred," Kate catches the fancy of a young woman in town. Kate and her admirer, Nelly, court, exchange "passionate" letters, and are on the verge of eloping when the local police and Nelly's father disclose Kate's dupe. When she actually returns the affection of this innocent young maid, Reade chastises her for no longer being "useful" to him. He writes that Kate's story, "served [him] for a character-study and if only the hussy had not chosen to deviate so widely from the lines of nature," might have been in one of his plays.[74] This is somewhat disingenuous since Reade's work, even before 1858, constantly deals with such erotically charged, contradictory female figures.

Reade does not abandon Kate at this juncture; rather, he continues his investigation, attends her trial, and purportedly meets her in person. It is this second stage of Kate's affair, the part most difficult to diffuse, that he finds most fascinating. Reade says that Kate's desire for Nelly ". . . is in truth, hybrid; perhaps morbid; perhaps insane; yet not outside the region of recorded fact. That it must yield nothing more satisfying than Dead Sea fruit does not militate against its existence" (p. 21). Such statements about this "real-life" situation reflect Reade's rationalization that such encounters "yield nothing" of permanence. Reade attempts to diffuse Kate's potential ability to usurp power by resorting to his belief that the culture's rules will regulate nature's aberrations. Nevertheless, an element of doubt about Kate's ability to resist scratching her feminine "itch for simulation" (p. 10) lingers at the end of the text.

In an article whose focus on cross-dressing actresses resembles Reade's narrative, his contemporary, theater critic Lyman Horace Weeks, argued:

In aspiring to rise superior to the limitations of sex, alike in her pleasures and in her employments, the enterprise of the fin-de-siècle woman is not altogether a modern instance. One hundred and fifty years ago the comedy of women in doublet and hose—a comedy that occasionally rose to the rank of dignified drama but more frequently fell to the lower range of pitiful farce—was much in vogue. Few [actresses] did not feel it incumbent to portray the male character.[75]

Weeks concludes his article by stating:

There seems to be no immediate danger that men will be supplanted in the privilege of depicting their sex before the footlights and it is far from likely that the stage will ever have any female Keans. . . . The spirit of to-day, if not opposed to such experiments, is at least indifferent to them, on the part of both the public and of the profession. Even the remarkable activity that distinguished the Cushman epoch in this respect quite failed to maintain itself and has exercised no deep or permanent influence. That episode, and others that preceded it, are now remembered only as the curious pages in the history of the English-speaking stage. (p. 94)

Weeks's reference to the "Cushman epoch," which is now "safely" passed, nevertheless attests to the profound and vaguely threatening power of the famous cross-dressing actress, Charlotte Cushman, who said, "How little do they see what *is*, who frame / Their hasty judgement upon that which *seems*."[76] Cushman—who had an enormous following, especially among women admirers—succeeded in both strong female roles, such as Lady Macbeth, and in male roles, such as Romeo, which she played opposite her sister, Susan. Cushman's transvestite roles (she played more than thirty throughout her career) may have appealed to some women viewers because of the acceptance

of romantic friendships that often flourished between women in the early and mid nineteenth century. Intense same-sex relationships were not subject to the heavy taboos and moral opprobium that were later visited upon them. Displays of affection between women and life-long relationships that approximated marriage seemed pure and worthy to contemporaries. Only in the 1880's and 1890's would romantic unions between women begin to be labelled "congenital inversion" or "perversion."[77]

Although Weeks dismisses such performances as transitory curios, he may have missed their larger cultural significance.

Weeks also says, "Women choose leading heavy roles of the trage- dies . . . as though they would annihilate at one bound the distinction between themselves and their male rivals."[78] This reference to the im- minent and immediate destruction of "natural" laws parallels the (too) rapid transformation of traditional values. Reade read some of these emerging themes in Kate's performance, which he labeled as "random, hybrid, mutated" events. Like Weeks, Reade naturalizes this process by deferring to evolutionary models that are a corrupt version of social Darwinian ideology. He posits that in the struggle for the survival of the fittest, women, as the weaker sex, are doomed to failure. The androgynous actress in these accounts is reduced to a mere curio—a buried and insignificant artifact that existed in history but exerted no historical influence, and most significantly, produced no healthy progeny. The categories seemed to be shifting or expanding. Nevertheless, Reade still fantasizes that he might control these changes, if they did not occur at the disturbingly rapid rate of contagion. In this battle of wills, the androgynous actress served patriarchy while challenging its authority. The threat such women posed to the basic structures of patriarchal society were real, but rarely realized. Looking the part was acceptable; playing too well was problematic.

In Victorian pantomimes, the female figure was contained safely because women were allowed to be the principal *boy*, but not the transformed male lover.[79] As David Mayer explains, the breeches role was a response to "significant alterations in English commercial and industrial life . . . specifically the employment of women." Mayer marks 1831 as the year the first successful breeches role in pantomime occurred, when a slender, rather "androgynous Miss Poole played Jack in the opening act."[80] He goes on to state that,

Woman is a rival, and the pantomime offers a fantasy means of setting aside her threat. The role of the principal boy, a creation of male anxiety, allows both men and women to confront and to contemplate female power, to admit in fantasy that an aggressive woman rivals a man even to the point of pursuing the girl who is to become Columbine. (p. 67)

This describes Kate's anomalous position well. What the culture does not allow, or rather has difficulty imaging and imagining, is sexual love between women. Such an event is dismissed by Reade and, indeed, Kate herself as "the impossible." And yet, Reade redeems Kate's "odd affair" because, ultimately, he believes that even before she "transformed herself into an affectionate wife and is said to have died of a broken heart,"[81] her love for Nelly was "true."

When she is pressed about the effect of the affair on Nelly, on a "girl who finds the man she is deeply in love with is a woman," Kate becomes dejected. Reade represents Kate's equivocal feelings about the incident with the following dialogue:

Kate: "When Nelly was told the truth I became hateful to her."
Reade: "She revolted from you?"
K: "Yes."
R: "What else could you expect?"
K: "What indeed!" (Tears.) "I wish I had let her into the secret. We might still be friends now."

"What indeed?" followed by tears (the only polite bodily secretion permitted in bourgeois discourse, which Reade consistently reads as evidence of "true womanhood") signifies the impossible, unspeakable, and unnamed desire between women, even in the age of romantic same-sex friendships. Reade professes to believe that Kate's tears are sincere, in earnest. Kate's answer is far from reassuring: she wished that she had let Nelly *in* on the secret. That is, Kate wanted to invite her to participate in an open secret as opposed to "never lying in the first place."[82] This distinction between open and closed secrets is again the difference between dissembling and simulation. According to this dialogue, Kate would have granted Nelly the power of the male observers—to have Nelly see her as merely masked, performing the mask, and not simulating. Once masculinity can be seen as merely a performance, her femininity is retroactively suspect as well. There is even the suggestion that Nelly, too, might have played a role.

Reade asks, but does not answer, the query: "Would Miss Nelly have wasted a single heart-string on Mrs. Kate Coombe, had that lady appeared in the regulation petticoat and corset?"[83] Because Reade poses this as a question, and not an unequivocal and disavowing statement, "Certainly such a thing is without doubt impossible," it leaves room for his readers to ponder the outcome of such a situation. Moreover, Reade says that Kate's affection for Nelly, because of its apparent veracity, must be valued and not uncritically denounced. Here we see Reade's commitment to the "actual"—to the sincerity of everyday, micropolitical reality. It is his desire to "report" the facts of this case, to bring it to light as a "true-case," that indeed makes his piece an "exceptional case in which the part simulated merged in realism" (p. 22).

He must deal with "an unnatural romance . . . [that is] wretchedly real. A wild growth of the erotic principle partly atoned for by its un-sullied purity" (p. 21). This is the paradox that Reade unravels in his essay, where the real, even or especially the wretchedly real, cannot be ignored. Such paradoxically pure passion makes Kate a heroine of sorts and allows Reade to treat her with a degree of fairness, or as he says, her exceptional case "convinces the critic to spare rather than squander sarcasm" (p. 25). Although Reade occasionally employs a con-demnatory tone, ultimately, the essay functions as an indictment of an inadequate system of representation. As he states: "the narrative [of] my theory of Mme. Coombe's escapade being due to an eccentricity of the entire system rather than to gross criminality" (p. 201) proves cor-rect. Here, Reade acknowledges that the "entire system" plays a role in regulating sex/gender relationships. Writing during the period in which "the [male] homosexual became a personage, a case history, a life form, and a morphology, with indiscreet anatomy and possibly a mysterious physiology," Reade is able to capture the shift between deviant acts in the juridical realm and the production of "deviant" modern sexual sub-jectivities and identities, such as "the mythic mannish lesbian."[84]

Kate's actions are from the outset disruptive to family structures. Changing genders involves shifts in class and familial status. One's class, family, and race bespeak one's gender—these aspects of identity are un-evenly imbricated. The family structures in this tale are from the incep-tion fractured. To begin with, Tom and Kate are cousins whose fathers are absent. Only Nelly possesses (or rather is possessed by) a father who rescues her, his issue and property, from deception. Androgynism presents a problem for any culture that benefits from creating and main-taining rigid gender distinctions. Although Reade's fascination with the problematic figure of the androgyne might have been the result of his interest in "real" narratives, his investigative (and perhaps voyeuristic) sensibilities, and his tendency toward "morbid" subjects, ultimately, his rendering of Kate's tale reveals how cultural rules are confronted by their own conflicting nature.

It also sets the stage for his broader claims about modern Western culture's inadequate system of sexual difference. According to Reade's reasoning, the current system is insufficient because it precludes "real" subjects, like Kate, who do not conform and who challenge the system's authority. As Francette Pacteau notes:

Discussions of Androgynism invariably . . . come up against a resistance
—not so much from the speaking subject, but from language itself. . . .
[L]anguage does not cater for the "neither . . . nor" of androgyny. . . .
[C]onfronted with the ubiquitous representations of the figure of the androgyne disseminated across visual and literary texts [these] definitions ask
for their own *dépassement*.[85]

When Kate admits her "true love" for Nellie, Reade contends that
"we are lost in haze."[86] This idea that questions the power of ocular perception has been interrogated throughout the entire dramatic account.
Reade has Kate proclaim: "If anyone thinks me what my things bespeak
me, that's no fault of mine" (p. 18).[87] This statement places the onus on
the viewer and exemplifies the belief that, "the androgyne does not exist
in the real; it is a symptom indicative of repressed desire."[88] Certainly,
this is one way to read both Reade's and Nelly's fascination with Kate.

In the beginning of his essay, Reade announces that men are the objects of women's jesting looks, that men are the most susceptible to the
inevitable falsehoods of sirens. Later, he claims Nelly as the quintessential myopic dupe. How else could he explain the fact that poor Nelly fell
in love with "a phantom, coat and trousers, *voilà tout*"?[89] After Kate's
costume has been shed, Reade surmises that "there is a flaw in the feminine iris, a variety of colour-blindness, or these amazing errors would
cease to be repeated from generation to generation" (p. 202). Reade's
allusion to "colour-blindness" is another instance of the imbrication of
race and sex. Reade writes that Nelly thought "that Fred was the very
most charming specimen of the hideous sex" (p. 20). This doubly ironic
statement sums up the spirit of Reade's commentary and exposes the
fissures in Victorian discourse about gender. Only Fred, "this beautiful
thing" and "a lady-killer" (this is, of course, literalized by Kate, who
kills the lady she was, to invent the "man" she portrays), could represent the best of the hideous sex because she is, in fact, not that sex. This
double gesture allows Kate to perform as a specimen of the hideous
male sex. She knows that "never has a man loved a women so" (p. 21),
and thus, Kate is and is not the exception to the rules of masculinity.

Reade tends to occlude his own leering interest in Kate's deceptive
body. At the end of the narrative when she finally puts on the regulation

petticoats, it is he who asks her to "extract" her incriminating "masculine properties," which Kate conveniently still kept in the "recesses of her wardrobe" (p. 210). The power of (put on/exchangeable) male properties is obscured by the culture that desires to keep such properties discretely closeted. The reference to Kate's "properties," when the very notion of married women's property was still in dispute, calls attention to another aspect of Kate's masculine presumptions. By endowing herself with "properties," she usurps or steals a masculine privilege: she assumes a false identity, which scathingly is revealed to be not false, but rather "falsely true" (p. 25).

As Reade explains it: "Folly plus deceit . . . is not vice, neither is it conspiracy to deprave, nor any crime recognised by human law" (p. 194). Reade says that, "Meeting Nelly Smith, Kate forgot her sex, accepting the illusion of her own manufacture as reality" (p. 194). Kate's damnation and salvation is marked at the moment her "play developed into earnest [when her] simulating merged with realism" (p. 22). Reade "rates her as a poet, rather than a scoundrel" (p. 212) because she repents and remains with her husband. He adds, "I don't doubt that the proper place for many poets may be an asylum, but not, if you please, a gaol" (p. 212). This statement is applicable, ironically, to Wilde's post-trial trials. While this may have been the case when Reade wrote Kate's story, the last decades of the century ushered in new taxonomic categories that produced new roles, which were both played and plagued. Kate's equivocal equation, "folly plus deceit," would become a serious charge.[90]

"An epoch that has invented the divided skirt need not be too severe on androgynism. Sexes, like classes, have a tendency to fuse and borrow each other's *differentia.*"[91] Reade appears to sanction, rather sarcastically, such mixing: he claims that it is natural in the wake of the proliferation and perversion of Darwinian ideology. Nonetheless, his anxiety is evident. In the next paragraph he labels such transformations "evil," writing:

Fred's short hair in 1860 was an outrage. . . . in 1883 the Kates one meets are cropped *à la militaire*, and parade with gold-headed sticks like bedells. The sex is following Fred to do evil, and at the rate of progress androgynism is making, the table of affinity will soon have to be enlarged by the addition of the prohibitive enactment, "A woman may not marry her grandmother." (p. 212) [92]

This quotation reflects the changing status of women in Victorian society as well as the potential need for restructuring Victorian values.

Reade's remarks prefigure the fears of degeneration that plagued the final decades of the century: "That is the story from prologue to climax. It needs only a real male lover, jilted in favor of Kate, to impart the essentials of a comedy of errors. In its existing form it might be described as serious farce, but for the anti-climax which was no laughing matter." [93] Indeed, the climax of such a "pathetic and piquant [or pruriently prudish]" (p. 11) tale could not be "a laughing matter." Had her tale, in dramatic terms, been a Shakespearean comedy whose topsy-turvy inverted center is righted in the end, it would not have exposed the seriousness of Kate's transgression. That is, Reade's pathetic anti-climax serves as just (and necessary) punishment for "the victimizer" (p. 212). Put differently, Reade ends this piece as he did his novel, *Peg Woffington*, with the actress shedding tears as a sign of her repentance. The reader of Kate's story is assured of her death as means of ending her otherwise endless oscillations.

At the conclusion of Reade's account, Kate seemingly succumbs to the law when she "transforms herself into an affectionate wife and . . . dies of a broken heart" (p. 212). But this report is hearsay, secondhand and perhaps unreliable. This statement does not assure of us of these facts and, indeed, like Kate's "closeted" costume, may only be the mask hiding her still hollow heart. Reade does say, after all, that Kate *transformed* herself into an affectionate wife. Does not this conversion also hint at her continuing aptitude for simulation and locomutation? This is the question that haunts not only Victorian visions of gender but also our own. The story ends with a return to an "original" order (that is to say, with each "family" intact), but not without some substantive epistemological shifts, and a sense that policing and prohibitions will be necessary to secure the current regime of radical difference. As Lewis Lapham explains, "The clarity of gender makes possible the human dialectic. Let the lines of balanced tension go slack and the structure dissolves into the ooze of androgyny and narcissism." [94]

It is an effort to control such women—it requires the continued assertions of inequality, and overt as well as covert practices (legislation, police intervention), to maintain the norm and exclude women's power. Reade acknowledges that these hybrid things exist and his use of them affirms (if not creates) their cultural value. As the narrator asserts in *Peg Woffington,* "these things would be incredible if they were not common."[95] Reade's concern for the (re)production of normative conditions serves as a harbinger to the "hybrid, morbid, insane new truths of the era."[96]

By backing up and looking backward, we can see Charles Reade and his collection of bachelors, deviants, odd figures, and his attention to identity as performance as Wilde's predecessor. If Reade's fictional works set up many of the issues about earnestness and acting in Victorian England, then Oscar Wilde might well be his theatrical heir. Wilde's now "legendary" epigrams and his antinatural style (he wrote in *An Ideal Husband* that, "to be natural is such a very difficult pose to keep up") are reminiscent of Reade's themes. Many important moments and characters that appear in Wilde's oeuvre were gleaned from Reade, who died well before Wilde's first play was even produced.

One might even look to the names of characters like Sybil Vane in *Dorian Gray* to map out a connection, since Reade himself had several characters named Vane in his work. So too, Reade's line, "A husband with a wife in Shropshire is so much like a bachelor," resembles Wilde's, "These days one cannot tell the difference between bachelors and husbands."[97] Both Reade and Wilde were figures who worked to blur the boundaries between art and life, mask and face, theater and home.

One difference between these theatrical men, besides that of temperament and talent, is the tenor of the times in which they wrote. Wilde's world (remember that he stood in symbolic relation to [his] age) was characterized by a cynicism that was only beginning to surface when Reade was writing at mid-century. Beatrice Webb described the society of the 1890s as having "no roots in neighborhood, in vocation, in creed, or for that matter race. . . . [We are like] a series of moving pictures—surface impressions without depth—restlessly stimulating in their variety."[98] Thus, Wilde's public was perhaps more comfortable with the glittering surfaces presented in his productions.

Wilde's play, *Lady Windermere's Fan,* presents a leading woman, Mrs.

Erlynne, who is like Peg, both comic and compassionate: "both very clever and very good."[99] Mrs. Erlynne is a fallen woman because she had an illegitimate daughter. The daughter, now Lady Windermere, is a respectable married woman who knows nothing of her own impure origins. The two women meet unexpectedly at a ball given at the Windermere mansion. Mrs. Erlynne's role in the play is similar to Peg's in *Masks and Faces*. She, too, elects to preserve a "perfect" patriarchal marriage by keeping the secret of her daughter's birth. In a line reminiscent of the pure wife Mabel Vane's reaction to Peg in act 1 of *Masks and Faces*, the "pure" woman, Lady Windermere, exclaims that "she abhors dreadful people and scandals," just before she is about to be entangled with both. Lady Windermere's rigid morality is eroded by her adventure with Mrs. Erlynne, who never discloses her true identity to her daughter. The similarities in plot between these two works include the fact that the two women switch identities and that the actress pretends to sacrifice herself for her sentimental "sister."

Peg and Mrs. Erlynne are also similar: both are drawn from "real" actresses (the latter is Wilde's version of Lily Langtry) and, indeed, both characters act sublimely. Mrs. Erlynne poses as a respectable lady and, later, as a moralistic mother. When Peg queries: "What have we to do with homes, hearths, or firesides? Have we not the play-house, its paste diamonds, its paste feelings. . . . Hearts?—beneath loads of paint and tinsel? Nonsense!" her answer is echoed by Mrs. Erlynne, who says, "A heart does not go with modern dress."[100] Mrs. Erlynne's cavalier attitude about her "heart" and her motherly feelings harken back to George Eliot's characterization of Princess Halm-Eberstein, Daniel Deronda's mother in the novel of the same name, in that both women choose independence over marriage and motherhood. Both *Masks and Faces* and *Lady Windermere's Fan* cut to the heart (pun intended) of dominant Victorian values. Both Peg and Mrs. Erlynne have the comic ability to cast off convention.

Women such as Peg and Mrs. Erlynne are hybrid because they combine passion—thought to be a masculine attribute—with purity—the ultimate feminine virtue. By being both clever and good, pure and passionate, these characters became exceptional figures who highlighted possibilities for reconceptualizing gender differences in Victorian culture. Mrs. Erlynne may be read as a more advanced Peg Woffington.

Although the former is not technically an actress, she is a "woman with twelve pasts," making her very much like an actress who has played and impersonated a number of parts with which she is identified.[101]

The ending of the original production of *Masks and Faces* leaves the audience with Peg having ended her affair with Vane and returning him to Mabel, while she herself dupes Pomander into giving her a cash bonus. That Peg will continue happily in her escapades is implicit. In *Lady Windermere's Fan*, however, the comic triumph of the heroine is explicit. Mrs. Erlynne states quite clearly that conventional men like Lord Windermere might "like [her] to retire to a convent . . . as people do in silly novels [an almost direct reference to Reade's ending to *Peg Woffington*]; but in real life . . . what consoles one now is not repentance but pleasure."[102] She marries Tuppy, a wealthy gentleman, and retires to the continent, where her more passionate nature will be in accord with the warmer climate, lush Renaissance art, and rampant Catholicism.

Lady Windermere learns that "people can no longer be divided into the good and the bad as though they belonged to separate races" (act 4). Indeed, this idea reverberates throughout other fin de siècle texts, such as Wilde's *The Picture of Dorian Gray*, Robert Louis Stevenson's *Dr. Jekyll and Mr. Hyde*, and H. G. Wells's *The Island of Dr. Moreau*. The confusion of supposedly discrete and distant entities seen in the conflation of the playhouse (the actors' workhouse) and the middle-class home, of black and white races, as well as male and female roles, seemed to substantiate Reade's claim that men and women, like classes, were "borrowing each other's differentia."[103]

Chapter Four
DEFORMING ISLAND RACES

Society is a pyramid . . . resting precariously upon an unstable
agglomeration of mixed materials, often decaying and rotting away, whose
corrupting influences are perpetually spreading upwards.
—Alexander Thompson, *Meloria*

Throughout the nineteenth century, Thomas Atkins, a menagerist at the
Liverpool Zoological Gardens, successfully bred lions and tigers. Advertisements for Atkins's ligers, tigons, or lion-tigers, to use the phrase
purportedly coined by William IV, read: "The greatest phenomenon . . .
in the history of these animals . . . once the most implacable enemies in
the forest . . . [is that] the Proprietor of these Gardens [has proven], that
under the dominion of man even the most savage spirits may be subdued."[1] Although Atkins effectively mastered his hybrid animals, many
other Victorian men succumbed to the power of the beast. The perceived similarity of man and beast flourished in the wake of Darwinian
ideology, and was viewed as a threat to and symptom of the dissolution
of the boundaries that distinguished not only the tame from the wild,
but also one race, sex, and/or class from another.

This chapter examines attempts to subdue savage man-beast hybrids,
and discusses ways in which many nineteenth-century critics conflated
monstrous hybrids and their white, "middle-class" male creators. More
specifically, this chapter explores ideas about hybridity, blackness, femininity, and monstrosity in H. G. Wells's novel, *The Island of Dr. Moreau*.[2]
This late-nineteenth-century text reflects the pervasiveness of the hybrid anxiety documented as being an important aspect of much Victorian discourse.[3] *The Island of Dr. Moreau* registers as well as reinscribes
the belief that the fate and status of the *English* race itself is in jeopardy
of becoming monstrously hybrid, blackened, and feminized.

Wells claimed to see his work as a response to Oscar Wilde's infamous trial.

There was a scandalous trial . . . the graceless and piteous downfall of a man of genius, and [my] story was the response of an imaginative mind to the reminder that humanity is but animal, rough-hewn to a reasonable shape and in perpetual internal conflict between instinct and injunction. The story embodies this ideal, but apart from this embodiment it has no allegorical quality. It was written just to give the utmost possible vividness to that conception of men as hewn and confused and tormented beasts.[4]

This statement shows how the "pure" English gentleman becomes bestial at the end of the century. What Wells was responding to may not only have been the trial, but also Wilde's *The Picture of Dorian Gray*, which mentions many "impossible" and "monstrous" things that "breed horrors," and has at least one "half-caste dressed in a ragged turban and shabby ulster grin[ning] a hideous greeting."[5] The fascination with unnatural hybrids reflects attitudes toward race, gender, and generation that were crucial in the age of imperialist trauma.

The degenerative transformations of the protagonist, Mr. Prendick, an upstanding Englishman, occur at the height of English imperial power and nationalistic supremacy. Indeed, many middle-class English*men* in this generation became newly aware of themselves as racialized beings. The representative Englishman questioned his ability to maintain the various boundaries (economic, geographic, gender, sexual, psychological) he created. In other words, as ideas about "little England" succumbed to Benjamin Disraeli's ideology of imperialism, and as England's geopolitical borders expanded, fears about maintaining English borders (both real and imagined) multiplied. Although in 1898 C. F. Adams asserted that imperialism "has saved the Anglo-Saxon stock from being a nation of half-breeds and miscengenates" (*OED*), as we have seen, the Anglo-Saxon race is always already a hybrid nation. Moreover, *The Island of Dr. Moreau* makes a black female puma, a defiant daughter, the source of the threatening downfall. The black female puma contrasts with the black tulip, the compliant daughter produced by Van Bearle.

Even though ideas about the invasion and influence of un-English "others" had always played a part in discussions of domestic policy and in definitions of English identity, the new economic and intellectual climate at the end of the century fueled and magnified these fears. Would the English nation be able to control its growing hybrid border-populations, such as the Irish Catholics, the Africans, and the Hindus? More important, would the strong Anglo-Saxon race survive the threats to its assumed racial purity when some of its own breed seemed to succumb to the power of the horrific hybridity "invading" England? Was man evolving or devolving? What role did his sexuality and heredity play in determining his position?

The magnitude of these queries results from the fact that ideas about "race" hardened as the nineteenth century "progressed." The Darwinian revolution made organizing disciplines such as taxonomy and other sciences available to a greater number of educated Victorians, who then disseminated and distorted, as well as reinforced, this Darwinian ideology. Wells is one of the major writers to elaborate corrupted versions of Darwinian thought, as his scientific fantasy, *The Island of Dr. Moreau,* demonstrates.

In order to discuss nineteenth-century reactions to "man-beast" hybrids, I present a brief overview of the relationship between man and animals in the British, Western tradition. That man himself was a unique being situated, by God's glory, halfway between the beasts and the angels was a common conception in early modern England. Indeed, this is the basic thesis of the Great Chain of Being. The Great Chain of Being dominated intellectual thought in the Renaissance and its imaginative power persisted throughout the nineteenth century.[6] Some scholars have argued that even Darwin only temporalized the theory, rendering it dynamic in our time rather than fixed.[7] Constructions (philosophical, economic, linguistic, and social) of the relationship between humans and animals throughout British culture concur with readings of the function of the hybrid in Victorian discourse. Various strategies of classification and categorization are an enduring part of the quest to define Englishness.

Before the nineteenth century, philosophers, members of the clergy, and other officials of nationally sanctioned bodies that produced dominant cultural ideology, attempted to "fix" ambiguous, nondiscrete categories into a stable, differentiated framework. This project went hand in hand with the Newtonian scientific revolution enterprise of stressing order, stability, and regularity. Earlier in the Renaissance, according to

Harriet Ritvo, bestiaries "made no attempt to group animals that were physically similar . . . such as the lion and the tiger; nor in arranging their contents did they employ the anthropocentric binary distinctions, such as edible-inedible, useful-useless, wild-tame, and beautiful-ugly. . . ."[8] These oppositional definitions began to appear during the seventeenth century with the development of empirical science, natural history, and more analytic systems of classification.[9]

Many Puritan thinkers believed that it was dangerous to pretend to be an animal on the stage, as this might be read as a desecration of man's godly image.[10] As John Stuart Mill, among many other Victorians who argued for the Sanitation Acts, said, cleanliness is essential because its absence, "more than anything else renders man bestial."[11] Other practices that were thought to render humans bestial were overindulgence of the sexual appetite, vivisection, and vaccination. But it was the act of bestiality that was believed, until 1861 when it was no longer illegal, to "turn man into a very beast . . . and was seen as the sin of confusion . . . the immoral mix[ing of] categories," according to Keith Thomas.[12] The decision to allow bestiality seemed to confirm the clarity of the species and, in some sense, lent humanity to the animals.

The mutability of this previously fixed barrier drives many late-Victorian fantasies that discuss man-beast hybrids. As Michel Foucault notes,

It is often said that the establishment of botanical gardens and zoological collections expressed a new curiosity about exotic plants and animals. In fact, these had already claimed men's interest. . . . What had changed was the space in which it was possible to describe them. To the Renaissance the strangeness of animals was spectacle: . . . the natural history room and the garden as created in the Classical period, replace the circular procession of the show with the arrangement of things in a table. What came surreptitiously into being between the age of the theatre and that of the catalogue was not the desire for knowledge, but a new way of connecting things both to the eye and to discourse. A new way of making history.[13]

The barriers become mutable as well through the loss of faith, changes in the economic structure of England that valued the symbolic cash nexus over more concrete material exchange, and increased imperial expansion. In *Past and Present,* Thomas Carlyle characterized his era as ". . . a great unintelligible PERHAPS."[14] The question of man, and especially the *English* man's place on the scale of human civilization, was vexed by conflicting social, scientific, and political theories.

The eighteenth-century naturalist Charles Bingley asserted, "How slender so ever it may appear . . . the barrier which separates men from brutes is fixed and immutable."[15] This assertion was challenged throughout the nineteenth century. The slender but assiduously maintained barrier that separated man from beast slowly eroded. New developments in the nineteenth century assailed the comparatively simple, dichotomous ordering so common in the seventeenth and eighteenth centuries. Although fears about man's place in the natural order predate Darwin, his science gave such anxieties new immediacy and legitimacy. Through the dissemination of Darwinian thought, the English gentleman had to work harder than ever to distinguish himself from his animal brethren (as well as "lower" beings—such as the Irish, black people, and women—and those associated with them). How successful were Victorians at "mov[ing] upward / working out the beast," to use Alfred Tennyson's suggestive phrase?[16]

Tennyson's classic poem, *In Memoriam*, addresses the effects of pre-Darwinian conceptions of evolution on man's place in nature. He writes:

They say the solid earth whereon we tread
In tracts of fluent heat began,
And grew to seeming-random forms
The seeming prey of cyclic storms,
Till at the last arose the man;

Who throve and branch'd from clime to clime,
The herald of a higher race,
And of himself in higher place,
If so he type this work of time

Within himself . . . and show
That life is not as idle ore . . .
Arise and fly
The reeling Faun, the sensual feast;
Move upward, working out the beast,
And let the ape and tiger die.

Tennyson's important statement about evolution posits that man is the harbinger of his own, more civilized future. Written in the imperative, the poem still contains elements of doubt. Man appears to be the "herald of a higher race," no longer a being "who throve and branch'd from clime to clime." But the statement is ambiguous. In one reading, the "original" tree of affinity served as a common way of imagining the growth of man. This statement might also refer to man's simian ancestry. In Tennyson's text, man's "life is not as idle ore"—it is not stagnant and idle; rather, man has the ability to move and progress. He walks upright, even flies upwards, working out the beast, the "Faun" (another version of Defoe's satyr) and "the sensual feast." Man's animal past of ape and tiger will surely die with man's ascendancy. Although the injunction is stated, time seemed to ravage this revision of the biblical origin.

In comparing Tennyson's famous verse about the origin of life to that of Defoe's satirical "A True-Born Englishman," both pre-Darwinian, we find two versions of human development, one overtly nationalistic, the other more general. Both acknowledge the random origins of life and both conclude with images of the *extraction* of the Englishman from this chaotic material. In *The Island of Dr. Moreau*, the mad scientist attempts to speed up this process through his vivisection experiments. Moreau's plan to "humanize" all the beasts seems to be a literal translation of Tennyson's utopic fantasy. Of course, Moreau fails—the ape and tiger stubbornly refuse to die or to be tamed, just as, it might be said, the Englishman fails to "[m]ove upward, working out the beast[ly]" aspects of his humanity.

What had changed from earlier in the century was man's control of science and technology. Indeed, by the end of the century, racial theories were aided by the predominance of imperialism and the birth of eugenics, which replaced "natural" (read random) selection with ideas about genetic transformation. The term *eugenics* was coined in 1883 by Darwin's cousin, Francis Galton, who defined it as "the study of agencies under social control that may improve or impair the racial qualities of future generations either physically or mentally."[17] The idea that racial populations could be controlled by human effort appealed to Victorian notions of progress and, although resisted by some, eugenic theory gained popularity. Certainly, it played a role in Wells's work.

Because evolutionary theorists had such an impact on Victorian cultural classifications, writers across a range of disciplines grappled with new representations of man's place in this endlessly transforming world. Wells, along with such other "empire boys" as Robert Louis Stevenson, Rider Haggard, and Rudyard Kipling, wrote in the aftermath of Darwin's astonishing assertions. As late-nineteenth-century intellectuals, these writers were interested in and influenced by scientific inquiry. Their work, almost as much as that of the evolutionary theorists, helped to seal the continuity between men and animals, and for many, even cemented the parallels between these (now more than ever) closely related species.[18] Their novels quite clearly reinterpret Darwinian ideas about man's relationship to animals. Wells's work, in particular, focuses on man's relationship to the animal within himself—in short, to the wild aspects of the tame English gentleman. References to and constructions of this "doubled" standard man are ubiquitous during the final decades of the century. Moreover, *The Island of Dr. Moreau* may be seen as a supreme example of "imperial gothic."[19]

The Island of Dr. Moreau describes the imagined *rapid* degeneration of the English race as a result of imperial expansion, scientific theories, and political and economic conflict. The birth of the hybrid (monstrous) middle-class Englishman in this book, and in late-Victorian culture in general, signals the break down of national boundaries. The heart of darkness invades what became known as "Darkest England."[20] This metaphoric contamination of Anglo-Irish and Anglo-Indian, as well as Anglo-Saxon, populations appears frequently in late-Victorian literature. As Patrick Brantlinger asserts:

Not only do stereotypes of natives and savages degenerate toward the ignoble and the bestial in late Victorian thinking, however; so do the seemingly contrasting images of European explorers, traders, and colonizers. . . . Robinson Crusoe held out manfully against the cannibals. . . . [L]ate Victorian literature is filled with *backsliders* who like Conrad's Kurtz themselves become white savages. (italics added)[21]

In the nineteenth century, the classification of animals changed. During this period, animals, like women, were divided into two categories: domestic (owned) and wild. When, as was the case in Regent's Park beginning in 1840, animals were arranged taxonomically, the exhibits showed "nature not only confined and restrained, but interpreted and ordered." [22] Of course, as has been suggested earlier, the absolute division between wild and tame is logically inconsistent, and therefore, difficult to maintain. Thus, anxiety remained about the measure of control one had over other creatures.

The numerous injunctions against ill-bred dogs and the negative descriptions of animal hybrids were similar to injunctions against the creation of human hybrids at the end of the century. Darwin made these connections explicit when he wrote, "the dichotomy between domesticated animals and wild animals is similar to that between the civilized and the savage human societies. The wildness often shown by hybrids of domestic species had the same cause as the wickedness that characterized human half-breeds." [23] Clarity of category and purity of breed were to be preserved, since that was one way of maintaining a distinctive, linear (if mythical) history of the English race.

The injunction against some kinds of hybridity and forms of hybridizing and the sanction of others raises the question of value. It seems that professional breeders, in response to patron's demands and market pressures (some of which they helped to foster), were rewarded, while natural hybridization led to the production of mongrels — especially in animals. Indeed, scientific hybridizers or eugenicists thought that their man-supervised hybridizing could be beneficial to society; they frowned, however, on "brute" miscegenation as evil, as untamed nature mixed too promiscuously. Only white Englishmen were able to strike the proportionate balance between variation and stability.

Responding to anxiety aroused by Darwin's *The Origins of Species by Means of Natural Selection, of the Preservation of Favoured Races in the Struggle for Life,* [24] "hybridizers" became obsessed with asserting man's dominance over lower animals and sought to prove their superiority by controlling the breeding of others. Eugenicists attempted to solidify stereotypical figures, thereby fixing forms forever. This desire is read most clearly in the development of dog pedigrees and the pervasiveness of dog shows, the purpose of which, as Harriet Ritvo explains, was to "improve various breeds, display model specimens, and to discourage the breeding of mongrels." [25] Nevertheless, she continues, "the desire to triumph over obstacles mounted by nature may also explain the Victorian fascination with hybrids, which explicitly violated natural categories" (p. 235). The differences between these two reactions to hybrid mongrels become sharper when the division between man and animal is more distinct. That is, hybrid animals produced under man's control could be fascinating, whereas randomly produced or indiscriminate hybrid humans were usually read as threatening to the social order.

When monkey hides were displayed in a booth at the Great Exhibition of 1851, viewers noted that "it was painful to think of the suffering the poor beasts must have undergone [yet some good was also shown since] the work of catching these animals civilizes the Africans."[26] This remark unwittingly provides evidence of the English propensity to equate civilized value with conquest. Some fifty years later, the 1908 Franco-British exhibit displayed "primitive" people of the British empire (including the Irish) as "savage spirits subdued."[27] So too, the frontispiece for an edition of Kipling's works published in 1900 depicts the author in a white suit, playing with his "colored" characters, who are portrayed as "lesser," smaller, colonized puppets—with strings attached. This is a clear representation of the white man's burden. Indeed, it is the hybridity of these tamed wild things that served as a "model for the double process of colonialism,"[28] to use Stallybrass and White's phrase.

One way in which this distancing occurred was the analogical labeling of low others as animalistic. The analogies made between the poor and pigs, between enslaved black bodies and unruly beasts, between apes and the Irish—did a disservice to all at the same time that it served to protect certain (mostly white male) individuals from contamination. The physiognomist Johann Casper Lavater believed that "those who wish to degrade man to beast caricature him to the rank of the orang-outang; and in idea, raise the orang-outang to the rank of man."[29] This formulation attests to the hierarchy established between man and animal, as well as to the slipperiness of the scale.

In these cases, as Ritvo describes, the controlled "wildness was attractive, not ugly. Wild animals, like peasants and exotic foreigners with whom they were classed [and displayed] evoked sympathy."[30] The attractive wildness of such creatures was a result of the increasing control over them by English imperialists. Certainly, this illusion of order, as well as the fixity of the other, worked to ease anxious English gentlemen. Such explanations suggest some of the fascination with hybrid others registered by Victorian observers.

Perhaps the most famous of all was Joseph Merrick, popularly, and erroneously, known as the Elephant Man.[31] As a captive beast paraded in menageries, Merrick exemplifies the Victorian hybrid. His journey from poor house to hospitable (if hospitalized) gentleman summarized the transformation of the hybrid in Victorian culture. Even Merrick's humane doctor, Frederick Treves, described the afflicted man as

a frightful creature that could only have been possible in a nightmare. It was the figure of a man with the characteristics of an elephant. The trans-figuration was not far advanced. There was still more of the man than the beast. This fact — that it was still human — was the most repellent attribute of the creature. . . . there was . . . the loathing insinuation of a man being changed into an animal. (p. 12)

Treves's identifies the Elephant Man's "asymmetry," his only partially finished transfiguration. The creature is especially hideous because these hybrid qualities that are synonymous with the gothic monstrosity suggesting the relationship between the discursive formation of race and the gothic. Treves fervently imagines that Merrick could only have been possible in a nightmare and his description of his patient makes use of the gothic, horror genre of which Wells's text is also a part.

Although trained to be an objective physician, even Treves categorizes the Elephant Man according to the prevailing ideology that named hybrids horrific. He makes it quite clear that the combination of Merrick's human (good English) qualities with his beastly (foreign and dirty) qualities is "the most repellent attribute of the creature." Such a formulation ensures that unions of opposites are always condemned.[32] Merrick is an unstable hybrid who shifts positions on the developmental hierarchy, thereby returning its manufactured order to chaos. He is an indeterminate figure and, therefore, as we have seen in so many other "true hybrid cases," must be read as a "loathing insinuation" that threatens supposedly solid and stolid John Bull figures.

In 1861, the ethnographer James Crawfurd stated that "at best we English are hybrids and not the worse for it,"[33] in a line that seems to echo Defoe's ideology in his poem, "A True-Born Englishman." Crawfurd's sentiment, however, proved to be problematic for the majority of Victorians. While anthropologists, ethnographers, and other "racialist" thinkers did acknowledge the "modern" fact that pure, aboriginal races no longer existed, they were clear in their belief that pure essences did

exist at some point and could still be detected, even in the ever changing present. Thus, the battle over control of the environment, a romantic and conservative movement to reclaim and preserve (to re-member)
pure races, became popular in many discourses. One exemplary expression of this Victorian sentiment is Edward Dicey's assertion (made
in 1863) that "hybridity insults the basic instinct of self-preservation"
(*OED*). Crawfurd and Dicey's statements were tested in a more public
forum during the Governor Eyre controversy of 1865.

One of the worst scandals that demonstrated whites' rule over blacks,
the controversy involved the English Governor Eyre and the leader of a
populist uprising, by George Gordon, a mulatto at Morant Bay, Jamaica.
Charles Kingsley, one of the Victorian critics who sided with Eyre's violent acts (he hanged the leader and massacred many others) against
the Jamaican subjects under his rule, said of the "native" inhabitants:
"Prove that it is *human* life. It is beast-life . . . you are beasts all the
more dangerous because you have semi-human cunning" (italics in
original).[34] This sentiment, also expressed in *Moreau*, echoes Treves's
description of the Elephant Man.

As one of the major incidents that crystallized the ideas of race and
empire at mid-century, the Governor Eyre controversy underscores the
importance of hybridity in debates about race and nation. During the
eighteenth century and the first half of the nineteenth century, two
incompatible scientific ideas about the origins of humankind existed.
Baldly stated, monogenesists believed that all humans were derived
from a single "racial" stock, whereas polygenesists believed humans
originated from several distinct types. The biological racism that pre-
dominated at the end of the nineteenth century was overwhelmingly
polygenesist. (Darwin was a monogenesist, as his beliefs about the web
of affinities between humans and his other theories indicate.)

Carlyle and Mill argued opposing sides in a debate on "the negro
question" that anticipated subsequent discussions about Eyre's violent
attack on the Jamaican revolters at Morant Bay in the 1860s.[35] As Catherine Hall asserts, Carlyle's agreement with Eyre's position was evidence
of the growth of "a more aggressive biological racism rooted in the assumption that blacks were not brothers and sisters [as abolitionist rhetoric claimed] but a different species, born to be mastered."[36] The more
liberal and progressive Mill, however, sympathized with the rebels.

Definitions of the term *race* shifted throughout the century.[37] If we define race like most Victorian intellectuals did, as lineage it applies to an English and Irish race, as well as a "negro" race. It is obvious even from these examples that the idea of race was inextricably connected to definitions of national identity. Victorian anthropologists and ethnographers commonly believed that geography, in some sense, produced racial variation. Edward A. Freeman's highly influential exhaustive six-volume *History of the Norman Conquest* [38] argued that although the English race had been mixed with other nations, an essential English type remained dominant. Thus, despite some disagreement, most of the "racial" historians of this period succeeded in their ultimate quest to give laudatory, essentialist descriptions of a *truly* true-born Englishman. As Freeman stated:

I will assume that what is Teutonic in us is not merely one element among others, but that it is the very life and essence of our national being; that whatever else we may have in us, whatever we have drawn from those whom we conquered or from those who conquered us, is no co-ordinate element, but a mere infusion into our Teutonic essence; in a word, I will assume that Englishmen are Englishmen, that we are ourselves and not some other people. I assume that, as we have had one national name, one national speech, from the beginning, . . . [that] we are an unbroken national being. (p. 554)

Freeman's representation of the purity of the English race, despite mixing, pays homage to the dominance of the Teuton strain and denigrates an imagined "co-ordinate," unstable (even broken), hybrid other. Freeman summons and holds up the image of a unified nation. His tautological formulation, "I will assume that Englishmen are Englishmen," openly contradicts the fact that the race is grounded only on "assumption." There is no origin, or rather, only an origin arbitrarily conceived. His formulation follows that of Wells's beast people, who ultimately revert to their original type. The belief in pure, if unseen essences allows England and the English—despite years of struggle for Irish, Welsh, and Scottish independence—to remain, at root, an unbroken nation and "nationality." The significance of the term *English* subsumes lesser British countries (not to mention colonies) under one corporeal cover.

Whig historical accounts such as Freeman's placed English civilization at the zenith of human achievement. The overwhelming rationale for the crowning glory of England's proven ability to govern was the Teutonic racial heritage of her inhabitants. The English were the fittest race when it came to ruling (in all senses of the word—measuring and delineating) others. This ideology is both reflected in and challenged by Wells's under-read classic, *The Island of Dr. Moreau*.

H. G. Wells's *The Island of Dr. Moreau* focuses on one Englishman's confrontation with an island of man-beast hybrids. The story documents Prendick's reactions to these odd amalgamations, whose evolution and rapid degeneration he witnesses while marooned on the island of the outcast vivisector, Dr. Moreau. The connections between Prendick and Moreau's beast-men converge as the tale progresses. These connections, made stronger by Darwinian ideology, trouble the text, and transform it into a terrifying thriller and a modern allegory.

In one of the very few discussions of this work, Jill Milling notes that:

The human beast composite is a special construction of the human mind that acknowledges an affinity between humans and animals and external-izes the fear of the animal that lurks behind the human mask. . . . The characteristics ascribed to these animals are the most confused and contra-dictory; the domesticated beast is . . . half-human and half-beast—created partly by the gods and partly by man. It is a constant reminder of human domination of nature; belonging both to the natural world and to human civilization, the humanized beast is, like its master, an ambiguous animal, removed from its natural origins and encaged in an artificial world it helped to create.[39]

As well as appealing to and attempting to allay Victorian fears about various forms of hybridity, *The Island of Dr. Moreau* dramatizes other important tensions, such as the fear of human intervention in natu-ral selection, man's ability to control "nature," ambivalences about the growing cultural prestige of "professional" doctors, and finally, the po-tential collapse of "racial" distinctions as markers of character or moral beings. It may also be read as an anti-idyll that locates its demonic ex-perimenter in a place that had already begun to be appropriated as the privileged site for the celebration of "primitive" (uninhibited) sexuality.

The issue of bestiality is defused, however, in *The Island of Dr. Moreau* since the main character, Prendick, makes it a point "to avoid intercourse with them [beast people] in every possible way."[40] Although Prendick may not mean or may not only mean intercourse in the carnal sense, it is mentioned in the context of a discussion of the wanton females who inhabit the island. Even though he never engages in sexual intercourse with the brutish beast women, Prendick's purity is not immune to the taint of the bestial. At specific moments in the text, discourses about hybridity and breeding, as well as race and gender, connect in culturally important and intriguing ways.

For example, the genre under which this text has been classified is itself a marker of its hybridity or "gothic monstrosity."[41] Traditionally termed a "scientific romance," it remains a difficult book to categorize. Michael Draper explains that "the term scientific romance . . . like science-fiction, yokes together two apparent opposites: science and art, knowledge and fantasy."[42] In short, it is a hybrid form and thus appropriate to Wells's content. The novel opens like *Dracula* or many other novels that use newspaper or documentary accounts to establish the "truth" of fabulous tales. In this sense, it is also in the tradition of *Frankenstein* (London, 1818), although Wells's beast people, unlike Mary Shelley's hybrid monster, do not have "souls." There are also some parallels with Defoe's *Robinson Crusoe* in that the remote islands in each text may be read ironically, as microcosms of England or Albion. So too, both of these novels open with a shipwreck.

In chapter 1 of *The Island of Dr. Moreau*, entitled "In the dinghy of the Lady Vain,"[43] recounts the desperate plight of three passengers from the wrecked Lady Vain who narrowly escape eating one another. Only Prendick is rescued by Moreau's assistant, Montgomery, whose "loose nether lip" is remarked on throughout the text. It is Prendick who narrates the bizarre tale of Dr. Moreau's island. The ship that saves Prendick is a trading vessel, the *Ipecacuanha* (a medicine used to induce regurgitation). The ship travels between "Arica and Callao," and therefore, is located halfway (like halfway houses) between two sites in a liminal, hybrid space. Indeed, at first glimpse, the ship is sailing as the "sun is midway down the western sky" (p. 18). One may read the text as an interrogation of the interstitial.

For example, Prendick describes the landscape as a space where "the interspaces in the trees, the gaps in the further vegetation . . . grew black and mysterious . . . [and] melted into formless blackness" (p. 60). The very first description of the island represents it as "a low-lying patch of dim blue in the uncertain blue-grey sea" (p. 23). Such depictions of the island as hybrid and unstable recur throughout the work. "The world was confusion, blurred with drifting black and red phantasms . . ." (p. 51). The ground on which Prendick walks is always "giving way," threatening to subsume him like the unstable foundation that grounded modern man's place on the hierarchy.

Contemporary reviews of the novel aptly compared it to Swift's *Gulliver's Travels*, Defoe's *Journal of the Plague Year*, Shelley's *Frankenstein*, and Stevenson's *Dr. Jekyll and Mr. Hyde*. Most of the reviewers had difficulty classifying the book. They admired Wells's skill but were unclear as to whether or not his subject was "fit for art." Critic Basil Williams wrote that "the horrors described . . . raise the question how far it is legitimate to create feelings of disgust in a work of art."[44] Most English reviewers felt that "Mr. Wells put out his talent to the most flagitious usury" (ibid.). Only the French critic Augustan Filon, writing in *Revue des Deux Mondes* (December 1904), gave a positive review. He surmised that, "whether because of the repulsive details with which it abounds, or because an anti-Christian symbolism was discovered in it, the book . . . has had very little recognition from the English public."[45] It could be argued that the text was too much of its time and expressed the most frightening dreams of precariously placed late-Victorian English gentlemen. Indeed, most of the contemporary reviews advised that those of a delicate constitution avoid the distressing, if engrossing, narrative altogether.

The chapter headings may be read as a synopsis of Prendick's journey from "The Dinghy of the Lady Vain" (from the womb) to "The Man Alone" (a kind of psychic death). Chapter 2, entitled "The Man Who Was Going Nowhere," reminds us of the unclear direction not only of the narrative itself, but of the telos of the entire post-Darwinian generation. There are two chapters with very similar titles, namely, chapter 8, "The Crying of the Puma," and chapter 10, "The Crying of the Man." Both of these creatures *cry*, and thus, have in common the ability to feel and express emotion. The conflation in the text of human and animal emotion leads the reader to reflect on the newly blurred distinction between human and animal.

Prendick's first reaction to the hybrid beasts he meets aboard the trading ship reveals that he does recognize them as related beings. He states: "I had never beheld such a repulsive and extraordinary face before, and yet—if the contradiction is credible—I experienced at the same time an odd feeling that in some way I *had* already encountered exactly the features and gestures that now amazed me."[46] Here, Prendick remembers an earlier version of himself—perhaps his ancestors on the developmental ladder. This statement clearly expresses his connection to the "beast folk" (the latter term resonates in late Victorian culture; when folklore studies began, and when the "discovery" and preservation of England's folk history became popular).[47]

In the middle of the text, Prendick comes upon "three grotesque human figures . . . bestial-looking creatures . . . [who are] reciting gibberish."[48] He exclaims, "Suddenly, as I watched their grotesque and unaccountable gesture, I perceived clearly for the first time what it was that had offended and had given me the two inconsistent and conflicting impressions of utter strangeness and yet of strangest familiarity" (p. 57). The hybrid creatures incite division in Prendick himself. He claims that what he saw, despite the creatures' human trappings, was the "irresistible suggestion of a hog, a swinish taint, the unmistakable mark of the beast" (ibid.). In order to maintain his status and identity, Prendick must maintain a "safe" distance, literally and figuratively, from the beasts. Prendick's first desire after this revelation is to distance himself in what has been deemed a typically bourgeois move.

This constant vigil produces the paranoid hysteric, the late-Victorian split subject who forever fears the fall. To quote Prendick at the end of the text,

They say that terror is a disease, and . . . I can witness that for several years now, a restless fear has dwelt in my mind, such a restless fear as a half-tamed lion cub may feel. My trouble took the strangest form. I could not persuade myself that the men and women I met were not also another, still passably human, Beast People, animals half-wrought into the outward image of human souls; and that they would presently begin to revert, to show first this bestial mark and then that. (p. 186)

This is an exemplary description of the hybridized Englishman as well as the infection of one island, dark and supposedly distinct, with another island—England itself.

During the years 1895–96, when Wells wrote *The Island of Dr. Moreau*, one of the most prominent political phrases and concepts (and policy) was "splendid isolation." This term, utilized by and associated with Lord Salisbury, twice prime minister in the final decades of the century, connotes that England was unique and justified in her isolated difference.[49] The notion is relevant to *The Island of Dr. Moreau* because this so-called splendid segregation was based on England's geographic and racial specialness. The conflation of Moreau's island with England and the English (as well as with the unstable Englishman Prendick) reflects the significance of the ideology of splendid isolation and of England's precarious island population. Tales like *Dr. Moreau* troubled imperial Britain's quest to maintain its circumscribed and idealized island identity while (or perhaps because) its actual geopolitical borders were expanding rapidly.[50]

Prendick's similarity to the hybrid beasts on the island, (one of whom is called Satyr man) and his ultimate inability to distinguish between English subjects living in London and the ghastly beasts he encountered on Moreau's island, recalls Dr. Jekyll's destabilizing breakdown in Robert Louis Stevenson's macabre classic, *The Strange Case of Dr. Jekyll and Mr. Hyde*. Like the afflicted and conflicted Jekyll, Prendick witnesses his own division and hybridity in a hysterical manner. Prendick describes himself as a bit of powerless "human flotsam," thus emphasizing the malleability of human flesh. In chapter 10 of the book, Prendick declares himself to be "in a state of collapse,"[51] thereby mirroring the comparable collapsing structures in Victorian society that also contribute to Dr. Jekyll's downfall.

There is a long passage at the end of *Dr. Jekyll and Mr. Hyde* in which the tormented doctor exhibits hybrid symptoms similar to those Prendick endures. There are many parallels in the trials of these "upstanding" gentlemen. Dr. Jekyll describes his dilemma as

. . . a dreadful shipwreck: man is not truly one, but truly two. . . . I hazard the guess that man will be ultimately known for a mere polity of multifarious, incongruous, and independent denizens. . . . I learned to recognize the thorough and primitive duality of man; I saw that, of the two natures that contended in my consciousness, even if I could rightly be said to be either it was because *I was radically both;* and from an early date, even before the course of my scientific discoveries had begun to suggest the most naked possibility of such a miracle, *I had learned to dwell with pleasure, as on a beloved daydream, on the thought of separation of these elements.* If each, I told myself, could *but be housed in separate identities life would be relieved of all that was unbearable;* the unjust might go his way delivered from the aspirations and remorse of his more upright twin; and the just could walk steadfastly and securely on his upright path . . . no longer exposed to disgrace and penitence by the hands of this extraneous evil. *It was the curse of mankind that these incongruous faggots were thus bound together that in the agonized womb of consciousness these polar twins should be continuously struggling.* (italics added) [52]

This passage exemplifies the late-nineteenth-century ideology that claims the Englishman's desire is for a single and singular identity devoid of "extraneous" evil material. So too, it reflects the desire to be definite in the "separate" categories of man and animal, to have a clear and complete distinction between man's inferior animal instincts and his superior human spirituality at the same time that it sadly acknowledges that "man is radically both." Indeed, it is the "daydream," the rational (national?) ideal that conceives a way to "house identities separately," that fantasizes about keeping each designated category inviolate. This perfectly compartmentalized construction functions as a metaphor for a number of late-Victorian "buildings" (in the most general sense). Certainly, it works for the bounded bodies of England, English (race and language), and the Englishman.

Thus, English fears of the invasion of the foreign extend not only to their language but also to race. Prendick fears "the contagion of these brute men, but deep down within [him] laughter and disgust struggled together." [53] The juxtaposition of the conflicting emotions of laughter and disgust again reflect hybrid sentiments that many English felt at the moment of confrontation with the other. This same disquieting reaction is iterated by those who peered at the Elephant Man. The tantalizing combination of these emotions is pleasurable and affirms the Englishman's identity. Again, like Jekyll, Prendick reveals his superior interiority that marks both his difference from and similarity to the hybrid beast people. The contrast between them, as with the ape-man, comes with internalized (psychological and contradictory) versus externalized (physical and apparently harmonious) hybridity.

Toward the end of the text, Prendick begins to speak in fragmented sentences. Later, he asks rhetorically, "Can you imagine language, once clear-cut and exact, softening and guttering, losing shape and import, becoming mere lumps of sound again?" (p. 174). Although many new forms enter the language as a result of the commingling of oppositional forms, such practices are discouraged by authoritarian regulatory discourses. Here, the negative aspects of linguistic "cross-breeding" are stressed.

In Victorian texts that discuss hybrids, there are a preponderance of hyphens that join not only "single" words, but also sentence fragments or semidependent clauses. For example, the first paragraphs of Kipling's Anglo-Indian classic, *Kim*, read:

He sat, in defiance of municipal orders, astride the gun Zam-Zammah on her brick platform opposite the old Ajaib-Gher-the Wonder House, as the natives call the Lahore Museum. Who hold Zam-Zammah, that "fire-breathing dragon," hold the Punjab, for the great green-bronze piece is always first of the conqueror's loot.
There was some justification for Kim, -he had kicked Lala Dinanath's boy off the trunnions, -since the English held the Punjab and *Kim was English*. Though he was burned black as any native; though he spoke the vernacular by preference, and his mother-tongue in a clipped uncertain sing-song; though he consorted on terms of perfect equality with the small boys of the bazar; *Kim was white*-a poor white of the very poorest. The half-caste woman who looked after him (she smoked opium, and pretended to keep a second-hand furniture shop by the square where the cheap cabs wait) told the missionaries that she was Kim's mother's sister; but his mother had been nursemaid in a colonel's family and had married Kimball O'Hara, a young colour-sergeant of the Mavericks, an Irish regiment. (italics added) [54]

The use of the hyphen throughout *Kim* is striking. In the first two paragraphs alone, there are eighteen hyphenated words and eight uses of the hyphen to segregate or amend subordinate clauses.

This opening passage from *Kim* has only two simple clauses, "Kim was English" and "Kim was white." These phrases are patently clear and appear to be more so in the context of "foreign" words and complex prose. What a different book this would be if we did not have Kim's racial history given to us so conspicuously on the first page. If this crucial information were not so privileged, if Kim's racial identity were more obscure, Kipling's masterpiece might not have been so popular. That is, in an era of doubt and dissemination, an era that tried vigorously to rear a new generation of white leaders, *Kim* might have been dismissed as a tale of a merely marginal man . . . but "Kim was white[;] Kim was English."

Although later in the text he does question his identity by asking himself, "Who is Kim-Kim-Kim?" (p. 167), the reader never doubts Kim's true destiny. The seeming stability of Kim's "English" identity (actually, he is Irish and poor, and this too might be evidence of the need for white men of all "cases" and "classes" to band together against a new and more powerful enemy) needs to be affirmed amid unstable others. Joseph Bristow notes, "The slippage between [Kim's] Englishness and Irishness indicates how Kim variously represents white superiority *and* white subordination. . . . This boy hero . . . bears the traces of competing discourses of national identity (Irish, Indian, British)."[55] He exemplifies the late-nineteenth-century "white" hybrid.

Kim seems to invert the famous phrase from the Song of Songs in the Bible (spoken by a woman), "Nigra sum, sed formosa."[56] The difference here is that Kim's blackness is superficial—he is not black, merely *burned* black. He has been *made* black and, thus, he is not a hybridized conundrum, he is not "white but black." Indeed, it is the task of the book "to make [him] de-Englished,"[57] even though he was never *truly* English. To this end, he learns from the Anglicized mimic Babu to speak like an Indian—that is, with hyphenated hesitations. The "test-sentence" (p. 165) is to be said as follows: "There is no caste when men go to—look for tarkeean. You stop a little between those words, to—look. That is the whole secret. The little stop before the words" (p. 165). Needless to say, this "time lag" is represented by a series of hyphens. They mark the Indian's struggle with and difference from the English.

One of the first Anglo-Indian dictionaries asserted, "Words of Indian origin have been insinuating themselves into English and are lying in wait for entrance into English literature."[58] Notice that in *Kim*, in distinct contrast to the geopolitical reality, it is the Indian terms that have "insinuated themselves" into *English* territory and forms—that, indeed, have "pounced" on the prose of Rudyard Kipling. In a linguistic study of Kipling's work, critic Asfar Husain pointed out that, "It is not all types of admixture of words [that offend]; it is hybridization in the verbal group and in words operating in the verbal group that has a jarring effect. And yet, hybridization . . . makes Kipling's work realistic."[59] He continues:

No special literary merit can be claimed for this kind of jugglery. . . . The admixture of words could not have failed to amuse the Urdu-knowing Anglo-Indian audience by whom the story was intended to be read. It was quite plainly journalism. . . . Kipling grew out of the habit. Indian words recur in other stories, but there is no attempt to mix them [with English words]. (p. 84)

Kipling's language in *Kim* is hybrid—a merely temporary style.

Kipling himself was read as a hybrid by his contemporaries. For example, in Holbrook Jackson's famous study, *The 1890s*, Kipling is portrayed as the versatile voice behind "children, animals, machines, . . . a genius . . . equally at home in the realm of fancy and on the borderland of human experience."[60] Jackson characterizes Kipling's accomplishments by stating that,

Everybody felt that a new force in a double sense had come to literature. [Kipling] was a new voice, a new accent, . . . a new language. . . . The critics found it impossible to locate [Kipling], even when they admitted that he had earned a definite place in the hierarchy of art. . . . There was overpraise and half-praise, as well as down-right opposition. . . . [H]e had no antecedents, so he belonged to no definite movement. (p. 282)

What occurs in *Kim* is an opposition not between English and Indian per se, but rather, and more significantly for the argument here, between English and un-English.

The recurring problem with excess meaning is another key aspect of hybrid representations that other critics acknowledge. Language has long been one of the main differences between humans and beasts (as well as the companion of empire). Like the opposable thumb, the ability of human beings to articulate thought has set them apart from the beast. Moreau's creatures, many of whom are endowed with the capacity for speech (even semiarticulate speech), are transformed into hybrids—between humans and animals—by this ability. In this sense, they resemble Anthony Trollope's description of "Jamaican Negroes [who] have no language of their own for they speak in broken English . . . [and] have no idea of country . . . no pride of race."[61] As Michael Draper has aptly stated, "The Beast People are animals corrupted by an impossible ideal."[62]

The scene in which Prendick meets the beast-people in their huts reveals his own kinship with them. When they see him, they exclaim, "It is a man, a man, a man."[63] They use the neuter "it" to describe him. This is one of the few times in the text in which Prendick himself becomes the object of the beasts' gaze. We also see the repetition and interpellation in Kipling's *Kim,* in which the hero's unstable identity is questioned, repeated, and affirmed all in the triplicate iteration of "a man, a man, a man."

In one of the first scenes of *The Island of Dr. Moreau,* the narrator notices a hideous red-haired man, who "went down like a felled ox, and rolled in the dirt among the furiously excited dogs. The red-haired man gave a yawp of exultation and stood staggering, and as it seemed to me, in serious danger of *either going up backwards down the cap-nion hatchway, or forwards upon his victim.*" (italics added).[64] As for the beast people themselves, Prendick explains that, "Each had been tainted with other creatures" (p. 92). The use of the negative term *taint* reveals its underlying ideology.

Hybridization and miscegenation are misguided affairs in English texts. "I saw with quivering disgust that it was like neither man nor beast [the neither/nor is an important hybrid formulation], but a mere shock of grey hair, with three shadowy overarchings to mark the eyes and mouth" (p. 83). This is Prendick's description of the "Sayer of the Law" and reminds us of Aubrey Beardsley's parody of Paula Tanqueray, the ex-prostitute protagonist in Pinero's problem play, *The Second Mrs. Tanqueray.* In Beardsley's drawing, entitled *The 252nd Mrs. Tanqueray,* the actress, Mrs. Patrick Campbell, appears as a mere skeletal creature, similar to Moreau's beast-man. Both of these hideous creatures are reduced, degenerate beings whose animal appetites have claimed their humanity (which, in both cases, was manufactured).

Dr. Moreau and the Evils of Vivisection

Did I request thee, Maker, from my clay
to mould me man? Did I solicit thee
From darkness to promote me?
—John Milton, *Paradise Lost* quoted as prologue to *Frankenstein*

I wanted to find out the extreme limit of plasticity in a living shape.
—H. G. Wells, *The Island of Dr. Moreau*

One of the odd and disturbing facts about Dr. Moreau's island for moralistic and capitalistic Englishmen is that it is not driven by a market economy. His creations do not serve any function; his wretched experiments do not benefit society. Rather, they are aesthetic creations whose value lies in "art for art's sake," or in Moreau's terms, "pain for pain's sake." This formulation not only feeds into the decadent self-image of the 1890s', but earlier tales of evil doctors from Faust to Frankenstein. And yet, there is an element of idealism that keeps Moreau from being a completely evil character. Although he oversteps his limits by "playing God," he nonetheless operates (pun intended) within the Victorian moral ideology of improvement and progress. In a sense, Moreau wants to transform all animals into upstanding English gentlemen. Is this not the dominant desire of education and colonization promoted by the Victorians? Indeed, it is; but Moreau's difficulties result from the fact that his chosen methods for the remodeling of God's unfortunate brute creations are improper.

Before we learn of Moreau's injections into the beasts, we see his assistant Montgomery revive Prendick by giving him a glass of icy, viscous liquid that "tasted like blood" (p. 15). The exchange of bodily fluids suggests the formation of kinship. Here, the unnatural exchange of blood between two men points to the homoerotic subtext of the novel. This act, according to Elaine Scarry, resembles "the rites of blood brothers who by opening the body and mixing their blood acquire the relationship normally acquired through the interior mechanism of biology alone. . . . [T]he rite itself is openly acknowledged to create rather than confirm the truth of the verbal assertion it accompanies."[65] The process of substantiating blood brotherhood mimics the structure of vivisection in that each act is a willed performance that seeks to ritualize what should be "natural." The infection of the beast-men and vice versa follows a ritually unnatural form of kinship. Each of these literally remade relationships aims to stabilize and make material what are otherwise tenuous relationships. In other words, the characters in *Dr. Moreau* are materialized in order to substantiate the unstable signifiers of the modern Englishman. It is through blood manipulation and transference of blood that nations, families, and "races" are perpetuated. The creatures Moreau creates make the relationship between human and beast material or literal.

Olive Schreiner envisioned something comparable to such vampiric transfusions of blood. She noted the increasing trend toward the separation of sex and reproduction, and thus, imagined a time when the human race could propagate itself by other means: "say by a mixture of human bloods drawn from the arm and treated in a certain manner, a mode analogous to the propagation of the rose tree by cuttings."[66] This example returns to the roots of scientific hybridizers, such as botanists, and to the description Dr. Van Bearle, the successful (that is, masterful and in control of his creations) hybridizer in Dumas's *The Black Tulip*.[67]

Moreau's transformations, like those of the vampire and "blood brothers," are too rapid and too violent for an age that paradoxically believed that there was a discrepancy between, as G. M. Young describes it, "the rapid rushing swiftness of intellectual advances [as well as technological ones] and the slow evolution of social [racial] and moral life."[68] Dr. Moreau's great sin, then, is tampering with the supposedly slow, tempered transformation of a nature that "made no leaps." His experiments (like the violence in the text) are read by contemporary critics as *excessive* acts.

Moreau believes too radically in replacing the stalwart laws of the era. Unwisely, in the eyes of his contemporaries, he believes: "In our growing science of hypnotism we find the promise of a possibility of replacing old inherent instincts by new suggestions, grafting upon or replacing the inherited fixed ideas."[69] This statement is the key to the entire novel, for it exposes the constructedness of all categories, even, or especially, "human nature." It is not only in the science of hypnotism that old instincts are being replaced by new suggestions, but also in religion, sexology, and nationalism—in short, in virtually every English cultural formation. It is this idea of uncontrolled transformations that makes Moreau (doctor and novel alike) unpalatable to English subjects.

Prendick recognizes Moreau's evil. He states: "A horrible fancy came into my head that Moreau, after animalising these men, had infected their dwarfed brains with a kind of deification of himself" (p. 82). He adds that these

> . . . certain Fixed Ideas implanted by Moreau in their minds . . . absolutely bounded their imaginations. They . . . had been told certain things were *impossible;* and certain things were not done, and these prohibitions were woven into the texture of their minds beyond any possibility of disobedience or dispute. . . . [C]ertain matters . . . were in less stable condition. (p. 113)

Moreau's experiments are evidence of the belief that, "A free resort to grotesque compounds favors the multiplication of even more grotesque hybrids." The quotation above refers less to the beast people than to the novel's English readers. It is also, quite obviously, an attack on fundamental and outmoded religious laws.

One failure of Moreau's experiments that makes the subtext less threatening is that the beast people ultimately revert to their beastliness. While this concurs with the ideas about degeneration that were circulating when Wells wrote *Dr. Moreau,* this reversion to type can be read in two ways. On the one hand, it quelled fears pertaining to the rapid transformation of lower forms into higher ones. On the other hand, such "failure" to transform, regulate, or control the low other might be interpreted as the Englishman's inability to maintain order and superiority. The key lies in exactly who is being transformed and for what purposes. Because the wild and tame are unfixed markers, any "reading" or representation of civilized or savage is never final. No boundary is secure; all are arbitrary and must be maintained assiduously. Nancy Leys Stepan writes:

> For Darwin, . . . it appeared reasonable to think that, just as natural selection produced *Homo sapiens* from animal forebears, so natural selection was the primary agent responsible for producing civilized races out of barbarity. As a result, Darwin's first general argument about man and evolution, for all its novelty concerning the descent of man from some ape-like

progenitor, did not disturb the assumption in race biology of a great chain of races. Indeed, evolution was fully compatible with it.[70]

The paradigm of pure types that resisted gross transformation re-inforced the idea that improper interbreeding was doomed to failure; in short, the stubborn beast flesh would not hold. In this context, efforts by low others to follow Samuel Smiles's "self-help" formula rarely succeeded.[71] Or put differently, the mutant and mutating hybrid figure is always mutilated (if not overtly murdered) in Victorian tales of transformation. This is the fate of Dr. Jekyll, Dorian Gray, and Prendick, who is unquestionably marred by his experience on Dr. Moreau's island.

Moreau's discussion of pain claims that, as a human category, it has lost its evolutionary function. The doctor asserts that the lower orders "may not even feel pain." He mutilates himself with a penknife and proclaims to Prendick, "It does not hurt a pinprick."[72] This returns us to the experimental use of slaves and other insensate "animals," who were supposed to be immune from pain. Indeed, in the fascinating exchange between Thomas Carlyle and John Stuart Mill about black slavery in *Fraser's Magazine* in 1849, competing ideas about pain were made explicit.[73]

Like Moreau, Carlyle mockingly denigrates what he imagines to be the overly humane goals of a "Universal Abolition of Pain Association." Mill's response to this most cynical suggestion reads:

Your contributor thinks that the age has too much humanity, is too anxious to abolish pain. I affirm, on the contrary, that it has too little humanity—is most culpably indifferent to the subject: and I point to any day's police reports as proof. I am not now accusing the brutal portion of the population, but the humane portion; if they were humane *enough*, they would have contrived long ago to prevent these daily atrocities. . . . An 'Universal Abolition of Pain Association' may serve to point a sarcasm, but can any worthier object of endeavour be pointed out than that of diminishing pain? Is the labour which ends in growing spices noble and not that which lessens the mass of suffering? . . . Is our cholera comparable to the old pestilence—our hospitals to the old lazar-houses—our workhouses to the hanging of vagrants . . . It is precisely *because* we have succeeded in abolishing so much pain, because pain and its infliction are no longer familiar as our daily bread, that we are so much more shocked by what remains of it than our ancestors were, or in your contributor's opinion we ought to be. (p. 49)

The problem of determining pain as a specifically human emotion prompted a debate among psychologists as well. Indeed, developments in the study of the nervous system occupied Darwin in his two-volume study on *Variations in Animals and Plants*.

Blackness and Slavery in *Moreau*

There is no sin in using a thing for the purpose for which it is. Now the order of things is such that the imperfect are for the perfect . . . and thus all animals are for man.
— St. Thomas Aquinas

Animals whom we have made our slaves we do not like to consider our equals.
— Charles Darwin

What on earth was he — man or animal? . . . The dim black Thing, the animal-man that blundered into me!
— H. G. Wells, *The Island of Dr. Moreau*

For many in the nineteenth century, black people of African descent were imperfect, enslaved, animalistic creatures equated with Irish and other "low" species. In the growing field of racial science, Africa and Africans played key roles in England's economic, political, and cultural life. As England's empire expanded, the question posed by Matthew Arnold in his lectures on Celtic literature, "And We, What Are We? What is England?" became more difficult to answer, since it now included a host of others both culturally and geopolitically distant. For the Victorians, explains George Watson,

race is more often a matter of cultural affinity and allegiance. . . . The Victorian interest in race is vastly in excess of that of any previous generation of Englishman, and it is the culminating of a long-developing interest that owes its beginnings to a fascination with regions and nations.[74]

We recall that Edward Dicey said, "in fact the instinct for self-preservation revolts at hybridism."[75] This negative view of "hybridity," understood here as a synonym for miscegenation, dominates future discussions about this phenomenon. If, as many feminist analyses of Victorian culture have argued, white women were demonized when they performed what were traditionally thought to be "manly projects," an obverse if similar process occurred when black men attended Royal College in the 1870s. In *Moreau*, Prendick damns the doctor by defining the beast people as "men whom you have infected with some bestial taint, men whom you have enslaved, and whom you still fear"[76] This statement reminds us of the nineteenth-century debates about the humanity of black people, who were thought to be both sickly and superior.

Surprisingly, none of the criticism of *The Island of Dr. Moreau* addresses the text's racialized (and occasionally racist) content or attempts to map the text's complicity with, or arguments against, Victorian racial theories. This is especially perplexing, since the racialized aspects of this novel are so explicit. For example, early in the text, Prendick bluntly asks Montgomery, "Your men on the beach . . . what race are they?" (p. 50). Montgomery answers evasively, stating, "Excellent men aren't they." This reply defines the beast people as belonging generally to "the race of men."

Also in the first chapters, Wells seems to model the trader vessel on slave ships, which, like the Lady Vain, were filled with chained, muzzled, and cramped life, as well as extreme filth. Although one of the characters describes Dr. Moreau's island, Arica, as a "seafaring village of Spanish mongrels [where one] hardly met the finest type of mankind" (p. 117), the fact that the island is called Arica seems also to suggest a connection with Africa. The other island mentioned is Calao similar to the word callaloo, a soup and staple of West Indian cuisine. So too, Prendick asks: "what are these beasts for? merchandise? curios? Does the captain think that he is going to sell them somewhere?" (p. 18). This litany of questions evokes the queries of abolitionists about the value of human cargo.

The slavery debates, or more accurately, the debates about the humanity and civility of black people, continued throughout the century. When Prendick observes a "misshapen man, short, broad, clumsy, with crooked back, hairy neck, and a head sunk beneath his shoulders . . . [who] turned with animal swiftness," he is quick to point out that "the black face . . . was a singularly deformed one. The facial part projected, forming something dimly suggestive of a muzzle, and the huge half-open mouth as big white teeth as I had ever seen in a human mouth. His eyes were blood-shot at the edges" (p. 62). This creature is known most often as "the black-faced man." For example, when Prendick pauses "halfway up the ladder, [he] looks back . . . at the grotesque ugliness of this black-faced creature" (p. 17). This creature is called "it" or the "black." Its external features are its most relevant attribute. Its loss of gendered humanity transforms it into "stark inhumanity" (p. 28).

Chapter 11, "The Hunting of the Man," makes explicit Prendick's implicit racialist perspective, for it is in this section that he encounters the simian creature he names "Ape-Man." This encounter with another creature who "walks upright and possesses language"—whose English accent was strangely good—is nonetheless labeled "far from human heritage" (pp. 76–80). The metaphoric use of temporal and spatial distance invokes the great chain of being, or the hierarchical scale of gradation that clearly delineated the different (and distinct) relation of each "type." Since "nature made no leaps," each creature was said to have a fixed place on the scale. Prendick is able to confront his past ancestry when he meets the ape-man. This affront from the past causes confusion because the separation is eerily indistinct; and yet, Prendick sees his own essential character in these confrontations.

The black ape-man in Wells's work is comparable to descriptions of black Africans in the racialist discourse of the period. As the tale progresses, and the animals regress, Prendick states that his "ape-like companion" is "no longer animal, or fellow-creature, [but] a problem" (p. 104). Another example of the text's reliance on metaphors of slavery/colonialism occurs when Prendick claims that, "like a missionary, I taught him [the ape-man] to read. He was the most imitative and adaptive of all the animals" (p. 106). This statement, in particular, may be read as a bare-bones version of the entire colonial project, whose subjects had indeed become "a problem" by the 1890s, prior to the outbreak of the Boer War.

The ape-man calls himself "a five man," in reference to his digits, and persistently compares himself to Prendick by pointing out their physical similarities. Yet Moreau's monkey man with five digits merely mimes speech as opposed to being fully articulate. We remember that Prendick's own speech becomes broken when he is on the island. The distinction between "broken beast speech" and pure English prose, or the division between hybrid (substandard) and proper (standard) English grammar, appears in this text as the contested site of language.

Dr. Moreau tells Prendick that the first man he made was from a gorilla. He "thought the gorilla-brain was a fair specimen of the negroid type. I made the thing read the alphabet and taught him the rudiments of English" (p. 105).[77] The emphasis on the brain and on negroid types is a direct paraphrase of racialist, nineteenth-century scientific naturalism that, as Peter Bowler describes, "popularized the view that a person's character was determined by the physical structure of his or her brain—not by a spiritual entity."[78] The various spurious investigations conducted by phrenologists, craneologists, and other nineteenth-century scientists resulted in added "evidence" for the vast chasm that divided human races by promoting the polygenetic origins of the world.

Among the most sophisticated of these theorists was Houston Chamberlain. Chamberlain had no problems with humankind's animalistic nature. Indeed, he rejected the notion that humans were completely unrelated to animals purely by virtue of "reason." Rather, he believed that people's ability to create "symbolic truths" placed them above other animals on a graded scale. Martin Woodroffe notes that, "For Chamberlain, in contrast to Darwin, the most striking characteristic of Nature was the permanency of form; [he believed] that the natural rule was conformity to type. [For him] race was a gestalt; miscegenation led to loss of gestalt, hence loss of life."[79]

The composer Samuel Coleridge-Taylor, himself racially mixed, held a different opinion:

It is amazing that grown-up, and presumably educated, people can listen to such primitive and ignorant nonsense-mongers. . . . An arrogant white man . . . dared to say to the great Dumas: "And I hear you actually have negro blood in you!" Yes, said the witty writer; my father was a mulatto, his father a negro, and his father a monkey. My ancestry began where yours ends![80]

This clever reversal of the descent of humankind was an exception to the dominant beliefs recorded elsewhere. As we have seen, a majority of Victorians popularly accepted the belief that hybridity was one of the worst aspects of modern England. Even Karl Marx adhered to this conservative view when he described his intellectual rival, Ferdinand Lassalle, as follows:

It is now perfectly clear to me that, as the shape of his head and the growth of his hair indicate, he is descended from the negroes who joined the flight of Moses from Egypt, unless his mother or grandmother on the father's side were crossed with a nigger. This union of Jew and German on a negro basis was bound to produce an extraordinary hybrid. The importunity of the fellow is also negroid.[81]

In the first volume of his socialist utopian trilogy, entitled *Anticipations,* Wells imagined that Jews would intermarry and "cease to be a physically distinct element in human affairs in a century or so."[82] Along with his or her physical traits, the Jew would also lose his or her characteristic usury. The belief that both distinct physical and social traits were specifically *racial* traits grew out of the polygenesist view of humankind. Here, Wells scapegoats the Jews for their propensity to interbreed, in direct contrast to Disraeli's or George Eliot's earlier assertions that the Hebrews were "that unmixed race of unsullied idiosyncrasy."[83]

Anticipations exemplifies the worst of the racist attitudes propounded in the late-nineteenth century. As Wells writes:

those swarms of black, and brown, and dirty-white and yellow people, who do not come into the new needs of efficiency? Well, the world is a world, not a charitable institution, and I take it they will have to go. The whole tenor and meaning of the world as I see it, is that they will have to go. So far as they fail to develop sane, vigorous and distinctive personalities for the great world of the future, it is their portion to die out and disappear.[84]

Wells sees the "dirty-white" beings as an insane swarm, as weak and undifferentiated personalities who will not have a place in the world of the future. A similar sentiment is expressed by this pronouncement: "Negroes in the Soudan are as black as ebony, not at all like the sickly hybrids one sees on Oxford Street" (*OED*). This statement echoes the ideology of the "pure" primitive advanced by *Dr. Jekyll and Mr. Hyde, The Picture of Dorian Gray,* and *The Island of Dr. Moreau.* The visible markers of race are kept inviolate in these texts as a means of keeping confusion, deception, and hypocrisy at bay.

It should be remembered that, as Lucy Bland explains,

Race tended to refer to the human race, the white race, the British race according to the context. The obsession with racial fitness needs to be seen in relation to the threat to Britain's imperial pre-eminence from Germany, Japan, and the United States. In relation to sex, the imperatives were for a practice geared towards healthy reproduction of race and nation. In its subordination to propagation, the sex instinct became known as the "racial" instinct.[85]

The inextricably related instincts of/for race and sex are the focus of the final section of *The Island of Dr. Moreau,* as well as this chapter.

Femininity and *The Island of Dr. Moreau*

Some contemporary reviews of *Dr. Moreau* noted the absence of women in the text (this also occurs in most other "boys" literature of the 1880s and 1890s). Of course, the glaring absence of "women" characters made them into a "present absence." *The Island of Dr. Moreau* is a quintessentially homosocial text in that it discusses the creation/birth of monstrous hybrid creatures. Indeed, that the births in these texts are monstrous may be read as a result of the fact that they are male births. Certainly, this is one way in which both *Frankenstein* and *Dr. Jekyll and Mr. Hyde* have been read.[86] In *Dr. Moreau,* the upstanding Englishman Prendick, as representative of his class, fears that the binary between human and animal is at risk, and points to the man-beast creatures on Moreau's island (several of whom are distinctly *black*) as proof of that impossible possibility. The beast people in Wells's scientific romance are virtually sterile: "They actually bore offspring, but these generally died."[87] The novel calls for eugenic coupling that, unlike the male-produced beast people, would produce "healthy English babies."

One contemporary critic began his review by stating: "We should have thought it impossible for any work of fiction to surpass in gruesome horror some of the problem-novels relating to the great sexual question which have been recently published, if we had not read *The Island of Dr. Moreau*." [88] This sentence explicitly links the book to that other decadent subject, the "new" woman.

The "new" woman emerged in the final decades of the century in popular venues, from *Punch* cartoons to numerous "new" women novels. Fictional heroines, such as George Gissing's Rhoda Nunn from his novel *The Odd Women* and Beth from Sarah Grand's semiautobiographical novel *The Beth Book*, displayed a new kind of passion for work outside the home. [89] These women were professionals—typewriters, teachers, clerks. They earned their own living and shared flats in the city. As Gissing's novel described, such a type possessed: "Will, Purpose . . . [for her] Passion had a new significance; her conception of life was larger, more liberal; she made no vows to crush the natural instincts. Where destiny might lead; she would still be the same proud and independent woman, responsible only to herself, fulfilling nobler laws [of] existence." [90] Other "new" women were educated, having been among the first to attend Sommerville or London University. These women were depicted as intelligent and athletic, biking in bloomers or playing golf.

A *Punch* cartoon characterizes the type as "Donna Quixote," waving the key of knowledge above her head (figure 15). The cartoon attests to the fact that novels of the day shaped other popular images of "new" women. The caption under this cartoon portrays Donna Quixote as crowding her imagination with "*disorderly* notions picked out of books." (italics added) She sits with her legs apart and her arm raised. Such a stance was not only unladylike, but would have been impossible in the constraining fashions of previous decades. It is significant, then, that a small woman in the background waves a flag printed with the words, "divided skirt." The cartoon stresses the "new" woman's desire to free herself (like Moreau's puma) from constricting social standards and the tyranny of "male" oppression. She is seen fighting for her dreams (Joan of Arc also appears in the background), even if her dreams are dismissed as foolish delusions (e.g., the allusion to Don Quixote). [91]

The powerful iconography associated with some of the depictions of the "new" woman was read by her opponents as a fall from power. In 1896, Eliza Lynn Linton warned:

15. *Donna Quixote.* ["A world of disorderly notions *picked out of books,* crowded into his (her) imagination."—*Don Quixote.*] *Punch,* circa 1896.

For a time now she has descended to be man's equal. And so let us again hope that she will be again on her old pedestal. In the minds of clear-thinking men, she has always been there. We have neither amused ourselves or been amused with the effort to create a "new woman." We cannot afford to trifle with the relations of the sexes and when fanciful ideas affect a deferential attitude of society-at-large, an attitude which means the protecting of women, the elevation of man, and the uplifting of the whole social body, we are tampering with something dangerous.[92]

This quotation demonstrates the fears associated with the new attempts at women's liberation—especially when those freedoms were sexually or politically radical. Thus, notes Cora Kaplan,

Although the men in these texts may threaten social coherence by their "hybrid" nature and their deceptive veneer of civilization, it often turns out to be the savage nature and original taint of the women who love them that are most profoundly disturbing. . . . Women end up responsible for the scandalous origins of sexuality and difference.[93]

When Dr. Moreau claims that, "the women were the first to revert," and that, much to his dismay, "the stubborn beast flesh would not hold," his language suggests the feminized "flaccidity" of his newly created creatures. In my reading of hybrid figures, such recurring, debased female figures have been read as the essence of instability. As in our earlier discussion, *The Island of Dr. Moreau* represents flexible or "flaccid" feminine figures. The book questions the fundamental function of the law (of the father), even revealing it to be obsolete and absurd. In a patriarchal culture that, like *Macbeth*, fantasizes about men "not of women born," the notion of creatures "born of man" becomes a frequently expressed alternative fantasy. Certainly, *Dr. Moreau* belongs to this subgenre of English literature. According to Diane Sadoff, "The insistence on the father, who is both an immediate and an uncertain origin, is a means of stabilizing the human record."[94]

Wells's book tries to stabilize the human record through the production of beings whose parents are a feminized nature and the masculine Dr. Moreau. Yet such a union of opposition produces only imperfect hybrids whose form will not hold. Moreau is penalized for his improper, unnatural manipulation of racial populations. His phallic power is revealed to be impotent against the true/original law of the real father of humankind. Still, this scenario is undercut by the end of the text, which leaves room for interpretations of the dominant rules to be reinstated by a "natural" law that disallows the reproduction of the mongrel.

Prendick also mentions the threat of these figures to the social order, as well as to prevailing law and custom. He claims that some of the women ". . . even attempted public outrages upon the institution of monogamy. The tradition of the law was clearly losing force."[95] Reminiscent of Reade's conclusions about androgynes or men-women, in which all familiar patterns break down, here also, it is the females in the text who are unable to keep their own bestial nature at bay, who are most severely criticized for their wantonness. They are also denounced for being sterile. The beast women were "actually able to bear offspring, but . . . these generally died" (p. 114), and thus, these females, like many "incomplete" and weak Englishwomen scapegoated in eugenic polemics, could not breed strong new members of the English race.

Elaine Showalter notes that both film versions of this story emphasize the imperial/colonial metaphors implied by the narrative. She describes these only as class revolution, thereby missing the explicit racial tension in the novel. Showalter accurately identifies the gender subtext of the story, in quoting Wells's intriguing line about the female puma "shrieking like an angry Virago." In this striking simile, the puma also wears red and white bandages, and therefore, recalls the many "red and white" purely passionate women. Moreover, these feminized figures are reminiscent of Tennyson's female "Nature red tooth and claw" in *In Memoriam*. If men were turning into monsters, certain women were and always had been more monstrous then men.[96]

The anomalous place of female sex as being both superior spiritual angel and inferior carnal creature is refigured in *Dr. Moreau*. The doctor's lecture on "man-making" confirms that it is easier to create man than it is to create a woman. Certainly, Moreau (like God) is more successful at making men than he is at making women. As Moreau tells Prendick, "Once or twice . . . [I tried to make a woman]."[97] The ellipses here represent the unrepresentable female subject. In the structure of the story, the female characters do not appear until the latter part of the text. This replicates the delayed arrival of Eve in the Bible; the female here is an afterthought and not necessarily a primary part of the plan. The females are the lesser copies of a more perfect (in the case of the beast men) original. Perhaps this is the reason that the half-finished female puma rebels and ultimately destroys Moreau.

Prendick, too, is guilty of denigrating and demonizing the females of the island. He fears that "the eyes of some lithe white-swathed female figure . . . these weird creatures, the females I mean, had in the earlier days of my stay an instinctive sense of their own repulsive clumsiness and displayed in consequence a more than human regard for the decencies and decorum of external costume" (p. 119). These females were more modest than the "androgynous" viragoes one met in the streets of London, or in Prendick's case, than the female cadavers he encountered in the medical theaters of London Hospital. Of course, one of the first signs of degeneration on the island is the women's desire to shed their protective garb. It does not surprise the reader (or Prendick) that the "females always are the first to go back" (p. 176). In other words, their flesh is the most plastic or viscous; they are the least able to hold higher forms. Such statements in the text affirm the increasing antifeminist discourse of the period.

Victorian discourse began to figure women as ferocious and wild animals in the 1860s, after they had begun to attend Somerville and to play more significant roles in the public arena. With the emergence of the "new" woman came increasing images of the vicious virago—"The Wild Women as Social Insurgents," to quote the title of Eliza Lynn Linton's series of anti-"new" woman articles that appeared in 1891. Thus, at a time when feminists and others were attacking beastly men or syphilis, the beast in man, many antifeminist authors were promoting the beastly woman.

Sheridan Le Fanu's haunting gothic novella, *Carmilla,* offers an example of this kind of animal woman.[98] Carmilla, the heroine, is described as "the prettiest creature . . . absolutely beautiful and [with] a sweet voice" (p. 83). Her beauty is "set-off" or rather compared with the "hideous black woman with a sort of colored turban on her head . . . gazing all the time from the carriage window, . . . grinning . . . with gleaming eyes and large white eyeballs . . ." (p. 83), who is also her double. The now stereotypical juxtaposition provides the reader with clues to Carmilla's beastly black nature.

The narrator, Laura, who may also be a vampire, states that "I did feel drawn to the beautiful stranger; but there was also something of repulsion. In this ambiguous feeling, however, the sense of attraction immensely prevailed" (p. 87). Here, we are reminded again of the viscous females in *Dr. Moreau.* Laura goes on to articulate the feeling of "pleasure mingled . . . with a vague sense of fear and disgust . . . adoration and abhorrence. This I know is a paradox" (p. 90).

Carmilla is constantly imbibing cups of coffee or chocolate—indeed, this is the only substance she ingests in the presence of others. Here, too, her characterization speaks to the exotic trade that saw in the combination of chocolate and sugar one of the many addictive substances of circum-Atlantic memory.[99] This gesture recalls Zoe's drinking of the poison to materially taint her body; so too, it makes Carmilla like Hillis Miller's parasite-virus in that she reproduces herself without eating—an odd trait that the other characters in the story note. Carmilla's story also provides us with an example of the too openly interpreted laws of the culture, which are concerned obsessively with maintaining the race through bloodlines, but can never admit that this is a factor (because it is artificial) in/for "natural" reproduction.

The climax of the story occurs when Laura reveals:

I saw something moving around the foot of the bed, which at first I could not distinguish. But I soon saw that it was a sooty-black animal that resembled a monstrous cat. . . . [I]t was to-ing and fro-ing with the lithe sinister restlessness of a beast in a cage. . . . Its pace was growing faster and the room rapidly darker and darker, at length, so dark that I could no longer see anything but its eyes. . . . I saw a female figure standing at the foot of the bed (p. 102).

She remembers vividly that ". . . the large black object very ill-defined spread itself" (p. 130) before her. The hideousness of the vicious and viscous object is the hideousness of the unstable hybrid. The resemblance of this monstrous black cat to the demonized, half-finished female puma in *The Island of Dr. Moreau* is striking. Both dark hybrid creatures embody the blackest fears of their male creators. In *Carmilla*, a doctor is impotent before this horrifying subject/object, as Dr. Moreau is powerless to transform his puma. As these detailed descriptions of the story reveal, *Carmilla* becomes the paradigmatic text of the (black) feminine hybrid. The story cunningly employs the iconography of the disturbing "black" woman so common in British culture and identifies the appalling appeal of such impossible figures, who are by turns, legitimate and illegitimate—those figures constantly "to-ing and fro-ing" until they are (momentarily) petrified.

Prendick especially seems to fear being seduced and subsumed by the increasingly indecent island women. He regards them with great suspicion. For example, he believes that "the Fox-Bear Woman's vulpine face [was] strangely human in its speculative cunning."[100] He too constructs and reflects on women's complex and conflicting "natural" disposition as animalized angel. Nancy Leys Stepan has argued,

So familiar and indeed axiomatic had the analogies concerning lower races, apes, and women become by the end of the nineteenth century that in his major study of male-female differences in the human species, Havelock Ellis took almost without comment as the standards against which to measure the typical female on the one hand, the child, and on the other the ape the savage and the aged human.[101]

In this quotation, we see the complexity of these metaphoric associations and understand how they become metonymic.

In trying to flee from the atrocious wailing of the female puma, Prendick, "turned about and walked in a direction *diametrically opposite* to the sound. This led me *down* to the stream, across which I stepped and pushed my way *up* through the *undergrowth beyond*" (italics added).[102] Prendick tries to escape, but inevitably falls back into the hybrid world of the island, which like the women in the text, is "rich and oozy." The language of black femininity recalls as well a description of the (black) new woman puma. When Prendick comes from the "undergrowth beyond," he is "startled by a great patch of vivid scarlet on the ground and going up to it found it to be a peculiar fungus branched and corrugated like a foliaceous lichen, but deliquescing into slime at the touch" (p. 54–55).

If, as noted earlier, woman was meant to be the hard and gemlike other against which man was to confirm his own subject position, what is the result of the confrontation between a highly unstable, black female hybrid body and its supposed "opposite," the white male body? One may read the travails of Prendick as a possible response to this dilemma. Prendick is unable to remain stable, since the lines of demarcation (however he may cut them—whether it be across the axis of race, place, or gender) will not remain rigid. "And so from the prohibition of these acts of folly," Prendick moves "on to the prohibition of what I thought then were the maddest, most impossible and most indecent things one could well imagine" (p. 81).

The novella ends with Prendick "withdrawing [himself] from confusing multitudes" (p. 137). The shrill cry of the black female puma conjures the heterogeneous city, which like the island, and identity, are revealed to be unstable, shifting, menacing signs of modern life. As Michel Foucault describes, "All these creatures redolent of decay and slime are slithering, like the syllables which designate them."[103] No longer could such female figures be trusted to reflect stolid Englishmen; now, the most horrific being imaginable was the black, monstrous, masculine "new" woman. The shrieking sister "deliquescing into slime" serves as perhaps the scariest manifestation of this new world order.

EPILOGUE

Who can tell us when the age of monsters which flourished in slime
came to an end? There must have been places and conditions which made
for greater longevity, greater size, greater strength than was usual. Such
over-lappings may have come down to our earlier centuries. Nay, are
there now creatures of vastness of bulk regarded by the generality of man
as impossible?—Bram Stoker, *The Lair of the White Worm*

Bram Stoker's novella, *The Lair of the White Worm*, tells the lurid tale
of an aristocratic Englishwoman named Lady Arabella March, who
doubles as the white worm alluded to in the story's title.[1] Like Stoker's
famous novel, *Dracula*, *The Lair of the White Worm* brings together an
assortment of Christian avengers to destroy a mysterious, murderous
monster; however, *The Lair of the White Worm* differs in several re-
spects from *Dracula*.[2] Although both Lady Arabella and Count Dracula
are highborn killers, Dracula is dark, foreign, and male, and his primary victims are white females; in contrast, Lady Arabella is white,
native English, and female, and her most significant victim is a black
male servant named Oolonga.

Set in the "real heart of the old kingdom of Mercia where the traces
of all the various nationalities which made up the conglomerate which
became Britain"[3] are present, the story begins in 1860 with the arrival
of the young hero, Adam Salton, from Australia. A kind of prodigal son,
Adam journeys to England to claim an inheritance from his bachelor
great-uncle, Richard Salton, whom he has never met. Adopting Adam
as a son and heir since the two men are "all that remain of [their] race
(p. 311), the uncle's actions demonstrate the artificial, tenuous, and unnatural construction of kinship.[4] Richard Salton *claims* kinship in the
first paragraph of the novella, thereby illustrating that pure patriarchal
descent often is a forced relationship.[5]

Adam, "heir to the old home,"[6] is another figure who, like the mulattaroon, travels at the behest of a powerful patriarch from a new country (the colony of Australia, which was an outpost for English criminals

and thus compromises Adam's origins) to the old country. Adam's transplanted roots are severed from English soil and yet, when replanted, flourish. A "salt of the earth" English gentleman and an expert on "The Romans in Britain," he is addressed with the following line: "To begin at the beginning Adam" (p. 315). Adam's arrival parallels his namesake's story in the Bible, for he, too, is a first man whose entrance into the narrative provides both a clear (if artificially constructed) beginning and the promise of the future propagation of the race. The forced, performative "nature" of such succession is suggested in the line, uttered by Adam, that reads, "history keeps . . . except in the making" (p. 315).

The young man's introduction to the area near Stafford includes a recounting of the hoary history of Diana's Grove, Lady Arabella's estate. The grove occupies land associated with England's ancient, pre-Christian roots; indeed, it "has no beginning" (p. 321). Timeless, amorphous, yet always already known to have been "invaded by—the Angles, the Saxons, the Danes, and the Normans" (p. 321). Stoker's description of the land is "feminized" because it has been invaded. The description invokes the impure roots of England characterized in Defoe's *A True-Born Englishman*. Adam, a latter-day Saint George, slays the white dragon personified by Lady Arabella and reclaims Diana's Grove with his own peculiar brand of muscular Christianity.[7]

Like the land on which she lives, Lady Arabella has been unnaturally invaded or impregnated by the white worm.[8] She combines characteristics not only of the primeval monster, but also of the "new" woman. A deviant, destructive animal woman of the type critiqued in *The Island of Dr. Moreau,* she is active, lithe, animate, and powerful. Descriptions of Lady Arabella suggest comparison not only with the female vampire Carmilla, but also with Thackeray's Becky Sharp. Both have "green eyes," adept acting ability, and are widows whose husbands died under mysterious circumstances. Moreover, the renderings of Becky Sharp as serpentine throughout the pages of *Vanity Fair* (she is depicted in illustrations holding snakes, and the text describes her as a siren and marine cannibal) are reproduced in representations of Lady Arabella.[9]

Lady Arabella enters the text dressed in her signature all-white outfit. She alights from a carriage, stepping over a pile of wriggling black snakes, "with a quick gliding motion . . . clad in soft white stuff, which clung close to her form showing to the full every movement of her sinuous figure."[10] Clearly, she is both woman and animal (it is Adam who becomes "fascinated by the idea of there being a link between the woman and the animal"), as well as white and impure. Her explicitly English mask of whiteness covers over and hides her monstrous form.

The whiteness of the worm, her alter ego, is merely a veneer of Englishness that conceals its un-English, black, snakelike interior.

The original "Worm" so-called, from which the name of the place came, had to find a direct way down to the marshes and the mud-holes. Now, the clay is easily penetrable, and the original hole probably pierced a bed of china clay. When once the way was made, it would become a sort of highway for the Worm. But as much movement was necessary to ascend such a great height, some of the clay would become attached to its rough skin by attrition. . . . [W]hen the monster came to view in the upper world, it would be fresh from contact with the white clay. (p. 403)

The worm's whiteness is skin-deep, painted on, and therefore, not intrinsic to the worm; rather, the white clay is the stuff of England itself. In a conversation in which Adam learns of the mythic origins of the "lair of the white worm," a character named Sir Nathaniel de Salis— geologist, natural historian, and president of the Mercian Archeological Society—explains that the whiteness of the worm derives from the white clay of Stafford, "where the great industry of china-burning was originated and grew. Stafford owes much of its wealth to the large deposits of the rare china clay found in it from time to time. . . . for centuries Stafford adventurers looked for the special clay, as Ohio and Pennsylvania farmers and explorers looked for oil" (p. 403). The valuable white substance contributes to the wealth of England; it is one of its most lucrative natural resources, comparable to the black oil of America. The ritual association between the wealth of England, figured as white, contrasts with the "black" wealth of America. Although England abolished African slavery if not imperial relations before America, during the nineteenth century, the painted figurine of Little Eva sitting on the knee of Uncle Tom was one of the best-selling pieces of Staffordshire china.[11] In short, the English still traded in black figurines.

Stoker's text trades explicitly on unequal, asymmetrical pairings of white and black, English and American, masculinity and femininity, Christian and heathen. These categories come together as the novella obsessively describes dangerous tropes of miscegenation. The African character, Oolonga, a servant of Caswell, an evil landowner on a neighboring estate, extracts the latent blackness of both Caswell and Lady Arabella. The mad Caswell's racial heritage is "early Roman. . . . [He has] hair of raven blackness, which grew thick and close and curly . . . eyes Black, piercing, almost unendurable . . . [and] strange, compelling qualities" with a suggestion of "demoniac possession."[12] Like the paranoid, late-Gothic "white" gentleman in danger of becoming black alluded to in *The Island of Dr. Moreau,* he looks "[like] a savage- [but he is still] a cultured savage. In him were traces of the softening civilization of ages—of some higher instincts and education of man" (p. 325). In contrast, his black servant Oolonga has a face "unreformed, unsoftened savage, and inherent in it were all the hideous possibilities of a lost, devil-ridden child of the forest and the swamp" (p. 325).

Lady Arabella is linked with Oolonga throughout the text. "Lady Arabella and Oolonga arrived almost simultaneously, and Adam was surprised to notice what effect their appearance had on each other. . . . He treated her not merely as a slave treats his master, but as a worshipper would treat a deity" (p. 325). This is a clue to the fact that Lady Arabella, in her guise of the white wyrm (the Old English spelling), was worshiped as a god in pre-Christian times, which the voodoo-practicing Oolonga recognizes. He prostrates himself before Lady Arabella, whom he views as the ultimate fetish. When Oolonga propositions Lady Arabella and proposes marriage to her, she is outraged. Lady Arabella answers in a scornful voice, which "sounded and felt—like the lash of a whip, 'You dared! you—a savage,—a slave— the basest thing in the world of vermin! Take care! I don't value your worthless life more than I do that of a rat or a spider. Don't let me ever see your hideous face here again, or I shall rid the earth of you'" (p. 363). In this scene, Lady Arabella seems to mimic the white mistress of a southern plantation, repulsed by the advances of a black inferior. The narrator notes that, "That combination of forces—the over-lord, the white woman, and the black man—would have cost some—probably all of them their lives in the Southern States of America. To us [the English characters, miscegenation] was merely horrible" (p. 349).

This statement is inaccurate, however, since not all forms of miscegenation are denigrated in the text. It is only unions between white

women and black *men* that are horrific, since a marriage between a
"black" woman and a white man is celebrated. Adam, Stoker's quintessentially English hero, takes Mimi Watford, a "mulattaroon" of Burmese
and English extraction, in a ceremony performed by the Archbishop of
Canterbury.[13] Described as "a good girl . . . as good as she is pretty,[14]
Mimi is born abroad and brought home to "the heart of England,"
where she grows up with her "pure" cousin, Lilla. The contrast between the girls is subtle: Lilla is "all fair, like the old Saxon stock from
which she is sprung . . . as gentle as a dove; Mimi . . . [shows] a trace of
her mother's race . . . [in] her black eyes that glow whenever she is upset" (p. 327). Mimi may be seen in the tradition of the whitened Eliza,
for both hybrid figures are purified by their association not only with
white characters, but also with idealized Christian symbols. Eliza (as
well as Eva and Tom) embodies all of the good, feminine, maternal instincts valorized by Stowe's Christian ethics. Similarly, Mimi embodies
the power of Christian purity and controls various mystical Christian
symbols, such as doves.

In the text, the primeval ooze of heathen England is covered over by
a nunnery called the House of Mercy. The word mercy is "a corruption or familiarization of the word *Mercia,* with a Roman pun included"
(p. 320). The nunnery, founded "in memory of Columba . . . Latin for
dove became a sort of signification for the nunnery" (p. 342).[15] Indeed,
"A cooing sob of doves which seemed to multiply and intensify with each
second,"[16] is heard as Mimi battles with the evil monster. The excessive
cleansing power of the doves, symbols of peace and purity, gathered by
the force of Mimi's own desire for purity, seems similar to the excessive landscape used to purify Eliza Harris in *Uncle Tom's Cabin.* Both
scenes glow with a transcendent whiteness that is simultaneously spiritual, material, and sublime.[17]

The exaggerated whiteness of the merciful and moral Mimi contrasts
with what must be the exaggerated blackness of the evil and immoral
Lady Arabella. Lady Arabella devours the lascivious negro in one of the
most frighteningly graphic scenes in the text. In the chapter entitled
"Exit Oolonga," Lady Arabella enacts her revenge. She literally incor-
porates Oolonga in a cannibalistic feast (his exit is an entrance into
monstrous whiteness, exemplifying Frantz Fanon's famous phrase, "For
the black man, there is only one destiny. And it is white.")[18] The incor-

poration of Oolonga's colonized black body feeds the ravenous imperial whiteness of the monster.[19] Lady Arabella emerges from the scene with blood dripping from the corners of her mouth. The suggestion that she has ingested Oolonga, then, permanently infects her with the taint of blackness. The logic for this association has been developed previously, since Lady Arabella and Oolonga are frequently conjoined in the text.

Once she has incorporated the black "racial" deviance of Oolonga, her sexual deviance increases. Not only does Lady Arabella aggressively pursue Caswell for his wealth, thereby violating Victorian rules of courtship, but her expressions of jealousy (the "green-eyed monster," which contributed to Othello's downfall), are directed at Adam Salton, who possesses Mimi. In a scene reminiscent of her destruction of Oolonga, Lady Arabella attempts to lure Mimi into the black hole, the lair of the white worm.[20] Perhaps, in a specifically British reading, the black hole refers to the Black Hole of Calcutta, an infamous prison where many British died in 1746.[21] Lady Arabella sets the scene of entrapment by inviting Adam, Sir Nathaniel, and Mimi to tea, in a chapter entitled, "In the Enemy's House."

Tea was in progress when suddenly Mimi started up with a look of fright on her face; at the same moment, the men became cognizant of a thick smoke which began to spread through the room—a smoke which made those who experienced it gasp and choke. . . . Denser and denser grew the smoke, and more acrid the smell. . . . [Mimi runs.] Adam . . . rushed forward . . . catching his wife by the arm. . . . It was well he did so, for just before her lay the black orifice of the well-hole . . . which was extremely slippery; something like thick black oil had been spilled where she had to pass. . . . [She slips, but is saved by Adam.] [T]hey fell together . . . outside the zone of slipperiness.[22]

In this scene, Lady Arabella vies with Adam for possession of Mimi; however, she loses the battle. In the scene that follows this one, Lady Arabella and her lair are obliterated violently by an explosion set by Adam that "leaves a vast bed of china clay" (p. 426). The resolution employs the technique of using "whiteness" to cover over the black deeds of the unstable and impure Lady Arabella, who is also a sign of the putrid, impure, miscegenated roots of England itself.

Toward the end of the novella, Adam and Sir Nathaniel describe the terrible remnants of the destructed lair. When close to the scene, they see that "a gray dust, partly of fine sand, partly of the waste of the fallen ruin, covered everything, and, though ghastly itself, helped to mask something still worse" (p. 426) — the possibility of "eruptions of funk" buried just beneath the thin veneer of civilization.[23]

The Worm's hole was still evident. A round fissure seemingly leading down into the very bowels of the earth. But all the horrid mass of slime and the sickening remnants of violent death were gone . . . the turmoil far below had not yet ceased. At short irregular intervals, the hell-broth seemed as if boiling up.[24]

The whiteness of purified Englishness momentarily masks the putre-faction of impurity. Only from a distance, both temporal and spatial, can the sickening remnants of violent death, like the purified history of England itself, appear as "a shining mass of white" (p. 426). The narrative ends with Mimi and Adam embarking on their honeymoon. The newly married Mimi now may shed her miscegenated history and produce a true-born Englishman, who will in turn inherit the purified earth of England.[25]

NOTES

Prologue: Complicating Categories

1. Known in Britain since the early eighteenth century, *Jack and the Beanstalk* was published anonymously as a satire in *Round about Our Coal Fire; or Christmas Entertainment* (London, 1734). Two nonsatirical versions were published in the nineteenth century: William Godwin, ed., *The History of Jack and the Beanstalk Printed from the Original Manuscript* (London: Benjamin Tabart, 1807); and John Harris, *The History of Mother Twaddle and the Marvellous Achievements of Her Son Jack* (London, 1807).

2. Written as a reply to John Tutchin's *The Foreigners*, Daniel Defoe's poem, *A True-Born Englishman: A Satyr*, was published in London in 1708. Citations here are from *Poems and Affairs of State*, ed. Frank Ellis, vol. 6 (New Haven, Conn.: Yale University Press, 1970).

3. Benedict Anderson has used Defoe's work in a similar manner. See his *Imagined Communities: Reflections on the Origin and Spread of Nationalism* (Baltimore, Md.: Johns Hopkins University Press, 1978).

4. Hippolyte Taine, introduction to *The History of English Literature* (London, 1871) in *Critical Theory since Plato*, ed. Hazard Adams (New York: Harcourt Brace Jovanovich, 1971), p. 614.

5. Linda Colley, *Britons: Forging the Nation, 1707–1837* (New Haven, Conn.: Yale University Press, 1992), p. 15. Colley argues that Defoe's use of satire is itself a sign of English confidence.

6. A satyr is a "class of woodland gods or demons in form partly human and partly bestial, supposed to be the companions of Bacchus" (*Oxford English Dictionary*, 2d ed. [New York: Clarendon Press]). The word is confused with and stands in for *satyric*, and has the rare secondary meaning of "ape or orang-utan, *simia satyrus*." An 1842 *Dictionary of Science* by William Thomas Brandes notes, "In zoology, the orang-outang is sometimes called satyr." Satyrs appear throughout Victorian literature. For example, chapter 2 of William Makepeace Thackeray's *Vanity Fair* opens with the minutely drawn visage of a satyr peering out from behind the letter *w*, and in Alfred Tennyson's *In Memoriam*, the author mentions the ". . . coarsest satyr-shape" (stanza xxxv).

7. Walter Benjamin, "Theses of the Philosophy of History," in *Illumina-*

tions: Essays and Reflections, ed. and intro. Hannah Arendt (New York: Schocken Books, 1968), p. 256.

8. In some ways, the poem is reminiscent of the anxiety about Othello and Desdemona's "monstrous" coupling in *Othello the Moor of Venice.* Their miscegenation is characterized by Iago as "making the beast with two backs" (I, i, 116) or "an old black ram . . . tupping a white ewe" (I, i, 88–89). Iago continues to fantasize about the monstrous outcome of such a coupling by claiming that Brabantio will have his daughter "covered by a Barbary horse; . . . [his] nephews neigh at [him], coursers for cousins, and gennets for germans" (William Shakespeare, *Othello the Moor of Venice,* ed. Gerald Eades Bentley [Harmondsworth, U.K.: Pelican, 1970], I, i, 110–13).

9. Hortense Spillers, "Interstices: A Small Drama of Words," in *Pleasure and Danger: Exploring Female Sexuality,* ed. Carol Vance (New York: Pandora Books, 1984), p. 207.

10. Lewis Carroll, *Alice in Wonderland,* in *The Annotated Alice* (New York: C. N. Potter, 1960), pp. 47–48.

11. Ibid., p. 30.

12. Kobena Mercer explains that, " 'Caucasian' was the name chosen by the West's narcissistic delusion of superiority: 'Fredrich Blumenbach introduced this word in 1795 to describe white Europeans in general, for he believed that the slopes of the Caucasus [mountains in Eastern Europe] were the original home of the most beautiful European species.' The very arbitrariness of this originary naming thus reveals how an *aesthetic* dimension concerning blackness as the absolute negation or annulment of 'beauty,' has always intertwined with the rationalization of racist sentiment." Kobena Mercer, *Welcome to the Jungle: New Positions in Black Cultural Studies* (New York: Routledge, 1994), p. 102. Moreover, the word "caucas" is itself an American import. This fact is noted in Daniel Bivona's *Desire and Contradiction: Imperial Visions and Domestic Debates in Victorian Literature* (Manchester: Manchester University Press, 1990), which contains a reading of *Alice* as an imperial text. Bivona argues that the caucas, "carries the implication of a meeting to iron out differences in order to present a united front for exerting political pressure—a local game of political accommodation within a larger adversarial context" (p. 54).

13. Salman Rushdie, *The Satanic Verses* (Dover, U.K.: Consortium, 1992), pp. 157–70.

14. In British political discourse, the most conservative members of the Tory Party are "dry" and the less conservative Tories, who presently favor Britain's increased involvement with the European common market, are called "wets."

15. One of the first studies that sought to "bridge the Atlantic" was Jonathan Arac's *Commissioned Spirits: The Shaping of Social Motion in Dickens, Carlyle, Melville, and Hawthorne* (New York: Columbia University Press, 1979), p. xviii. See also the influential 1986–87 special issue of *Critical Inquiry* edited by Henry Louis Gates Jr.—later reissued, in book form, as *"Race," Writing, and Difference* (Chicago: University of Chicago Press, 1986)—which initiated conversations among critical theorists working in the fields of Colonial, Postcolonial, Victorian, African, and African American studies.

16. Paul Gilroy, *The Black Atlantic: Modernity and Double-Consciousness* (Cambridge, Mass.: Harvard University Press, 1993).

17. Joseph Roach, *Cities of the Dead: Circum-Atlantic Performance* (New York: Columbia University Press, 1996), p. 4.

18. For a discussion of other historical aspects of miscegenation in Victorian culture, see Helen Callaway, "Purity and Exotica in Legitimating the Empire: Gender, Sexuality, and Race," in *Gender, Culture and Empire: European Women in Colonial Nigeria* (Urbana: University of Illinois Press, 1987), pp. 31–61. H. L. Malchow, *Gothic Images of Race in Nineteenth-Century England* (Palo Alto: Stanford University Press, 1996), and Ann Stoler, *Race and the Education of Desire: Foucault's "History of Sexuality" and the Colonial Order of Things* (Durham, N.C.: Duke University Press, 1996) provide related material about the Dutch colonization of Java.

19. There is valuable work to be done on "actual" black people in Britain, such as Mary Seacole, the "mulatta" nurse who volunteered her services in the Crimea after Florence Nightingale rejected her petition to be a nurse. See Mary Seacole, *Wonderful Adventures of Mrs. Seacole in Many Lands*, ed. Ziggy Alexander and Audrey Dewjee (1857; Bristol: Falling Wall Press, 1984); and Amy Robinson, "Authority and the Public Display of Identity: *Wonderful Adventures of Mrs. Seacole in Many Lands, Feminist Studies* (fall 1994): 537–57. The absence of black British women's historiography is discussed by Ziggy Alexander in "Let It Lie upon the Table: The Status of Black Women's Biography in the UK," *Gender and History* 2, no. 1 (spring 1990): 25. Gretchen Gerzina's book, *Black London: Life before Emancipation* (New Brunswick, N.J.: Rutgers University Press, 1995), contains a chapter entitled, "What about Women?" on actual black women in London. Adelaide M. Cromwell's book, *An African Victorian Feminist: The Life and Times of Adelaide Smith Casely Hayford, 1868–1960* (Washington, D.C.: Howard University Press, 1986), is a fine biography and Amina Mama's study, *Beyond the Masks: Race, Gender, and Subjectivity* (London: Routledge, 1995), has biographical interviews. Important treatments

of black people in Britain include Folarin Shyllon, *Black Slaves in Britain* (Oxford: Oxford University Press for the Institute of Race Relations, 1974); Peter Fryer, *Staying Power: The History of Black People in Britain* (London: Pluto Press, 1984); and Winthrop Jordan, *White over Black: American Attitudes toward the Negro, 1550–1812* (Chapel Hill: University of North Carolina Press, 1968). For an analysis that "questions the somewhat arbitrary boundaries between 'history' and 'literature'," see Kim Hall, "Reading What Isn't There: 'Black' Studies in Early Modern England," *Stanford Humanities Review* 3, no. 1 (winter 1993): 23.

20. Building on the historical framework provided by Douglas Lorimar's 1978 study, *Colour, Class, and the Victorians: English Attitudes to the Negro in the Mid–Nineteenth Century* (Leicester: Holmes and Meier Publishers, 1978), I discuss the relevance of black *femininity* for certain forms of Victorian Englishness. Femininity is highlighted here because Lorimar explores mostly masculine stereotypes. A source that examines feminine stereotypes is Anne McClintock's, *Imperial Leather: Race, Gender, and Sexuality in the Colonial Contest* (New York: Routledge, 1995).

21. This key text was published for the Anthropological Society of London. See C. Carter Blake, ed., *On the Phenomena of Hybridity in the Genus Homo* (London: Longman, Green, Longman, and Roberts, 1864). Subsequent references to this edition are noted in the text.

22. Hortense I. Spillers discusses the hybrid mulatto/a figure as being "stranded in cultural ambiguity [that] conceals the very strategies of terministic violence and displacement that have enabled a problematic of alterity regarding the African American community in the United States." She notes further that the mulatto/a "seems to disappear at the end of the nineteenth century." As such, it appears to be a specifically nineteenth-century phenomenon (Spillers, "Notes on an Alternative Model: Neither/ Nor," in *The Difference Within: Feminism and Critical Theory*, ed. Elizabeth Meese and Alice Parker [Philadelphia: John Benjamin Publishing, 1989], p. 176). Subsequent references to this article are noted in the text.

23. Kobena Mercer, "Skin Head Sex Thing," in *How Do We Look? Essays on Queer Film and Video*, ed. Bad Object Choice (Seattle, Wash.: Bay Press, 1991), p. 205.

24. Kim Hall's book, *Things of Darkness: Economies of Race and Gender in Early Modern Culture* (Ithaca, N.Y.: Cornell University Press, 1995), stands out as an exemplary model for this kind of criticism.

25. Kimberle Crenshaw, "Whose Story Is It Anyway? Feminist and Anti-racist Appropriations of Anita Hill," in *Rac-ing Justice, En-gendering Power*, ed. Toni Morrison (New York: Pantheon Books, 1992).

26. For an excellent overview of the current field of black feminist studies, see Ann duCille, "The Occult of True Black Womanhood," *Signs* 19, no. 3 (1994): 591–629. DuCille's article discusses the American (U.S.) black studies; however, a growing movement of British black feminist studies is documented in the works of Pratibha Parmar, Inderpal Grewal, Karen Caplan, Sylvia Wynter, Jacqui Alexander, Amina Mama, and Lola Young. See also *Reconstructing Womanhood, Reconstructing Feminism,* ed. Delia Jarrett-Macauley (London: Routledge, 1996) and *Black British Feminism,* ed. Heidi Safia Mirza (London: Routledge, 1997). To write a genealogy of black feminists, black feminisms, and black feminist theories is well beyond the scope of this project. However, a founding document that provides the foundation for such thinking is the Combahee River Collective Statement published in the United States in 1977, which also explicitly used the term "black feminism." See *Words of Fire: An Anthology of African-American Feminist Thought,* ed. Beverly Guy-Sheftall (New York: New Press, 1995).

27. Hortense J. Spillers, introduction to *Comparative American Identities* (New York: Routledge, 1991), p. 5.

28. Toni Morrison, *Playing in the Dark: Whiteness and the Literary Imagination* (Cambridge, Mass.: Harvard University Press, 1992), p. 7. Subsequent references to this edition are noted in the text.

29. Ibid.

30. In other words, the work seeks "to expose the catechresis at work in the [representation of blacks, blackness, and black femininity] to read the Negro [*sic*] as a trope, indeed, as a misapplied metaphor . . . [marking a shift] from complex matrices of power to comprehensible categories of natural difference. The overbearing motif of this occultation is the exclusion of the African from the space of Western history and the marginal inclusion of the Negro as negativity" (Ronald A. T. Judy, *(Dis)forming the American Canon: Afro-Arabic Slave Narratives and the Vernacular* [Minneapolis: University of Minnesota Press, 1993], p. 94).

31. Franz Heinrich Stratmann, *A Middle-English Dictionary* (London: Oxford University Press, 1891), p. 74. Ralph Hanna notes that the translation of terms is "a matter of interpretation." He claims that he struggled over whether or not a figure turns "black" or "pale" in his translation of the line, "That al [thorn] i burly body is blaknet." (*Awntyrs off Arthure at the Terne Wathelyn,* ed. Ralph Hanna [Manchester: Manchester University Press, 1974), p. 73.

32. Other suggestive meanings cited in the *OED* of the word *black* include:

total absorption, white, total reflection of light . . . perfect blackness being a rare attribute of objects . . . dirt, dirty, soiled, foul . . . having dark or deadly purposes, malignant, pertaining to or involving death . . . baneful, disastrous, sinister . . . indicating disgrace, censure, punishment . . . black in the face—strangled, having the face made dark crimson, made purple by passion . . . violent effort . . . black print on white paper . . . black painting, dye, pigment. (*OED*)

As is the rule in English, nouns may also be used as verbs. The verb "to black" or "to be or become black" is glossed in relation to these other definitions: "to put black color on"; "to black out—to obliterate with black"; and "to stain, sully, defame, or represent as 'black.'"

33. Excellent sources on the meaning of blackness in England include Anthony Gerard Barthelemy, *Black Face, Maligned Race: The Representation of Blacks in English Drama from Shakespeare to Southerne* (Baton Rouge: Louisiana State University Press, 1987); and Hall, *Things of Darkness.*

34. Robert Young, *Colonial Desire: Hybridity in Theory, Culture, and Race* (London: Routledge, 1995).

35. Joseph Roach, *Cities of the Dead: Circum-Atlantic Performance* (New York: Columbia University Press, 1996), p. 6.

36. "Categories of difference are protean, but they appear as absolutes. They categorize the sense of self, but establish an order—the illusion of order in the world" (Gilman, *Difference and Pathology: Stereotypes of Sexuality, Race, and Madness* [Ithaca, N.Y.: Cornell University Press, 1985], p. 29).

37. Harryette Mullen, "Optic White: Blackness and the Production of Whiteness," *diacritics* 24, nos. 2–3 (summer–fall 1994): 80.

38. As James Baldwin notes, "It is impossible to couple with a Black woman and describe the child you have both created as a mulatto—either it's your child, or *a* child, or it isn't. It is impossible to pretend that you are heir to, and therefore, however inadequately or unwillingly, responsible to, and for, the time and place that give you life—without becoming a dangerous disoriented human being" (Baldwin, *The Evidence of Things Not Seen* [New York: Henry Holt and Co., 1985], p. 31).

39. Henry Mayhew, *London Labour and the London Poor*, ed. Peter Quennell (London: Bracken Books, 1984), pp. 306–14.

40. Michel Foucault, *The Order of Things* (New York: Vintage Books, 1973), p. xvi.

41. Patricia Williams, *The Alchemy of Race and Rights* (Cambridge, Mass.: Harvard University Press, 1991), p. 102.

Chapter One: Miscegenating Mulattaroons

1. *The Woman of Colour: A Tale in Two Volumes* (London: Black, Parry, and Kingsbury, 1808), pp. 1–2.

2. In their sociological study, *Black, White, or Mixed Race? Race and Racism in the Lives of Young People of Mixed Parentage* (London: Routledge, 1993), authors Ann Phoenix and Barbara Tizard comment on the common transportation of mixed-race people from the colonies to the metropolitan centers during the nineteenth century. They note that, more often than not, people of color who went to London "were distinguished by 'wealth' rather than achievement. These were the offspring of rich White West Indian planters and black women, sent to England to be educated and finished" (p. 10).

3. The scholarly historiography of the 500-year-old trade in "black" Africans is vast. Important texts include David Brion Davis, *The Problem of Slavery in the Age of Revolution, 1770–1823* (Ithaca, N.Y.: Cornell University Press, 1975); and Sterling Stuckey, *Slave Culture* (New York: Oxford University Press, 1987).

4. One of the best sources on the tortuous terminology of amalgamation is Jack Forbes's *Black Africans and Native Americans: Color, Race, and Caste in the Evolution of Red-Black Peoples* (Oxford: Blackwell Publishers, 1988).

5. For a chronological list of "American novels of miscegenation" written between 1792 and 1914, see James Kinney, *Amalgamation! Race, Sex, and Rhetoric in the Nineteenth Century American Novel* (Westport, Conn.: Greenwood Press, 1985); and Werner Sollers, *Neither Black Nor White Yet Both* (New York: Oxford University Press, 1997). Throughout the nineteenth century, according to my research, the mulattaroon served as the sacrificed subject and desired object of at least twenty-five plays licensed by the lord chamberlain's office.

6. The term *miscegenation* is the title of an anonymously published tract that appeared in the United States in 1864. The subtitle, *A Theory of the Blending of Races: White Men and Negroes,* provided the definition of the term. See Joel Williamson, *New People: Miscegenation and Mulattoes in the United States* (New York: Free Press, 1980). This decidedly *colonial* practice was never illegal in England. Indeed, its prohibition originated on what was American soil when Maryland passed a statute in 1661 that criminalized marriage between white women and black men. The 1662 Virginia colonial law recorded as Act XII reads: "Children got by an Englishman upon a Negro woman shall be bond or free according to the condition of

the mother, and if any Christian shall commit fornication with a Negro man or woman, he shall pay double the fines the former act." See Leon Higginbotham Jr., *In the Matter of Color: Race and the American Legal Process, the Colonial Period* (Oxford: Oxford University Press, 1978).

Attitudes toward interracial marriage, in particular, were never uniform. Although intermarriage may have been actively discouraged by many, historically, a number of "interracial" marriages flourished. For example, black sailors in the bustling seaport of Liverpool (where Harriet Beecher Stowe first arrived in England) often intermarried with white women living in the city.

7. Unlike Latin American narratives of the mulatta, in which this figure is frequently represented with and referenced through her quadroon mother, most Anglo-American narratives situate and cite the mulatta in conjunction with her white father. The interesting aspect of this maneuver, the "right and rite of rape," is the often overt preference for the "biologized" dark daughter over that of the enslaved mother. The purifying "white" blood of the father made the "mulattaroon" more acceptable since it was she, and not her mother, who was guaranteed to retain the cleansing trace of the father. We must try to attend to differences of all types and kinds —even at the level of the individual, who is divisible. So, in contrast to most mulat*tas*, many male mulattoes appear in antagonistic relationships with their "white" fathers and in conjunction, as well as in sympathy, with their African "mothers." Examples include Frederick Douglass's *Narrative of the Life of Frederick Douglass: An American Slave* (New York: Mentor Books, 1845); James Weldon Johnson's *Autobiography of an Ex-Colored Man* (New York: Penguin, 1912); and Langston Hughes's play *Mulatto* (1935). Of course, narratives of male "mulattoes" who are the sons of black fathers, arguably a more recent phenomenon, perform this problematic differently. In southern American and some French representations, this is not usually the case. See Vera Kutzinski's superb study, *Sugar's Secrets: Race and the Erotics of Cuban Nationalism* (Charlottesville: University Press of Virginia, 1993), especially the chapter entitled "Caramel Candy for Sale," pp. 43–80, in which she compares the lithograph *La Mulata* by Victor Patricio Landaluze to Manet's *Olympia*. See also the series known as *Las Castas*, discussed in Richard Powell, *Black Art and Culture in the Twentieth Century* (London: Thames and Hudson, 1997).

8. The eminent African American writer Sterling Brown noted this in his essay on "Negro Character as Seen by White Authors": "octoroon," has come to be a feminine noun in popular usage." English, of course, is a language in which nouns are *not* gendered—thus, this phrase itself hints

at the gendered use of the term that is "invisible" but spoken (*Journal of Negro Education* 2 [January 1933]: 191). More recently, Philip Brian Harper claims that "the mulatto [*sic*] is a decidedly *feminine* character." See his *Are We Not Men? Masculine Anxiety and the Problem of African-American Identity* (New York: Oxford University Press, 1996), p. 103.

9. Autobiographical narratives of actual women of color who made the journey from (North) America to England in the nineteenth century include the slave narrative, *The History of Mary Prince, a West Indian Slave* (London: Pandora Books 1831); *Wonderful Adventures of Mrs. Seacole in Many Lands* (1857); and later in the century, *Crusade for Justice: The Autobiography of Ida B. Wells* (Chicago: University of Chicago Press, 1970), by an American journalist and antilynching activist.

10. Frederick Douglass, *The Narrative of the Life of Frederick Douglass: An American Slave*, in *The Classic Slave Narratives*, ed. Henry Louis Gates Jr. (1845; New York: Mentor Books, 1987).

11. Unlike French forms of citizenship, "the West Indian does not by being born in England, become an Englishman" (Paul Gilroy, *Ain't No Black in the Union Jack* [London: Hutchinson Press, 1987], p. 46).

12. See Valerie Smith, *Self-Discovery and Authority in Afro-American Narrative* (Cambridge, Mass.: Harvard University Press, 1987).

13. This play was penned by an unknown author under the name Captain Williams. Whereas *The Woman of Colour* beckoned the enslaved octoroon to Britain's benevolent shores, in the 1980s, the deportation of blacks signaled a change in the direction of democratic asylum.

14. It was more common for people of the lower classes to "intermarry," as did the black mariners who took white wives in Liverpool, which to this day has the highest population of "mixed-race" people in Britain. Even the popular black American actor Ira Aldridge, whose portrayal of Othello made him one of the greatest Shakespearean actors of the nineteenth century, married a white Englishwoman offstage.

15. See Ann duCille, *The Coupling Convention: Sex, Text, and Tradition in Black Women's Fiction* (New York: Oxford University Press, 1993), for a related discussion of William Wells Brown's *Clotel, or the President's Daughter: A Narrative of Slave Life in the United States* (New York: Carol Publishing Group, 1989). *Clotel*, the first published novel by an African American and a former slave, was printed in London in 1853. The involved plot of the novel is not addressed here.

16. I am indebted to Marsha Gordon for this insight.

17. In her study *Ambiguous Lives: Free Women of Color in Rural Georgia, 1789–1879* (Fayetteville: University of Arkansas Press, 1991), Adele Alexan-

der notes that her mixed-race family had separate living quarters. Similarly, there is no known complete family portrait of my grandmother's illegitimate mixed-race family.

18. Audrey Fisch, " 'Repetitious Accounts So Piteous and So Harrowing': The Ideological Work of American Slave Narratives in England," *Journal of Victorian Culture* (1994).

19. An example of this kind of noble chivalry is demonstrated by Dr. Gresham in Frances Ellen Watkins Harper's novel, *Iola Leroy, or Shadows Uplifted* (Philadelphia: Garrigue Brothers, 1892).

20. William Blake, *Songs of Experience,* quoted in *The Poetry and Prose of William Blake,* ed. David Erdman (New York: Doubleday Press, 1970), p. 24.

21. For a discussion of abolitionist discourse, rhetoric, and emblems, see Karen Sanchez-Eppler, "Bodily Bonds: The Intersecting Rhetorics of Feminism and Abolition," in *The Culture of Sentiment: Race, Gender, and Sentimentality in Nineteenth-Century America,* ed. Shirley Samuels (New York: Oxford University Press, 1992), pp. 92–114.

22. These terms appear in quotation marks in order to question their status. They are imaginary terms whose efficacy must not be assumed.

23. Nancy Armstrong, "Why Daughters Die: The Racial Logic of American Sentimentalism," *Yale Journal of Criticism* 7, no. 2 (1994): 9.

24. As Frederick Douglass noted in his slave narrative, 1845, with particular force for his own story: "Slaveholders have ordained, and by law established that the children of slave women shall in all cases follow the condition of their mothers, and this is done obviously to administer to their own lusts, and make a gratification of their wicked desires profitable as well as pleasurable; for by this cunning arrangement, the slaveholder, in cases not a few, sustains to his slaves the double relation of master and father" (Douglass, *The Narrative of the Life of Frederick Douglass: An American Slave,* in *The Classic Slave Narratives,* ed. Henry Louis Gates Jr. [New York: Mentor Books, 1987], pp. 256–57; first published in 1845).

25. My reading of Miss Swartz is indebted to my participation on the 1995 Interdisciplinary Nineteenth-Century Studies Conference panel, "Thackeray's London: The Imperial Culture of *Vanity Fair,*" with Alison Booth, Jennifer Otsuki, Sabina Sawhney, and Susan Zlotnick.

26. Peter Stallybrass and Allon White, *The Politics and Poetics of Transgression* (Ithaca, N.Y.: Cornell University Press, 1986).

27. There is another mulatta named Miss Pye and a mulatto named Lord Crawley's compatriot in Parliament, "Mr. Quadroon with carte-blanche on the Slave question" (p. 101). The most frequently referenced black charac-

ter is the servant Sambo, who makes an appearance in the second sentence of chapter 1.

28. Jane Austen's unfinished manuscript *Sandition* (1817) contained a character named "Miss Lambe," a wealthy mulatta heiress sent to London to school.

29. *Vanity Fair* stands out in Thackeray's oeuvre as the only novel he wrote that has women as main characters.

30. In an edition of *Vanity Fair*, John Sutherland asserts that Thackeray may have borrowed the idea for his theatrical preface from Alfred Bunn, manager of Drury Lane, who wrote a biography, published in 1840, entitled *The Stage, Before and Behind the Curtain.*

31. See, for example, Harold Bloom, ed., *Modern Critical Interpretations: Thackeray's "Vanity Fair"* (New York: Chelsea House Publishers, 1987); Arthur Pollard, ed., *Thackeray: "Vanity Fair," a Casebook* (London: Macmillan Publishers, 1978); or M. G. Sundell, ed., *Twentieth Century Interpretations of "Vanity Fair"* (Englewood Cliffs, N.J.: Prentice-Hall, 1969).

32. Françoise Basch, *Relative Creatures: Victorian Women in Society and the Novel* (New York: Schocken Books, 1974), p. 87.

33. Hazel Carby asserts, "Historically, in terms of narrative plot, the figure of the mulatta . . . was a device of mediation. . . . [She] allowed for movement between two worlds, white and black, and acted as a literary displacement of the actual increasing separation of the races" (Carby, *Reconstructing Womanhood* [Oxford: Oxford University Press, 1987], pp. 89–90).

34. Richard Altick, *The Shows of London* (Cambridge, Mass.: Belknap Press of Harvard University Press, 1978), pp. 268–73.

35. Homi K. Bhabha, "Location, Intervention, Incommensurability: A Conversation with Homi Bhabha," *Emergencies* 1 (1989): 64–88.

36. George P. Davies, "The Miscegenation Theme in the Works of Thackeray," *Modern Language Notes* 76 (April 1961): 326–31. Significantly, this is the first and only article on this topic. In this piece, Davies neither contextualizes nor analyzes the import of this "theme" in Victorian culture; rather, he discusses its significance solely in terms of Thackeray's "autobiography." He offers the fact that Thackeray resented his half sister, Sarah Blechynden, who was "half black," as "evidence" of the author's seemingly "morbid" fascination with "mixed race" characters. In short, Davies argues that the numerous references to mulattoes and miscegenation in Thackeray's oeuvre are essentially personal and not ideological. This explanation of the mulatto/a presences in Thackeray's fiction is insufficient given the larger implications of these figures in Victorian cultural discourse.

37. Toni Morrison's notion of whiteness was first articulated in her 1989

essay, "Unspeakable Things Unspoken: The Afro-American Presence in American Literature," *Michigan Quarterly Review* 28, no. 1 (1987): 1–34, and expanded in her lecture series collected as *Playing in the Dark: Whiteness and the Literary Imagination* (Cambridge, Mass.: Harvard University Press, 1992).

38. Catherine Peters, *Thackeray's Universe* (Oxford: Oxford University Press, 1987), p. 168.

39. See James Walvin, *Black and White: The Negro and English Society, 1555–1945* (London: Orbach, 1975), especially chapter 10, "Black Caricature: The Roots of Racialism."

40. Martin Meisel's study, *Realizations: Narrative, Pictorial, and Theatrical Arts in Nineteenth-Century England* (Princeton, N.J.: Princeton University Press, 1983), has a chapter on Thackeray and Denis Diderot, but does not discuss the illustrations of Miss Swartz. He does note, however, that of all the major Victorian novelists, only Thackeray illustrated his own works. For more on his illustrated novels, see Judith Fischer, "Image Versus Text in the Illustrated Novels of William Makepeace Thackeray," in *Victorian Literature and the Victorian Visual Imagination*, eds. Carol Christ and John Jordan (Berkeley: University of California Press, 1995).

41. John Harvey uses this illustration to exemplify how the "imaginary world of the novel becomes visually precise in a moment of sudden movement . . . and spontaneous response" (Harvey, *Victorian Novelists and Their Illustrators* [New York: New York University Press, 1971], p. 93).

42. Rebecca's association with the demonic mermaid will have implications for the final chapter of *Impossible Purities*, where Lady Arabella March, a character from Bram Stoker's *The Lair of the White Worm* (New York: Orion), is revealed to be an ancient Christian demon with a feminine guise. See also, Nina Auerbach's discussion of mermaids in her *Woman and the Demon: The Life of Victorian Myth* (Cambridge, Mass.: Harvard University Press, 1982), pp. 93–95.

43. These comic references to the conflicts between color, class, and caste will be repeated almost verbatim in the various black-faced minstrel shows that were so enormously popular in Victorian England. Thackeray's work as a sketch artist for *Punch*, which was founded in 1840, seems to parallel scripts for many of the minstrel shows performed during the nineteenth century.

44. Harriet Ritvo, "Professional Scientists and Amateur Mermaids: Beating the Bounds of Nineteenth-Century Britain," *Victorian Literature and Culture* 19 (1991): p. 277.

45. Jennifer Otsuki, "Commodity Culture and the Hottentot Venus" (un-

published paper presented at the Interdisciplinary Nineteenth-Century Studies Conference, Santa Cruz, Calif., April 1995).

46. Winthrop Jordan, *White over Black: American Attitudes Toward the Negro, 1550–1812* (Chapel Hill: University of North Carolina Press, 1968).

47. In her important discussion of the intersectionality of black women, Kimberle Crenshaw argues, "While the fallen-woman imagery that white feminists identify does represent much of black women's experience of gender domination, given their race, black women have in a sense always been within the fallen-woman category" (Crenshaw, "Whose Story Is It Anyway? Feminist and Anti-racist Appropriations of Anita Hill," in *Race-ing Justice, En-gendering Power,* ed. Toni Morrison [New York: Pantheon Books, 1992], p. 414).

48. Frantz Fanon, *Black Skin, White Masks* (New York: Grove Wedenfeld Books, 1967), p. 63.

49. J. Hillis Miller, "The Critic as Host," in *Deconstruction and Criticism,* ed. Geoffrey Hartman (New York: Continuum Books, 1990), p. 218. Subsequent references to this edition are noted in the text.

50. It is interesting to speculate about the origin of the term *mulatto,* which is most likely Arabic. See Ann duCille, "The Unbearable Darkness of Being: 'Fresh' Thoughts on Race, Sex, and the Simpsons," in *The Birth of a Nationhood: Gaze, Script, and the Spectacle in the Simpson Case,* ed. Toni Morrison (New York: Pantheon, 1997), pp. 319–20.

51. *The Creole,* a drama by Reece and Farnie with music by Jacques Offenbach, was performed in London at the Holbern Theatre in September 1877.

52. Dion Boucicault, *Plays by Dion Boucicault,* ed. Peter Thompson.

53. An exception to these more common readings is Harley Erdman's essay, "Caught in the Eye of the Eternal: Justice, Race, and the Camera, from *The Octoroon* to Rodney King," *Theatre Journal* 45 (1993): 333–48. This interesting article discusses Boucicault's novel use of the camera and photographic evidence. He concludes his look at visual technology with the 1992 videotaped beating of Rodney King by the Los Angeles Police Department.

54. Zoe, as a hybrid herself, seems to implicitly understand Wahnotee, the "red-skin" who speaks a "mash up of Indian, French, and Mexican" (p. 109). She also wholeheartedly endorses Wahnotee's love for a young slave boy, Paul: it is she who exclaims that the Indian is "a gentle, honest creature . . . [who] loves the boy with the tenderness of a woman" (p. 109). Here, noble savages recognize one another as belonging to a class

apart from the unnamed chorus of "little niggers [sic], black trash or varmin [who] steal bananas . . . dem tings, dem darkies" (p. 135). Indeed, all of the named characters, with the exception of Wahnotee, who was played by Boucicault himself, who are not white, are described as "octoroon, quadroon, or yellow." The "yellow" slave boy, Paul, was played in both London and New York by a female actress, thereby complicating the play's homoerotic representation.

55. Dion Boucicault, unpublished manuscript. Theatre Museum, Covent Garden, London, 1861.

56. Harriet Beecher Stowe, *The Key to Uncle Tom's Cabin* (Salem, N.H.: Arno Press, 1968).

57. Among the most prolific and popular nineteenth-century dramatists, Boucicault's work is well-known by theater historians in both the United States and Britain. It was also frequently performed throughout the early decades of this century. See the introduction to the play in Myron Matlaw, ed., *Nineteenth-Century American Plays* (New York: Applause Theatre Book Publishers, 1967), pp. 97–99.

58. Joseph Roach, *Cities of the Dead: Circum-Atlantic Performance* (New York: Columbia University Press, 1996), p. 215.

59. Ibid., p. 179.

60. This is a slogan for the ultracontemporary Cross-Colors clothing company, owned by black youth in Los Angeles. The company's self-styled moniker reads: "Clothing without Prejudice: Post Hip-Hop Academic Hardware for the Next Generation."

61. William Shakespeare, *The Sonnets of William Shakespeare* (New York: Heritage Press, 1941), Sonnet 147.

62. A similar confession occurs in a climatic moment in Bram Stoker's *Dracula* (New York, 1897), when the newly hybridized heroine, Mina, is branded with a red scar by Dr. Van Helsing. At this moment, when conflicting Christian and vampire signs meet on Mina's body, the vampirized woman wails, "Unclean! Unclean! Even the Almighty shuns my polluted flesh! I must bear this mark of shame upon my forehead until Judgment Day!" (chapter 22, p. 296). Like Zoe, Mina's wretched condition does not preclude her from marrying a pure, upstanding, middle-class man. Moreover, Cain has been seen as the first "amalgamationist."

63. The "happy ending" was written in 1861 in response to British audiences, who were disappointed with Zoe's tragic death in the 1859 version. For a fuller account of the politics of the different productions, see Dion Boucicault, introduction to *Plays by Dion Boucicault*, ed. Peter Thompson (Cambridge: Cambridge University Press, 1984), p. 9.

64. Unpublished playbill. Dick's plays. Theatre Museum, London.

65. Eva Saks, "Representing Miscegenation Law," *Raritan* 8, no. 2 (fall 1988): 39–69.

66. D. A. Miller, *The Novel and the Police* (Berkeley: University of California Press, 1988).

67. *Cora, the Octoroon Slave of Louisiana.* British Museum manuscripts, Lord Chamberlain's Collection, dated 1861.

68. Kent Anderson Leslie, *Woman of Color, Daughter of Privilege: Amanda America Dickson, 1849–1893* (Athens: University of Georgia Press, 1995), p. 1. Subsequent references are noted in the text.

69. Josiah Nott, *An essay on the natural history of mankind, viewed in connection with Negro slavery* (Mobile, Ala.: Dade, Thompson, 1851).

70. Hortense J. Spillers, "The Permanent Obliquity: In the Time of Fathers and Daughters," in ed. Cheryl Wall *Changing Our Own Words* (New Brunswick, N.J.: Rutgers University Press, 1989).

71. Quoted in John Mencke, *Mulattoes and Race Mixture: Images, 1865–1918* (Ann Arbor: UMI Research Press, 1976), p. 18.

72. Roach, *Cities of the Dead*, p. 10.

73. Russ Castronovo, *Fathering the Nation: American Genealogies of Slavery and Freedom* (Berkeley: University of California Press, 1995), pp. 9–10.

74. Miller, "The Critic as Host," p. 221. Subsequent references to this essay are noted in the text.

75. J. A. Rogers, *Sex and Race: Negro and Caucasian Mixing in All Ages and Levels* (St. Petersburg, Fla.: Helga M. Rogers, 1968), p. 204.

76. White middle-class women marked or ironically displayed their racial, class, gender, and national identities by remaining on the pedestal built for them by patriarchal ideology, as well as by following the injunction to "suffer and be still." See Martha Vicinus, ed., *Suffer and Be Still: Women in the Victorian Period* (Bloomington: University of Indiana Press, 1972).

77. William Starbuck, *A Woman against the World* (1864), quoted in *Sexuality and Victorian Literature*, ed. Richard Cox (Knoxville: University of Tennessee Press, 1984), p. 69.

78. Spillers, "Neither/Nor," p. 183.

Chapter Two: Casting the Dye

1. Note also that the epigraph for this chapter is from Martin Meisel, "The Material Sublime: John Martin, Byron, Turner, and the Theater," in

Images of Romanticism: Verbal and Visual Affinities, ed. Karl Kroebler and William Walling (New Haven, Conn.: Yale University Press, 1978), p. 211.

2. Alexandre Dumas père, *The Black Tulip,* trans. Marcel Girard (London: J. M. Dent, 1960). First published in 1850. Subsequent references to this edition are noted in the text.

Also, the subheading for this section is taken from Toni Morrison, *Playing in the Dark: Whiteness and the Literary Imagination* (Cambridge, Mass.: Harvard University Press, 1992), p. 87.

3. H. G. Wells, *The Island of Dr. Moreau* (New York: Lanser Books, 1968).

4. Richard Jenkyns, *Dignity and Decadence: Victorian Art and the Classical Inheritance* (Cambridge, Mass.: Harvard University Press, 1992), p. 107.

5. G. B. Shaw, *Pygmalion* (Baltimore: Penguin, 1951). First published in 1913.

6. Historically, botanists were the first successful hybridizers. What was achieved in the rarified realm of horticulture was then translated into more complex organisms. Darwin's book, *The Variation of Animals and Plants under Domestication* (London: J. Murray, 1868), discusses flowers and "graft-hybrids" as does his earlier tract, *The Origin of Species* (London: Penguin Books, 1859).

7. Harriet Beecher Stowe, *Uncle Tom's Cabin* (New York: Penguin Classics, 1986). First published in 1852. Subsequent references to this edition are noted in the text. Topsy is the black-faced female character who "balances" this representation. Numerous white actresses made their careers playing this quintessential black-faced role. See, for example, Edward Marks, *They All Had Glamour* (New York: Messner Books, 1944), pp. 71–74.

8. Angela Y. Davis, *Women, Race and Class* (New York: Vintage Books, 1983), p. 27.

9. George Aiken, *Uncle Tom's Cabin: or, Life Among the Lowly. A Domestic Drama, in Six Acts* (New York: Samuel French, n.d.), p. 17. In *Last Supper at Uncle Tom's Cabin/The Promised Land,* choreographer Bill T. Jones restages Eliza's escape by having five different dancers perform her part. One "Eliza" soloist, a black male, wears a white miniskirt and white high-heeled shoes—an homage to the play's cross-dressed origins and to Eliza's whitened femininity. See VHS tape of the 9 November 1990 performance at the Brooklyn Academy of Music.

10. Edmund Burke, *A Philosophical Enquiry into the Origin of Our Ideas of the Sublime and the Beautiful* (London: R. and J. Dodsley, 1764).

11. Robert Young, *Colonial Desire: Hybridity in Culture, Theory, and Race* (London: Routledge, 1995), p. 26.

12. Joy S. Kasson, "Narratives of the Female Body: *The Greek Slave,*" in

The Culture of Sentiment: Race, Gender, and Sentimentality in Nineteenth-Century America, ed. Shirley Samuels (New York: Oxford University Press, 1992), p. 173.

13. Ibid., p. 178.

14. Quoted in Jenkyns, *Dignity and Decadence,* p. 116.

15. Henry James quoted in Oliver W. Larkin, *Art and Life in America* (New York: Holt, Rinehart and Winston, 1960), p. 181.

16. Henrik Ibsen quoted in Bernard F. Dukore, ed., *Dramatic Theory and Criticism: Greeks to Grotowski* (New York: Holt, Reinhart, and Winston, 1974), p. 560.

17. Walter Benjamin, "The Work of Art in the Age of Mechanical Reproduction," *Illuminations: Essays and Reflections* (New York: Schocken Books, 1968), p. 220.

18. Jenkyns, *Dignity and Decadence,* p. 107.

19. Anonymous review in *Lucas Guardian and Hitchin Advertiser.* Unpublished manuscript, 12 May 1853.

20. See Robert C. Toll, *Blacking Up: The Minstrel Show in Nineteenth Century America* (New York: Oxford University Press, 1974); Eric Lott, *Love and Theft: Blackface Minstrelsy and the American Working Class* (New York: Oxford University Press, 1993); and Saxton, *The Rise and Fall.*

21. Townsend Walsh, *The Career of Dion Boucicault* (New York: Dunlop Society, 1915), p. 71.

22. One of the first scholars to tackle this subject was the eminent theater historian, Jacky S. Bratton. Bratton contends that "very little of what explains [the black minstrel shows'] success in America is relevant to its success in Britain; and yet this was almost as great." (Bratton, "English Ethiopians: British Audiences and Black-Face Acts, 1835–1865," *The Yearbook of English Studies* 11 [1981]: 128.)

23. The account is taken from the Thursday, May 12, 1853 "edition" of the *Lucas Guardian and Hitchin Advertiser,* and was transcribed on Tuesday, May 21, 1996 at the Hereford County Records Office with the assistance of Derek Forbes and Nick Wood. Reginald Hines, author of *Hitchin Worthies: Four Centuries of English Life* (London: George Allen and Unwin, 1932), explains the history of this local paper. Begun by the Hitchins—a farming and brewing Quaker family—it was handwritten. The paper marks the entrance of the Derbyites into power, and it sought to promote legal as well as sanitary reforms.

24. See Joan D. Hendrick's biography, *Harriet Beecher Stowe: A Life* (New York: Oxford University Press, 1994).

25. Figure is based on an examination of the collection of theatrical pro-

ductions approved by the Lord Chamberlain's office, which is held at the archives of the British Library. Citations that follow come from my own transcription of handwritten documents.

26. *Uncle Tom's Cabin or the Negro Slave: A Drama in Two Acts*, from Lord Chamberlain's Collection (London: British Library).

27. *Uncle Tom's Cabin: A Nigger Drama in Two Acts* from Lord Chamberlain's Collection (London: British Library).

28. Other specifically English additions to Stowe's text include: representing Topsy as a West Indian or Spanish American character who wears a turban or a mantilla rather than a wig of wiry hair and having a woman play the part of Harry. The audience for minstrels was not exclusively working-class. Productions at St. James Hall were popular with middle-class audiences and Queen Victoria herself was fond of the entertainment, to which the command performances staged at Balmoral Castle attest.

29. *Uncle Tom's Crib, or Nigger Life in London.* L. C. Collection. Squash-top has overheard the entire declaration and sings to his comrade, Dark Joe, the still-popular American folk song:

Dar's somebody in the house with Dinah
Dar's somebody in the house we know
(repeats) playing on de old Banjo

This scene illustrates how American tunes and elements were incorporated and translated into the British context, underscoring the complex cultural commerce between the two nations. The entire drama ends with a "grand nigger dance."

30. Michael Pickering, "Mock Blacks and Racial Mockery: The 'Nigger' Minstrel and British Imperialism," in *Acts of Supremacy: The British Empire and Stage*, ed. Jacky Bratton (Manchester University Press, 1991), p. 183.

31. Barthes, *Mythologies*, p. 152. Other excellent readings of mimesis include: Michael Taussig, *Mimesis and Alterity: A Particular History of the Senses* (New York: Routledge, 1993); and Judith Butler, *Bodies That Matter: On the Discursive Limits of "Sex"* (New York: Routledge, 1993).

32. Thomas Carlyle, *Occasional Discourse on the Nigger Question.* In *Thomas Carlyle, The Nigger Question; John Stuart Mill, the Negro Question,* ed. Eugene August (New York: Meredith Corporation, 1971), p. 7. First published in 1849, p. 7.

33. Lott, *Love and Theft,* p. 15. This point supports James Baldwin's polemical reading of the novel in his essay, "Everybody's Protest Novel," in *Notes of a Native Son* (Boston: Beacon Press, 1955), p. 195.

34. Anonymous news article from the Harry Birdoff Collection, Stowe-Day Library, Hartford, Conn.

35. *Uncle Tom in England; Or, a Proof That Black's White* (London: William Tyler, 1852). Subsequent references are noted in the text.

36. P. Merritt, *Flip, Flap, Flop.* Surrey Theatre, London. L. C. Collection, British Library. Sept. 19, 1883.

37. A superb reading of the significance of such performances appears in Annemarie Bean, "Transgressing the Gender Divide: The Female Impersonator in Nineteenth-Century Blackface Minstrelsy," in *Inside the Minstrel Mask: Readings in Nineteenth-Century Blackface Minstrelsy,* ed. Annemarie Bean, James Hatch, and Brooks McNamara (Hanover: Wesleyan University Press, 1996), pp. 245–56. For readings of late-twentieth-century performances of "blackface cross-dressing" that may be relevant, see Carole-Anne Tyler, "Boys Will Be Girls: The Politics of Gay Drag," in *Inside/Out: Gay and Lesbian Studies,* ed. Diana Fuss (New York: Routledge, 1994). See also commentaries on Jennie Livingston's film, *Paris is Burning,* especially Peggy Phelan, "The Golden Apple," in *Unmarked: The Politics of Performance* (New York: Routledge, 1993).

38. William Craft, *Running a Thousand Miles for Freedom; or, The Escape of William and Ellen Craft from Slavery* (Miami, FL: Mnemosyne, 1969). First published in 1860.

39. Paul de Man, "Hypogram and Inscription," in *The Resistance to Theory* (Minneapolis: University of Minnesota Press, 1986), p. 44.

40. It was not until later in the century that actual negro performers, such as the Fisk Jubilee Singers, were valued for their "authenticity." It is no accident that Ralph Ellison wrote about minstrelsy in his collection of essays *Shadow and Act* (New York: Random House, 1964), given this particular relation established in such performances.

41. Barbara Johnson, *The Critical Difference: Essays in the Contemporary Rhetoric of Reading* (Baltimore, Md.: Johns Hopkins University Press, 1980), p. 5.

42. G. W. Moore, *The St. James's Hall Veritable and Legitimate Christy's Minstrels Christmas Annual* (London: J. E. Allard, 1868).

43. Sir Walter Scott, *The Heart of Midlothian* (Edinburgh: Anna C. Black, 1887).

44. James Snead, *White Screens, Black Images: Hollywood from the Dark Side,* eds. Colin McCabe and Cornel West (New York: Routledge, 1994), p. 71.

45. The metonymic use of the term *blond,* epitomized in scenes from the *Invisible Man,* shows both how this term was femininized and juxtaposed

with a notion of black masculinity. So too, does the infamous description in Ellison's novel of the "optic white" paint, whose pure whiteness contains the fatal drop of black dope. See Ralph Ellison, *Invisible Man* (New York: Random House, 1952).

Similarly, the English-born Alfred Hitchcock notoriously transformed the heroines of his films into blondes.

46. See Richard Dyer, *White* (London: Routledge, 1997), p. 1.

47. Moreover, Snead observes that when Dietrich emerges from her gorilla suit in the infamous "Hot Voodoo" number, she "does not use her own hair, but instead wears a *blonde* Afro wig. The frizzy blonde hair, and her harmony with the 'African' women in the chorus line indicate that, despite having entirely removed the gorilla suit, she has now assumed some of the attributes of her 'black' get-up. Indeed, the subtle joke intended here is that, as a blonde *femme fatale* she is conceivably more threatening to the white male than a black gorilla would be" (*White Screens*, p. 72; italics in the original).

48. Lois Banner, *American Beauty* (Chicago: University of Chicago Press, 1983), p. 121. The subsequent reference is noted in the text.

49. Wendy Cooper, *Hair: Sex, Society, Symbolism* (New York: Stein and Day Publishers, 1971), p. 75. For a related discussion of the blond wig as an erotic commodity, in this case in the performance of Dietrich in *Blonde Venus*, see Mary Ann Doane, *Femmes Fatales: Feminism, Film Theory, and Psychoanalysis*.

50. Banner, *American Beauty*, p. 123.

51. Lydia Thompson has been memorialized, appropriately, in a Mardi Gras song.

52. Ibid., p. 125.

53. We must remember that a different system of racialization and differing models of citizenship emerged in France. France never had a "colonial" policy in the Americas—even today, French citizens need not reside on "French" soil to be considered part of the metropolitan center. Baldly put, France offered its *citoyens* a model of full assimilation from afar, whereas England hailed members of the commonwealth differently. See Lisa Lowe, *Critical Terrains: French and British Orientalisms* (Ithaca: Cornell University Press, 1991).

Novelist Caryl Phillips asserts that, "[m]ore than any other European colonial power, France exported a culture that aimed to embrace blacks. They tried to make West Indians in particular but also Africans feel that they had a shared history, and they could have equality in Frenchness if nothing else. . . . British racists have much to learn from the French."

(Phillips, *The European Tribe* [Boston: Faber and Faber, 1987], pp. 64–65.)
As Michel Fabre notes, France has been a refuge of sorts for black writers
and intellectuals from the eighteenth century to the 1980s. Arabs, Jews,
and Algerians were another matter. Today, Paris, like London, must deal
with a black urban presence—immigrants, now unwelcome, who are seen
as infringing on a delicate economy.

54. The French actress Eugenie Doche, who originated the role of Camille on stage, had blond hair (Alexandre Dumas fils, *La Dame aux Camellias*, trans. David Coward [Oxford: Oxford University Press, 1986]; first
published in 1852).

55. See the Académie française special edition translated by William Walton and illustrated by Eugene-Andre Champollion, Pierre-Augustin Masse,
and Albert Lynch (Philadelphia: Barrie and Sons, 1897), p. 64. This text
contains a drawing of Marguerite's disinternment that closely resembles
Bram Stoker's lurid description of the execution of the vampirized Lucy
Westenra in his 1897 classic, *Dracula* (Oxford: Oxford University Press,
1983).

56. Dumas, *La Dame aux Camellias*, trans. Coward, p. 64. Subsequent
references to this edition are noted in the text.

57. We recall that Miss Swartz, another object of fascination, also wore
expensive diamonds.

58. The term *cloaca* means a passage for wastes, a privy, or a water closet.

59. G. W. Griffin, *Camille, an Ethiopian Interlude* (New York: Happy
Hours Company, ca. 1880). Subsequent references to this edition are noted
in the text.

60. For a detailed discussion of Punch and Judy, and the text of one of
the shows that includes Jim Crow, see Peter Quennell, ed., *Mayhew's London* (London: Bracken Books, 1984), pp. 445–70.

61. Griffin, *Camille*, p. 8.

62. Purportedly, "a beautiful brown-skin actress in a Midwestern stock
company . . . always played *Camille* in white makeup and a blond wig. To
cover her arms throughout the play, the dark star wore long white gloves.
One night during the death scene . . . when she reached up to hug her beloved Armand, the sleeves of her lovely lace nightgown fell so far down
toward her shoulders that the upper portion of each dusky arm was exposed
[prompting an audience member to howl in ridicule and disbelief]." See
Langston Hughes and Milton Meltzer, eds., *Black Magic: A Pictorial History of African-American Performing Arts* (New York: DaCapo Press, 1990),
p. 123. The play has been filmed numerous times and was reincarnated
in the 1980s by camp performer Charles Ludlum in New York City in a

production that featured several black actors. See *The Complete Plays of Charles Ludlum* (New York: Harper and Row Publishers, 1973).

63. Originally entitled *The Lesbians* when advertised in 1846, there were several versions of Baudelaire's poems described, and in some cases printed, before the official publication of the book in 1857. Indeed, the 1857 version was promptly banned on publication and revised, with excisions, in 1861. For more on the publication history, see Charles Baudelaire, *Charles Baudelaire: The Flowers of Evil*, trans. James McGowan (New York: Oxford University Press, 1993). It is beyond the scope of this chapter to elucidate the full complexity of Baudelaire's crucial work; rather, he is cited in the context of "French" obsessions with "black femininity."

64. If, as Lynda Hart has asserted, the lesbian entered discourse as always already white, but connected parenthetically to women of color, then we can begin to see the imbricated notion of a black femme fatale—of the femme fatale as "black." As I argued in Chapter 1, the connection between Rebecca Sharp and Rhoda Swartz rethinks blackness and femininity as specific tropes of race and sexuality that were related in Anglo-American culture. See Lynda Hart, *Fatal Women: Lesbian Sexuality and the Mark of Aggression* (Princeton, N.J.: Princeton University Press, 1994).

65. J. A. Rogers claims that Baudelaire "gave Jeanne [Duvall] a blonde maid," suggesting yet another link between 'blackness' and 'blondeness.'" (J. A. Rogers, *Sex and Race: Negro-Caucasian Mixing in All Ages and Lands Vol. I* [St. Petersburg, Fla.: Helga M. Rogers, 1967] p. 257).

66. Linda Nochlin, *Realism* (London: Penguin Books, 1971), p. 203.

67. The close relations have been refigured famously in Larry Rivers's *I Like Olympia in Black Face* (1970), which has been described by Richard Powell as a *"tableau vivant* burlesque of Manet's *Olympia"* (see Richard Powell, *Black Art and Culture in the Twentieth Century* [London: Thames and Hudson, 1997], pp. 146–47). For a brilliant review of contemporary nineteenth-century cartoons, see "Olympia's Choice," T. J. Clark, *The Painting of Modern Life: Paris in the Art of Manet and His Followers* (Princeton, N.J.: Princeton University Press, 1984), in which a courisiane is defined as "something between a femme honnête and a prostitute" (pp. 109–11). In Pablo Picasso's 1901 (per)version of the painting, Olympia is re-presented "as" black in an exaggeration of the elements suggested more subtly in the original and confirmed by the numerous nineteenth-century cartoons of the picture. The American artist Herb Hazelton's *Marilyn Monroe* (1964) depicts the blond bombshell as Olympia with an Aunt Jemima-like figure bearing a stack of pancakes.

68. Lorraine O'Grady, "Olympia's Maid: Reclaiming Black Female Subjectivity," *Afterimage* (summer 1992): 14.

69. Charles Bernheimer's reading of the painting, in "Manet's *Olympia:* The Figuration of Scandal," helps to explain the appeal of this portrait. His chapter provides numerous nineteenth-century interpretations of the picture. He notes that contemporary accounts called Olympia "a sort of female gorilla, a grotesque in India rubber outlined in black; a naked and cold . . . monster of banal love [who] inspires a scared horror . . . the impure par excellence (p. 113). Some form or other . . . a sort of monkey mocking the pose and the movement of the arm of Titian's Venus, with a hand shamelessly flexed (p. 116). That Hottentot Venus with the black cat (p. 120)." Charles Bernheimer, *Figures of Ill Repute* (Cambridge, Mass.: Harvard University Press, 1989), p. 104.

70. Thomas Hood, *The Poetical Works of Thomas Hood* (Boston: Crosby and Nichols, 1864), p. 23.

71. Jean-Paul Sartre, *Being and Nothingness* (New York: New York University Press, 1956), p. 777.

72. A paradigmatic example of the early Victorian fallen woman comes from Countess Blessington's *Heath's Book of Beauty* (London: Longman and Co., 1836). The book includes the story of "Agnes," an evangelical country girl who is seduced by an aristocratic cad and abandoned with their child. Ultimately, she throws herself into a river, aptly named "The Serpentine," never to emerge again. Notable, also, is the fact that in the popular narrative *Clotel* (New York: Carol Publishing, 1989), the heroine jumps into the Potomac River.

73. Sander Gilman, "I'm Down on Whores: Race and Gender in Victorian London," in *The Anatomy of Racism*, ed. David Goldberg (Minneapolis: University of Minnesota Press, 1990), p. 146–47.

74. Carroll coins "slithy" in *Through the Looking Glass* (1871). In the preface to the 1896 Christmas edition, Carroll instructs his readers to "[p]ronounce slithy as if it were the two words "sly, the" (p. 171). The word spelled *slythy* is glossed as smooth and active, as well as a compounded form of lithe and slimy. It is supposed to be an Anglo-Saxon term. It is also related to *sleathy,* an obsolete word meaning slovenly. Carroll's slithy hybrid beings, which combine incompatible elements like oil and water, are similar to Sartre's notion of the slimy.

75. *Lithe* means active and, according to Nina Auerbach, "Victorian literature conveys a covert fear that any activity smacks of acting" (Auerbach, *Private Theatricals: The Lives of the Victorians* [Cambridge, Mass.: Harvard University Press, 1990], p. 4).

76. William Acton, *Prostitution Considered in Its Moral, Social, and Sanitary Aspects in London* (London: Cass, 1972), p. 108. First published in 1857. See also Parent-Duchâtelet, *De la prostitution dans la ville de Paris*, 2 vols. (Paris, 1836).

Chapter Three: Masking Faces

1. Charles Reade was the successful author of twenty-seven novels, most notably, *The Cloister and the Hearth* (London: Trubner, 1861). He also wrote, produced, and/or adapted more than twenty plays. He was compared to other dramatic, sensation novelists—such as Dickens, Mary Braddon, and Wilkie Collins. He was appointed to the Royal Commission on Copyrights. For more on Reade, see Wayne Burns, *Charles Reade* (New York: Bookman Associates, 1961).

2. See Charles Reade, *Plays by Charles Reade*, ed. Michael Hammet (Cambridge: Cambridge University Press, 1986); Charles Reade, *Peg Woffington* (London: Bradbury, Evans, and Company, 1868); and Charles Reade, "Androgynism; or, Woman Playing at Man," *English Review* (1911): 10–29, 191–212.

3. The London Library, a private lending library rather than a manuscripts collection, houses the nearly seventy notebooks compiled by Reade during his career.

4. Octave Uzanne, "Notes on the Portraits of Alexandre Dumas the Elder," in *The Black Tulip*, trans. Richard Garnett (New York: Collier and Son, 1902). Uzanne's "descriptive notes" conclude this edition of *The Black Tulip* and exemplify the commodification of the author.

5. Quoted in Wayne Burns, "More Reade Notebooks," *Studies in Philology* 42 (October 1945): 838.

6. Reade may have been among the first to articulate in explicit terms the value of *American* literature (which was not thought to exist before the publication of *Uncle Tom's Cabin*).

7. Charles Reade, undated notebook, circa 1860, Parrish Collection, Firestone Library, Princeton University. Reade wrote something similar to these lines in his novel about prison reform, *It's Never Too Late to Mend* (London: Chatto and Windus, 1894). In their article, "Uncle Tom and Charles Reade," *American Literature* 17, no. 4 (January 1946): 334–47, Wayne Burns and Sutcliffe discuss the influence of Stowe's method on Reade's fiction.

8. W. E. B. DuBois, *The Souls of Black Folk* (Chicago: A. C. McClurg and Company, 1903).

9. For a reading of the play's imperial context, see Michael Hays, "Representing Empire: Class, Culture, and the Popular Theatre in the Nineteenth Century," *Theater Journal* 47, no. 1 (1995): 65–82.

10. Reade's collection is reminiscent of Sir Arthur Munby's documentation of his "secret marriage" to his servant (who played the part of his slave), Hannah Cullwick. This information was revealed "after the fact" in Hannah's diaries, along with the discovery of Munby's obsessive drawings and photographs of working-class women dressed in working*men*'s attire. Apparently, he preferred the women to be begrimed with evidence of their "unsexing" labor. For more on Munby, see Hannah Cullwick, *The Diaries of Hannah Cullwick* (New Brunswick, N.J.: Rutgers University Press, 1984); and Anne McClintock, *Imperial Leather: Race, Gender, and Sexuality in the Colonial Contest* (New York: Routledge, 1995).

11. According to Wayne Burns, Reade believed that "in fiction (as in life) the mask became the person, the idea the Baconian reality. At least this is what he attempted when he began to write. . . . He drew upon everything from Parliamentary oratory to Pre-Raphaelite painting to develop a new and more extreme form of documentary realism" (Burns, *Charles Reade*, p. 85).

12. Cross-dressing was a common practice among eighteenth-century actresses. One of the most famous of such figures was Charlotte Charke, the actor Colley Cibber's daughter. Charke wore male attire not only on the stage, but more infamously, on the streets of London. For more information on Charke and this practice, see Kristina Straub, *Sexual Suspects: Eighteenth Century Players and Sexual Ideology* (Princeton, N.J.: Princeton University Press, 1992).

13. Reade, *Peg Woffington*, p. 11.

14. Reade, "Androgynism," p. 202.

15. Quoted in John Coleman, *Charles Reade as I Knew Him* (New York: Dutton and Co., 1903), p. 103.

16. Judith Halberstam, *Skin Shows: Gothic Horror and the Technology of Monsters* (Durham, N.C.: Duke University Press, 1995).

17. Oscar Wilde, "An Ideal Husband," in *The Plays of Oscar Wilde*, intro. John Lahr (New York: Vintage, 1988).

18. See Nina Auerbach's similar interpretation of Ellen Terry's "boy" parts in *Ellen Terry: Player in Her Time* (New York: W. W. Norton and Co., 1987).

19. Here I concur with Susan Carlson's thesis that British comedy is not necessarily a liberating genre for women and implicitly reject Northrop Frye's liberationist reading. See Susan Carlson, *Women and Comedy: Re-*

writing the British Theatrical Tradition (Ann Arbor: University of Michigan Press, 1991).

20. Charles Reade, *Plays by Charles Reade.*

21. Martin Meisel, *Realizations: Narrative, Pictorial, Theatrical Arts in Nineteenth-Century England* (Princeton, N.J.: Princeton University Press, 1993).

22. For a discussion of changes in Victorian theater, see Michael R. Booth, *Theatre in the Victorian Age* (Cambridge, England: Cambridge University Press, 1991); Richard Altick, *The Shows of London* (Cambridge, Mass.: Belknap Press of Harvard University Press, 1978); and George Rowell, *Nineteenth Century Theatre* (New York: Oxford University Press, 1956). Reformers took on a more active role at the very end of the century when a form of "homosexual" panic proliferated. See the archive in the Greater London Records Office that includes petitions to the Lord Chamberlain by a Mrs. Laura Chant on the topic of sodomites and prostitution.

23. Clement Scott quoted in David Mullin, ed., *Victorian Actors and Actresses in Review* (London: Greenwood Press, 1983), p. 252.

24. Ibid.

25. Ibid.

26. George Farquhar's famed play *The Female Officer* was not performed in the years commonly claimed as Victorian (1830–1901), thus Peg's famous breeches role was not revived in the nineteenth century.

27. Reade quoted in Sheila Stowell, "Actors as Dramatic Personae: Nell Gwynne, Peg Woffington, and David Garrick on the Victorian Stage," *Theatre History Studies* 8 (1988): 129.

28. See Charles Bernheimer, *Figures of Ill Repute: Representing Prostitution in Nineteenth Century France* (Cambridge, Mass.: Harvard University Press, 1989), p. 5.

29. Reade quoted in Coleman, *Charles Reade as I Knew Him*, p. 93.

30. Pompey's role in the drama is less significant than it is in the novel. In *Masks and Faces*, Pompey plays the "angel of darkness" to Peg's "angel of light" (act 2). He serves as a kind of comic relief, appearing on stage only twice. The conventional representation of the black servant in both painting and drama is discussed by Kim Hall, *Things of Darkness: Economies of Race and Gender in Early Modern Culture* (Ithaca, N.Y.: Cornell University Press, 1995).

31. This scene might be compared to the masculine tradition of school flogging. Floggings were standard in Victorian pornography as well as in the British navy. Certainly, such scenes were familiar in the antislavery literature, also called "printed sadism," that flourished in both England and

America. For example, in the *The Narrative of the Life of Frederick Doug-lass*, a best-seller in England, Douglass describes a scene in which the Maryland slaveholder, Mrs. Hamilton, whips her slave, Mary. As the "eye-witness" of the cruel beatings in which Mary is "cut to pieces," Douglass provides his readers with lurid details that are meant to elicit sympathy for "pecked" Mary and to illustrate that slavery even corrupts white women in the North. That both Reade and Douglass locate the nadir of a corrupt cul-ture in the figure of the "white woman who whips" suggests the extent to which white women were to be revered (thus their debasement is the most disturbing symbol). Of course, a major difference between Reade's account and that of Douglass is that the latter focuses less on the figuration of the white woman with a "black heart" and more on Mary, the object of her abuse. The tortured Mary that Douglass describes is not a battered *body*, but rather, mere raw and mutilated "flesh." Here I allude to Hortense J. Spillers' distinction between the body and flesh of the enslaved woman in "Mama's Baby, Papa's Maybe: An American Grammar Book," *diacritics* 17, no. 2 (summer 1987): 65–80.

32. See the "classic" essay by Gayle Rubin, "The Traffic of Women: Notes on the Political Economy of Sex," in *Toward an Anthropology of Women*, ed. Rayna R. Reiter (New York: Monthly Review Press, 1975). See also Eve Sedgwick, *Between Men: English Literature and Male Homosocial Desire* (New York: Columbia University Press, 1985).

33. Reade, *Peg Woffington*, p. 45. Subsequent reference is noted in the text.

34. See, for example, Mary Prince's narrative, *The History of Mary Prince, a West Indian Slave*, ed. Moira Ferguson (London: Pandora Books, 1987). First published in 1831.

35. Reade's sweeping knowledge of the culturally marginal and of "whip-ping women" includes an article about Ashantee women who whip men in the tribe into going to war.

36. Reade, *Peg Woffington*, p. 141.

37. The connection between the Irish and hybrids (the Black Irish) goes back at least to Ben Jonson, who is quoted in the *OED* as describing "a wilde Irish girl and a hybride." For more information, see L. Perry Curtis's classic study, *Apes and Angels: The Irishman in Victorian Caricature* (Wash-ington, D.C.: Smithsonian Institution Press, 1971), an early and very good example of popular culture scholarship.

38. Reade referenced Othello in nearly all his work. For more on mon-strous couplings and miscegenation in Victorian England, see Howard L. Malchow, *Gothic Images of Race in Nineteenth-Century Britain* (Palo Alto,

Calif.: Stanford University Press, 1996). So too, we might think here of Elizabeth Gaskell's character Ruth (from the novel of the same name) and her deformed Welsh protector, Mr. Benson; of Catherine and Heathcliff in *Wuthering Heights,* and Ayesha and the baboonish narrator of Rider Haggard's *She.*

39. Reade, *Peg Woffington,* p. 68.

40. Thomas Love Peacock, *Melincourt, or Sir Oran Haut-ton,* quoted in *Culture and Comedy: 1820–1900,* Roger Henkle (Princeton, N.J.: Princeton University Press, 1980).

41. Two other examples are Ellean and Paula, the second Mrs. Tanqueray in Pinero's play of the same name; and Jeanie and Effie Deans in Scott's *Heart of Midlothian.*

42. Reade, *Peg Woffington,* p. 121. Subsequent references are noted in the text.

43. Oscar Wilde, *The Picture of Dorian Gray,* in *The Portable Oscar Wilde,* eds. Richard Aldington and Stanley Weintraub (New York: Penguin Books, 1981), p. 390. First published in 1890.

44. It is significant that she is called Margaret only rarely, since her "pet" name emphasizes her objectification so well.

45. These notebooks are housed at the London Library. Interestingly, the American author Mark Twain wrote a series of "transvestite tales," to use Marjorie Garber's term, during this same period.

46. Reade, "Androgynism."

47. See Judith Butler, *Gender Trouble: Feminism and the Subversion of Identity* (New York: Routledge, 1990).

48. Teresa DeLauretis, *Technologies of Gender* (Bloomington: Indiana University Press, 1987), p. 25.

49. This section contributes to the growing scholarship in gender and queer studies by focusing on a "case of the congenitally epicene" in nineteenth-century England. Both Marjorie Garber's *Vested Interests: Cross-Dressing and Cultural Anxiety* (New York: Routledge, 1991), and Julia Epstein and Kristina Straub, eds., *Body Guards: The Cultural Politics of Gender Ambiguity* (New York: Routledge, 1991) discuss what might be termed "congenially epicene" figures; neither study, however, devotes any significant space to *Victorian* representations of the "ambiguous/transvestite body" (although Straub has an excellent discussion of eighteenth-century cross-dresser Charlotte Charke). One might speculate that Victorian representations about such figures have not received much attention because, as both of these books argue, Victorian culture has erroneously been seen as

achieving the solidification of boundaries that were relatively indistinct in earlier periods, such as the eighteenth century and the Renaissance.

50. Reade, "Androgynism," p. 11. Subsequent references are noted in the text.

51. In many ways, the actual Peg Woffington found herself in the vanguard of this debate. Her first breeches role as Sylvia in *The Female Officer* won her good notices; however, it was her performance as Sir Harry Wildair, the male lead in Farquhar's drama, *The Constant Couple,* that won her fame. Among the other actresses to play leading men were Madame Vestris, who performed in MacHeath in *The Beggar's Opera,* and Sarah Bernhardt, who played Hamlet in 1899.

52. William Makepeace Thackeray, *Vanity Fair,* ed. and intro. John Sutherland (Oxford: Oxford University Press, 1983), p. 812.

53. For more on the blush in Victorian literature, see Mary Ann O'Farrell, *Telling Complexions: The Nineteenth-century English Novel and the Blush* (Durham, N.C.: Duke University Press, 1997).

54. Emily Dickinson, "One Need Not Be a Chamber to Be Haunted . . . ," in *The Complete Poems of Emily Dickinson,* ed. Thomas Johnson (Boston: Little, Brown, and Co., 1960), p. 333.

55. Jean Howard, "Cross-Dressing, the Theater, and Gender Struggle in Early Modern England," *Shakespeare Quarterly* 39 (1988): 432.

56. Tracy Davis, *Actresses as Working Women: Their Social Identity in Victorian Culture* (London: Routledge, 1991), p. 113.

57. Ann Rosiland Jones and Peter Stallybrass, "Fetishizing Gender: Constructing the Hermaphrodite in Renaissance Europe," in *Body Guards,* Epstein and Straub, p. 106.

58. Reade, "Androgynism," p. 205.

59. Reade, *Peg Woffington,* p. 269.

60. Peter Stallybrass and Allon White, *The Politics and Poetics of Transgression* (Ithaca, N.Y.: Cornell University Press, 1986), p. 200.

61. Reade, "Androgynism," p. 22. Subsequent references are in the text.

62. Theresa DeLaurentis, *Technologies of Gender* (Bloomington: Indiana University Press, 1987), p. 4.

63. One of the first accounts of a cross-dressed actress that includes its racial aspect states: "If this [cross-dressing of women] bee not barbarous, make the rude *Scithian,* the untamed *Moore,* the naked *Indian,* or the wilde *Irish* Lords and Rulers of well-governed cities" (quoted in Howard, "Cross-Dressing," p. 112).

64. Carol Hanbery Mackay, *Dramatic Dickens* (New York: St. Martin's Press, 1989), p. 81.

65. Jean Baurillard, *Simulations*, trans. P. Foss, P. Patton, and P. Beitchman (New York: Semiotext(e), 1983). Subsequent reference is noted in the text.

66. For more on the theoretical aspects of "androgyny," see Kari Weil, *Androgyny and the Denial of Difference* (Charlottesville: University Press of Virginia, 1992).

67. Nina Auerbach, *Private Theatricals: The Lives of the Victorians* (Cambridge, Mass.: Harvard University Press, 1990), p. 4.

68. Reade, "Androgynism," p. 205. Subsequent reference is noted in the text.

69. Hillis Miller, "The Critic as Host," in *Deconstruction and Criticism*, ed. Geoffrey Hartman (New York: Continuum Books, 1990).

70. Reade, "Androgynism," p. 15. Subsequent references are noted in the text.

71. Wilde, *Dorian Gray*, p. 144.

72. Reade, "Androgynism," p. 19.

73. Francette Pacteau, "The Impossible Referent: Representations of the Androgyne," in *Formations of Fantasy*, eds. Victor Burgin, James Donald, and Cora Kaplan (London: Methuen Books, 1986), p. 70.

74. Reade, "Androgynism," p. 19. Subsequent references are noted in the text.

75. Lyman Weeks, "Women in Doublet and Hose," *Blackwood's Magazine* (1896): 88. Subsequent reference is noted in the text.

76. For an account of Cushman's appeal, see Faye Dudden, *Women in the American Theater: Actresses and Audiences, 1790–1870* (New Haven, Conn.: Yale University Press, 1994), p. 97.

77. For a related reading, see Elizabeth Reitz Mullenix, "Acting between the Spheres: Charlotte Cushman as Androgyne," *Theater Survey* 37 (1996): 22–65.

78. Weeks, "Women in Doublet," p. 90.

79. R. J. Broadbent's *History of Pantomime* (London: Simpkin, Marshall, Hamilton, Kent, and Co., 1901) explained that Bernadin de St. Pierre observes "miming" as the "first language of man; it is known to all nations; and is so natural and expressive that the children of white parents learn it rapidly when they see it used by the negroes" (p. 15).

80. David Mayer, "The Sexuality of Pantomime," *Theater Quarterly* 4 (1974): 61. Subsequent reference is noted in the text.

81. Reade, "Androgynism," p. 212.

82. Kate exemplifies Jacques Lacan's reading of the phallus when she

says, "I suppose the girl supplied a certain want [desire and lack] to a child-less woman's heart. Perhaps I craved for something to cuddle and cherish, and pet and look down upon. You see, I am accustomed to look up to my husband" (Reade, "Androgynism," p. 211). Reade tells us that this last statement about her husband "may have been sarcasm" (p. 211). See Kaja Silverman, *Male Subjectivity at the Margins* (New York: Routledge, 1992).

83. Reade, "Androgynism," p. 21. Subsequent references are noted in the text.

84. Michel Foucault, *The History of Sexuality, Volume One*, trans. Robert Hurley (New York: Random House, 1978), p. 43.

85. Pacteau, "Impossible Referent," p. 64.

86. Reade, "Androgynism," p. 192. Subsequent reference is noted in the text.

87. Pacteau, "Impossible Referent," p. 62.

88. For more on the visual as an epistemological guarantor in West-ern culture, see Amy Robinson, "It Takes One to Know One: Passing and Communities of Common Interest," *Critical Inquiry* (summer 1994); and Peggy Phelan, *Unmarked: The Politics of Performance* (New York: Rout-ledge, 1993).

89. Reade, "Androgynism," p. 20. Subsequent references are noted in the text.

90. In fact, Reade's Kate provides a paradigmatic example of Havelock Ellis's idea of the "congenitally inverted lesbian" subject. It is important to remember here, and in the comparison made earlier between Reade's re-port and Wilde's trial, that Reade died in 1885 and could not have known either of Ellis's work or of Wilde's controversial fin de siècle imprisonment.

91. Reade, "Androgynism," p. 212. Subsequent reference is noted in the text.

92. A similar construction of the ultimate limit appears in Toni Morri-son's *Sula* (New York: Plume Books, 1973), pp. 145–46. The paragraph reads: "After all the old women have lain with the teen-agers; when all the young girls have slept with their old drunken uncles; after all the black men fuck all the white ones; when the guards have raped all the jailbirds and after all the whores make love to their grannies; after all the faggots get their mother's trim; when Lindbergh sleeps with Bessie Smith and Norma Shearer makes it with Stepin Fetchit; after . . . every weathervane on every barn flies off the roof to mount the hogs . . . then there'll be a little love left over for me." More apt, perhaps, is a minstrel song by Joseph Mackay called "I Am My Own Grandfather." The lyrics for the song are:

I am the most related man that walks the earth to-day,

.   .   .   .

I am my own grandfather, and I'll prove it now to you:
I won the winsome widow, while one winter we were wed,
She had a daughter whom my father to the altar led;
Just see what strange relationship we bear to one another,
My father is my son, and now my daughter is my mother.

Chorus—
And I have no hesitation when I make this declaration
Not a nation in creation can produce another man,
In this trying situation—introduce him if you can.

.   .   .   .

My wife is now my grandmama for she's my mother's mother,
When daddy did my daughter wed of course you'll all agree
That I became his father, 'tis as plain as A B C,
If I'm my father's father, 'tis a fact without a flaw,
I am my own grandfather then according to the law.

Joseph Mackay, "I Am My Own Grandfather," in *Moore and Burgess Minstrels Programme and Words of Songs* (London: Hill, Siffken and Company, 1896), p. 6.

93. Reade, "Androgynism," p. 212. Subsequent references are noted in the text.

94. Lewis Lapham quoted in Elaine Showalter, *Sexual Anarchy: Gender and Culture in the Fin de Siècle* (London: Penguin Books, 1990), p. 13.

95. Charles Reade, *Peg Woffington* (London: Ballantyne Press, 1852).

96. The threat such women would later pose to the basic structures of "white (hetero)patriarchy" is described by Lynda Hart as follows: "If desire always verifies masculinity, so does crime. And it is the wedding of these two discourses that produces the paradoxical object—the 'impossible' lesbian, who was always already a criminal." Not until 1921, when Lord Desart opposed an act of Parliament that instituted legal sanctions against lesbianism, would the (im)possibility of Kate's actions gather force. When they did so, "The paradox of this situation was that the virtual content necessitating a concealment was precluded. Thus, the lawmakers were prompted to perform the paradoxical act of prohibiting the impossible" (Hart, *Fatal Women: Lesbian Sexuality and the Mark of Aggression* [Princeton, N.J.: Princeton University Press, 1994], pp. 1–11).

97. Reade, *Peg Woffington*, p. 164; and Oscar Wilde, *A Woman of No Im-*

portance from *The Plays of Oscar Wilde,* (New York: Vintage, 1956). First published in 1893. See also Reade, "Androgynism."

98. Beatrice Webb quoted in Regina Gagnier, *Idylls of the Marketplace: Oscar Wilde and the Victorian Public* (Stanford, Calif.: Stanford University Press, 1986), p. 113.

99. Oscar Wilde, *Lady Windermere's Fan,* in *The Complete Works of Oscar Wilde* (New York: Harper and Row, 1966). First published c. 1892.

100. Reade, *Masks and Faces,* p. 116; and Wilde, *Lady Windermere's Fan,* act IV.

101. The stock character of "the woman with a past" satirized in Jerome K. Jerome's *Stageland* appeared with increasing frequency on the Victorian stage. Among the most popular were Lucy Graham of *Lady Audley's Secret,* Isabel Vane of *East Lynne,* and Paula Tanqueray from Pinero's *The Second Mrs. Tanqueray.*

102. Wilde, *Lady Windermere's Fan,* act IV. Subsequent reference is noted in text.

103. Reade, *Peg Woffington,* p. 212.

Chapter Four: Deforming Island Races

1. Harriet Ritvo, *The Animal Estate: The English and Other Creatures in the Victorian Age* (Cambridge, Mass.: Harvard University Press, 1987), pp. 236–37.

2. H. G. Wells, *The Island of Dr. Moreau* (New York: Lanser Books, 1968). First published in 1896.

3. John MacKenzie's reading of Victorian culture's shift from "domestic class conflict and towards racial and international conflict . . . [in which] the melodramatic villain became an externalised . . . barbarous 'fuzzy-wuzzy' or black, facing a cross-class brotherhood of heroism," informs this chapter. See John MacKenzie, ed., *Propaganda and Empire: The Manipulation of British Public Opinion* (Manchester: Manchester University Press, 1984), p. 45.

4. Wells quoted in Elaine Showalter, *Sexual Anarchy: Gender and Culture in the Fin de Siècle* (London: Penguin Books, 1990), p. 178.

5. Oscar Wilde, *The Picture of Dorian Gray,* in *The Portable Oscar Wilde,* ed. Richard Aldington and Stanley Weintraub (New York: Penguin Books, 1981), p. 352. First published in 1890.

6. See Arthur Lovejoy, *The Great Chain of Being: The Study of the History of an Idea* (Cambridge, Mass.: Harvard University Press, 1966).

7. See Gillian Beer, *Darwin's Plots: Evolutionary Narrative in Darwin, George Eliot, and Nineteenth-Century Fiction* (London: Routledge, 1983), p. 28.

8. Ritvo, *Animal Estate*, p. 13.

9. See Michel Foucault, *The Order of Things: An Archeology of the Human Sciences* (New York: Vintage Books, 1973).

10. William Prynne in Keith Thomas, *Man and the Natural World* (New York: Pantheon Books, 1983).

11. John Stuart Mill, *Essays on Ethics, Religion, and Society*, ed. J. M. Robson (Toronto: University of Toronto, 1969). First published in 1864.

12. Keith Thomas, *Man and the Natural World* (New York: Pantheon Books, 1983), p. 39.

13. Foucault, *The Order of Things*, p. 131.

14. Thomas Carlyle, *Past and Present*, ed. Richard Altick (New York: New York University Press, 1965), p. 139.

15. Quoted in Thomas, *Man and the Natural World*, p. 35.

16. Alfred Tennyson, *In Memoriam*, ed. Robert Ross (New York: W. W. Norton, 1973). All subsequent references are from this edition. First published in 1842.

17. Francis Galton quoted in Nancy Leys Stepan, *The Idea of Race in Science* (London: Macmillan Publishers, 1982), p. 111.

18. Such works include *Kim, Dr. Jekyll and Mr. Hyde, The Picture of Dorian Gray*, and *She*. For a full explication, see Joseph Bristow, *Empire Boys: Adventures in a Man's World* (London: Unwin Hyman, 1991).

19. Patrick Brantlinger quoted in Howard L. Malchow, *Gothic Images of Race in Nineteenth-Century Britain* (Palo Alto, Calif.: Stanford University Press, 1996).

20. This refers to the many texts that employ the metaphor of an ominous dark cloud over England, including Dickens's *Bleak House*, Booth's *In Darkest England* (the title originally from Blake), Conrad's *Heart of Darkness*, and others too numerous to name.

21. Patrick Brantlinger, *Rule of Darkness: British Literature and Imperialism, 1830–1914* (Ithaca, N.Y.: Cornell University Press, 1988), p. 39.

22. Ritvo, *Animal Estate*, p. 218.

23. Charles Darwin, *The Variation of Animals and Plants under Domestication* (London: J. Murray, 1868).

24. Charles Darwin, *The Origins of Species by Means of Natural Selection, of the Preservation of Favoured Races in the Struggle for Life* (London: Penguin, 1859).

25. Ritvo, *Animal Estate*, p. 101. Subsequent reference is noted in the text.

26. Thomas, *Man and the Natural World*, p. 30.

27. *Ibid.* p. 30.

28. Peter Stallybrass and Allon White argue similarly in a chapter on "exotic" creatures who performed civilized tasks at carnivals and fairs. See their chapter, "The Fair, the Pig, and Authorship," in *The Politics and Poetics of Transgression* (Ithaca, N.Y.: Cornell University Press, 1986).

29. Johann Casper Lavater, *Essays on Physiognomy*, quoted in Perry L. Curtis, *Apes and Angels: The Irishman in Victorian Caricature* (Washington, D.C.: Smithsonian Institution Press, 1971). It should be noted that the original meaning of the word "orang-outang" is "wild man," derived from Malay. See the definition in the *Oxford English Dictionary*.

30. Ritvo, *Animal Estate*, p. 3.

31. Joseph Merrick suffered from a congenital disease now known as neurofibromatoses. The appellation, "The Elephant Man," has encouraged a confusion of this disease with elephantiasis, a disorder transmitted by mosquitos (Michael Howell and Peter Ford, *The True History of the Elephant Man* [London: Penguin Books, 1980], p. 141). Subsequent reference is noted in the text. The protagonist of Stevenson's *The Strange Case of Dr. Jekyll and Mr. Hyde* shifts positions in the hierarchy, like the Elephant Man. Although most readings of this tale see Jekyll/Hyde as the "horrible double man," in fact, a close analysis of the text reveals that it is Jekyll himself who is divided and horrific, whereas Hyde (the low other is expected to be hybrid) remains alive at the end of the text because he is "whole." See Robert Louis Stevenson, *The Strange Case of Dr. Jekyll and Mr. Hyde*, ed. Jenny Calder (London: Penguin Press, 1979). First published in 1886. So too, in *The Island of Dr. Moreau*, Prendick says, "These men were in truth only bestial monsters, grotesque travesties of men, and filled me with a vague uncertainty of their possibilities that was far worse than any definite fear" (p. 11).

32. Homi Bhabha's formulation of the "not quite, not white" of postcolonial populations provides us with an example of this phenomenon. See "Of Mimicry and Man," *The Location of Culture* (London: Routledge, 1994).

33. James Crawfurd, quoted in *OED*.

34. Charles Kingsley quoted in Walter Houghton, *The Victorian Frame of Mind: 1830–1870* (New Haven, Conn.: Yale University Press, 1957), p. 212. Howard L. Malchow discusses the mulatto and revolts in *Gothic Images of Race in Nineteenth-Century Britain* (Palo Alto, Calif.: Stanford University Press, 1996).

35. Eugene August, ed., *Thomas Carlyle, the Nigger Question; John Stuart Mill, the Negro Question* (New York: Meredith Corporation, 1971).

36. Catherine Hall, "The Economy of Political Prestige: Thomas Carlyle, John Stuart Mill, and the Case of Governor Eyre," *Cultural Studies* (New York: Routledge, 1992). Also on this topic, see Bernard Semmel, *The Governor Eyre Controversy* (London: Macgibbon and Kee, 1962); and Arvel Erickson, "Empire or Anarchy: The Jamaica Rebellion of 1865," *Journal of Negro History* 44, no. 2 (April 1959): 99–122.

37. The question of "race" in Victorian England is taken up in the following texts: Michael Banton, *Racial Theories* (Cambridge, England: Cambridge University Press, 1987); Henry Louis Gates Jr., ed., *"Race," Writing, and Difference* (Chicago: University of Chicago Press, 1986); Brantlinger, *Rule of Darkness*; Ashley Montagu, ed., *The Concept of Race* (London: Collier-Macmillan, 1964); Stepan, *The Idea of Race*; George Stocking, *Victorian Anthropology* (New York: Free Press, 1987); and Elsie Michie, *Outside the Pale* (Ithaca, N.Y.: Cornell University Press, 1993).

38. Edward Freeman, *History of the Norman Conquest* (Oxford: Clarendon Press, 1870–79). This is a wonderful narrative of *English* (not Anglo-Saxon) history.

39. Jill Milling, "The Ambiguous Animal: Evolution of the Beast-Man in Scientific Creation Myths," in *The Fantastic in World Literature and the Arts: Selected Essays from the Fifth International Conference on the Fantastic in the Arts*, ed. Donald E. Morse (New York: Greenwood Press, 1987), p. 111. Milling's piece compares Moreau with three twentieth-century science fiction pieces, and does not focus on issues of Victorian sexuality or race.

40. Wells, *Dr. Moreau*, p. 138.

41. *The Island of Dr. Moreau*, as Judith Halberstam argues, exemplifies the idea of "gothic monstrosity . . . in which boundaries between good and evil, health and perversity, inside and outside dissolve and threaten the integrity of narrative itself" (Halberstam, *Skin Shows: Gothic Horror and the Technology of Monsters* [Durham, N.C.: Duke University Press, 1995], p. 2).

42. Michael Draper, *H. G. Wells* (New York: St. Martin's Press, 1982), p. 35.

43. Wells, *Dr. Moreau*, p. 7. Subsequent references are noted in the text.

44. Basil Williams, *Athenaeum* (May 1896), quoted in Patrick Parrinder, ed., *H. G. Wells: The Critical Heritage* (London: Routledge and Kegan Paul, 1972).

45. Augustan Filon, in *H. G. Wells: The Critical Heritage*, ed. Patrick Parrinder (London: Routledge, 1972), 314.

46. Wells, *Dr. Moreau*, p. 77.

47. Thomas Hardy was an avid collector of folklore and one of the first members of the society. For more information on folklore in Victorian England, see Stocking, *Victorian Anthropology*, pp. 53–56.

48. Wells, *Dr. Moreau*, p. 56. Subsequent references are noted in the text.

49. Christopher Howard, *Splendid Isolation: A Study of Ideas Concerning Britain's International Position and Foreign Policy during the Later Years of the Third Marquis of Salisbury* (London: Macmillan, 1967).

50. For a brief but excellent account of the English as an "island" people, see Gillian Beer, "The Island and the Aeroplane: The Case of Virginia Woolf," in *Nation and Narration*, ed. Homi K. Bhabha (New York: Routledge, 1990), pp. 269–72.

51. Wells, *Dr. Moreau*, p. 66.

52. Stevenson, *Dr. Jekyll and Mr. Hyde*, p. 82.

53. Wells, *Dr. Moreau*, p. 81. Subsequent reference is noted in the text.

54. Rudyard Kipling, *Kim* (New York: Bantam Books, 1983), p. 1. Subsequent reference is noted in the text.

55. Bristow, *Empire Boys*, p. 198.

56. This can be translated as, "I am black, but beautiful."

57. Kipling, *Kim*, p. 166. Subsequent references are noted in the text.

58. Colonel Henry Yule and A. C. Burnell, *Hobson-Jobson: A Glossary of Colloquial Anglo-Indian Words and Phrases, and of Kindred Terms, Etymological, Historical, Geographical, and Discursive* (London: John Murray, 1903), p. xv. First edition published in 1886.

59. Asfar Husain, *The Indianness of Rudyard Kipling: A Study in Stylistics* (London: Cosmis Press, 1983), p. 84. Subsequent reference is noted in the text.

60. Holbrook Jackson, *The 1890s* (London: Cresset Library, 1988), p. 282. First published in 1913. Subsequent reference is noted in the text.

61. Trollope.

62. Draper, *H. G. Wells*, p. 44.

63. Kipling, *Kim*, p. 80.

64. Wells, *Dr. Moreau*, p. 19. Subsequent references are noted in the text.

65. Elaine Scarry, *The Body in Pain: The Making and Unmaking of the World* (Oxford: Oxford University Press, 1985), pp. 394–95.

66. Olive Schreiner quoted in Elaine Showalter, *Sexual Anarchy: Gender and Culture in the Fin de Siècle* (London: Penguin Books, 1990), p. 175.

67. Robert Young makes a similar point when he comments that "hybridity . . . implies a disruption and forcing together of any unlike living things, grafting a . . . rose on to a different root stock, making difference into sameness. Hybridity is making one of two distinct things, so that it be-

comes impossible for the eye to detect the hybridity of a geranium or a rose. Nevertheless the rose exists like the vine, only in so far as it is grafted onto the different stock. Neglect to prune either and the plant eventually reverts to its original state. In the nineteenth century . . . a common analogous argument was made that the descendants of mixed-race unions would eventually relapse to one of the original races, thus characterizing miscegenation as temporary in its effects as well as unnatural in its very nature" (Young, *Colonial Desire: Hybridity in Theory, Culture, and Race* [London: Routledge, 1995], p. 26).

68. G. M. Young, *Portrait of an Age* (Oxford: Oxford University Press, 1983), p. 145.

69. Wells, *Dr. Moreau*, p. 101. Subsequent references are noted in the text.

70. Stepan, *The Idea of Race*, p. 58.

71. The last chapter of Samuel Smiles's tract, *Self-Help* (London: J. Murray, 1859), is entitled, "Character: The True Gentleman," which foregrounds the ability of humans to constitute themselves performatively.

72. Wells, *Dr. Moreau*, p. 103.

73. For a detailed discussion of these essays, see August, *Thomas Carlyle.* Subsequent reference is noted in the text.

74. George Watson, *The English Ideology: Studies in the Language of Victorian Politics* (London: Allen Lane, 1973), p. 200.

75. Edward Dicey, *Egypt and England* (London: Darf, 1986), p. 208. First published 1881.

76. Wells, *Dr. Moreau*, p. 92. Subsequent references are noted in the text.

77. Although in a footnote Elaine Showalter claims that the two film versions of Wells's tale deal with imperial readings of Moreau, I was struck by the absence of any ape or dealings with race in the 1977 version—even though the makeup was done by the same artist who did the *Planet of the Apes* television series, the creatures hardly seem to be racial stereotypes. One interesting moment in the film occurs when "Prendick" (his name is changed to Braddock) miraculously, after being literally animalized and then reverted back to type, begins his human tale with the classic slave narrative opening, "I was born . . . home is England." Fatimah Rony discusses the 1933 film version, *The Island of Lost Souls*, in *The Third Eye: Race, Cinema, and the Ethnographic Spectacle* (Durham, N.C.: Duke University Press, 1996). John Frankenheimer's film version (1996) of the book alludes to incest and miscegenation in several scenes. The Black Panther woman, Aissa, who dies at her "mulatto" brother's hand is played sympathetically in the tradition of the tragic mulattaroon. The choice of Marlon

Brando to play the part of Dr. Moreau in exaggerated whiteface makeup also fits nicely with the reading of the novel presented here.

78. Peter Bowler, *The Mendelian Revolution: The Emergence of Hereditarian Concepts in Modern Science and Society* (Baltimore, Md.: Johns Hopkins University Press, 1989), p. 153.

79. Martin Woodroffe, "Racial Theories of History and Politics: The Example of H. S. Chamberlain," in *Nationalist and Racialist Movements in Britain and Germany before 1914*, eds. Paul Kennedy and Anthony Nicolls (London: Macmillan Publishers, 1981), p. 146–47.

80. Samuel Coleridge-Taylor quoted in Jane Beckett and Deborah Cherry, eds., *The Edwardian Era* (London: Phaidon Press and Barbican Art Gallery, 1987), p. 49.

81. Karl Marx in an 1862 letter to Friedrich Engels quoted in Watson, *The English Ideology*, p. 211. Engels agreed with Marx's description of their rival, Lassalle, that the latter's "thirst to push his way into polite society, *de parvenir*, to smear over the dirty Breslau Jew, for appearance's sake, with grease and paint, was always revolting" (ibid.). Engels's comments here reconstitute the discussion about the parvenue players and actresses who were allied with "painted ladies."

82. H. G. Wells, *Anticipations of the Reaction of Mechanical and Scientific Progress Upon Human Life and Thought* (London: Chapman and Hill, 1901) p. 317.

83. Benjamin Disraeli, *Coningsby, or the New Generation* (London: Penguin Books, 1983), p. 12.

84. Wells, *Anticipations*, p. 317.

85. Lucy Bland, "Sex and Morality: Sinning on a Tigerskin or Keeping the Beast at Bay," in *The Edwardian Era*, ed. Jane Beckett and Deborah Cherry (London: Phaidon Press and Barbican Art Gallery, 1987), p. 89.

86. See Elaine Showalter, Eve Sedgwick, David Halperin, and Christopher Lane for readings of the homosexual subtext of these book.

87. Wells, *Dr. Moreau*, p. 114.

88. Unsigned review, *Speaker* (18 April 1896), quoted in *H. G. Wells: The Critical Heritage*, H. G. Wells (London: Routledge and Kegan Paul, 1972).

89. See Martha Vicinus, *Independent Women* (Chicago: University of Chicago Press, 1985).

90. George Gissing, *The Odd Women* (New York: Macmillan Publishing Co., 1893), p. 291.

91. See Patricia Stubbs, *Women and Fiction: Feminism and the Novel, 1880–1920* (London: Methuen Books, 1979).

92. Eliza Lynn Linton, "A Social Sign of the Time," *Ladies Home Journal* (May 1896): 16.

93. Cora Kaplan, "The Thorn Birds: Fiction, Fantasy, Femininity," in *Formation of Fantasy,* ed. Victor Burgin, James Donald, and Cora Kaplan (London: Methuen Books, 1986), p. 163.

94. Diane Sadoff, *Monsters of Affection,* quoted in Gillian Beer, "Origins and Oblivion in Victorian Narrative," in *Sex, Politics, and Science in the Nineteenth Century Novel,* ed. Ruth Yeazell (Baltimore, Md.: Johns Hopkins University Press, 1986), p. 35.

95. Wells, *Dr. Moreau,* p. 176. Subsequent reference is noted in the text.

96. In *Woman and the Demon: The Life of Victorian Myth* (Cambridge, Mass.: Harvard University Press, 1982), Nina Auerbach suggestively argues that the numerous angels who populated Victorian representations were actually divine/demonic mermaids whose power had to be bound and suppressed.

97. Wells, *Dr. Moreau,* p. 100. Subsequent references are noted in the text.

98. Sheridan Le Fanu, *Carmilla* (London: 1871). Subsequent references are noted in the text.

99. For more on this idea, see Joseph Roach, *Cities of the Dead: Circum-Atlantic Performance* (New York: Columbia University Press, 1996), p. 4.

100. Wells, *Dr. Moreau,* p. 118.

101. Nancy Leys Stepan, "Race and Gender: The Role of Analogy in Science," *Isis* 77 (1986): 275.

102. Wells, *Dr. Moreau,* p. 54. Subsequent references are noted in the text.

103. Michel Foucault, *The Order of Things* (New York: Vintage Books, 1973), p. xvi.

Epilogue

1. Bram Stoker, *The Lair of the White Worm* in *Bram Stoker's Dracula Omnibus,* ed. Fay Weldon (London: Orion Books, 1992), p. 331. First published in 1911.

2. For excellent discussions of "race" in *Dracula* see Howard L. Malchow, *Gothic Images of Race in Nineteenth-Century Britain* (Palo Alto, Calif.: Stanford University Press, 1996); and Judith Halberstam, *Skin Shows: Gothic Horror and the Technology of Monsters* (Durham, N.C.: Duke University Press, 1995).

3. Stoker, *White Worm,* p. 315. Subsequent reference is noted in the text.

4. For a brilliant reading of the homosocial/homosexual associations of

the aunt and/or uncle, see Eve Sedgwick, "Tales of the Avunculate: Queer Tutelage in *The Importance of Being Earnest*," in *Professions of Desire: Lesbian and Gay Studies in Literature*, ed. George Haggerty and Bonnie Zimmerman (New York: Modern Language Association of America, 1995), pp. 191–209.

5. See Hortense J. Spillers, "Mama's Baby, Papa's Maybe: An American Grammar Book," *diacritics* 17, no. 2 (summer 1987): 65–80, for a discussion of the complications of paternity and maternity under slavery.

6. Stoker, *White Worm*, p. 313. Subsequent references are noted in the text.

7. Stoker was an avid collector of English history and folklore. So too, he knew Greek myth and was well-versed in Christianity. The many allusions implicit in the text merit fuller discussion than provided here.

8. For an interesting comparison with the "white heart" of England, see Thomas Hardy, *Tess of the D'Urbervilles: A Pure Woman* (New York: New American Library, 1963; first published in 1891). The "Vale of Blackmoor [where Tess grows up] was once known as the Forest of the White Hart, according to a legend about a subject of King Henry III who killed a white hart." As the narrator notes, "many old customs linger in a metamorphasized or disguised form" (p. 23).

9. See, for example, the opening illustrations for chapters 44 and 63 in *Vanity Fair*.

10. Stoker, *White Worm*, p. 324. Subsequent references are noted in the text.

11. "Victorian Staffordshire figurines were manufactured in huge quantities throughout Queen Victoria's reign." Harriet Bridgeman and Elizabeth Drury, eds., *The Encyclopedia of Victoriana: A Sotheby's Publication* (New York: Macmillan, 1975), p. 111.

12. Stoker, *White Worm*, p. 318. Subsequent references are noted in the text.

13. Howard L. Malchow mentions an actual Edwardian marriage between a African black man, Peter Loben, and a white English woman, Kitty Jewell. This marks a shift in the representation of miscegenation.

In the twentieth century, relationships between black men and white women increase statistically and otherwise (e.g., in Britain, black male/white female marriages outnumber black female/white male marriages by two to one). See the anonymous article, "Integrated but Unequal," *Economist* (8 February 1997): 58–60.

14. Stoker, *White Worm*, p. 327. Subsequent references are noted in the text.

15. That mercia is almost an anagram of "america," which was founded by Columbus and represented by the figure Columbia, may be yet another way in which the text references America.

16. Stoker, *White Worm*, p. 350.

17. In nineteenth-century stage productions of *Uncle Tom's Cabin*, white doves were released to mark the death of the pure, white Little Eva.

18. Frantz Fanon, *Black Skin, White Masks* (New York: Grove Wedenfeld Books, 1967).

19. See Mary Ann Doane, *Femmes Fatales: Feminism, Film Theory, and Psychoanalysis* (New York: Routledge, 1991), especially her chapter entitled "The Dark Continents: Epistemologies of Racial and Sexual Difference in Psychoanalysis and Cinema."

20. The black hole is surely suggestive of a vagina dentata. See Barbara Creed, *The Monstrous-Feminine: Film, Feminism, Psychoanalysis* (New York: Routledge, 1993), especially chapter 8, "Medusa's Head: The *Vagina Dentata* and Freudian Theory."

21. Thackeray mentions the Black Hole of Calcutta in chapter 60 of *Vanity Fair*.

22. Stoker, *White Worm*, p. 398. Subsequent reference is noted in the text.

23. Toni Morrison uses the phrase "eruptions of funk" in an interview. See Susan Willis, "Eruptions of Funk: Historicizing Toni Morrison in *Black Literature and Literary Theory*, ed. Henry Louis Gates Jr. (New York: Methuen, 1984).

24. Stoker, *White Worm*, pp. 425–26. Subsequent reference is noted in the text.

25. In the mid-1980s, just after the Wandsworth riots, British director Ken Russell made a film version of *The Lair of the White Worm*. The overt references to blackness employed in the novel as signifiers of deviance and monstrosity are erased in the film, which is updated to take place in the late twentieth century. The translation to the screen omits the character Oolonga along with all references to racial miscegenation. Oolonga's Africanized body, overtly absent from the film, has been transmuted and reduced so that its only remnant may be the dildo-like appendage worn at the end of the film by the character playing Lady Arabella. This pornographic image recalls Fanon's phrase, "The negro *is* a penis." The trope of blackness provides supplemental material additions to Lady Arabella's monstrous whiteness.

The selection of specifically English actors—Catherine Oxenberg, Amanda Donahoe, and Hugh Grant—to star in the film replicates the attempt to repress the foundational blackness of whiteness. The blond, green-eyed Oxenberg, an actual aristocrat, plays the part of the mulatta-roon Mimi; Donahoe plays Lady Arabella as a blackened, phallic woman (she has played a number of "sexually deviant" women, including the part of the lesbian lawyer on the popular television series *L.A. Law*); and in a tryst of fate, Grant, who plays Adam, blackened himself offscreen when he was arrested for soliciting the services of an African American prostitute whose working pseudonym was Divine Brown.

Two interesting readings of the import of Grant's mésalliance are framed as follows:

"As the question of why Hugh Grant did it, there can be one answer: He's English. Without a doubt, the English came up with their wonderful language, high tea and chintz couches to disguise what dirty little minds they all have. In fact, their greatest triumph is the widespread notion that it is the French who are oversexed." (Richard Cohen, "Don't Laugh at Hugh," *Washington Post*, 4 July 1995).

In an editorial comparing the interracial sexual scandals of O. J. Simpson, Susan Smith, and Grant, Judy Mann asked: "Grant picked up a black hooker and woke up the next day to find his mug shot next to hers everywhere. Would the play have been the same if she had been white?" See Mann's "Summer Seething," *Washington Post*, 21 July 1995, sec. E 3.

BIBLIOGRAPHY

Manuscript Collections Consulted

Billy Rose Theater Collection. New York Public Library for the Performing Arts.

London Library. St. James Square. London.

Lord Chamberlain's Collection. British Library. London.

Parrish Collection. Firestone Library. Princeton University.

Stowe-Day Library. Hartford, Connecticut.

Theatre Museum. Covent Garden. London.

Primary Sources

Acton, William. *Prostitution Considered in Its Moral, Social, and Sanitary Aspects in London.* London: Cass, 1972. First published in 1857.

Aiken, George L. *Uncle Tom's Cabin: or, Life Among the Lowly. A Domestic Drama, in Six Acts.* New York: Samuel French, n.d.

Allen, Grant. "Plain Words on the Woman Question." *Fortnightly Review* 46 (1889): 448–58.

Austen, Jane. *Sandition.* Oxford: Clarendon Press, 1925. Unfinished manuscript, 1817.

Baudelaire, Charles. *Charles Baudelaire: The Flowers of Evil.* Trans. James McGowan. New York: Oxford University Press, 1993.

Blake, William. *The Poetry and Prose of William Blake.* Ed. David Erdman. New York: Doubleday Press, 1970.

Blessington, Countess. *Heath's Book of Beauty.* London: Longman and Co., 1836.

Booth, William. *In Darkest England, and the Way Out.* London: International Headquarters of the Salvation Army, 1890.

Boucicault, Dion. *Plays by Dion Boucicault.* Ed. Peter Thompson. Cambridge, England: Cambridge University Press, 1984.

Broadbent, R. J. *A History of Pantomime.* London: Simpkin, Marshall, Hamilton, Kent, and Co., 1901.

Broca, Paul. *On the Phenomena of Hybridity in the Genus Homo.* Ed. C. Carter Blake. London: Longman, Green, and Longman, and Roberts, 1864.

Brontë, Charlotte. *Jane Eyre*. New York: Hyperion, 1996. First published in 1847.

Brontë, Emily. *Wuthering Heights*. Ed. Jack Ian. Oxford: Oxford University Press, 1995. First published in 1847.

Brough, William. *Those Dear Blacks*.

———. *Uncle Tom's Cabin; or, Nigger Life in London*.

Brown, William Wells. *Clotel, or the President's Daughter: A Narrative of Slave Life in the United States*. New York: Carol Publishing Group, 1989. First published in 1853.

Bunn, Alfred. *The Stage: Both before and behind the Curtain*. London: R. Bentley, 1840.

Burke, Edmund. *A Philosophical Enquiry into the Origin of Our Ideas of the Sublime and the Beautiful*. London: R. and J. Dodsley, 1764.

Carlyle, Thomas. *Past and Present*. Ed. Richard Altick. New York: New York University Press, 1965.

Carroll, Lewis. *The Annotated Alice: "Alice's Adventures in Wonderland" and "Through the Looking Glass."* Ed. Martin Gardner. New York: C. N. Potter, 1960.

Cauldwell, Charles. *Thoughts on the Original Unity of the Human Race*. New York: E. Bliss, 1830.

Coleman, John. *Charles Reade as I Knew Him*. New York: Dutton and Co., 1903.

Craft, William. *Running a Thousand Miles for Freedom; or, The Escape of William and Ellen Craft from Slavery*. Miami: Mnemosyne, 1969. First published 1860.

Cullwick, Hannah. *The Diaries of Hannah Cullwick, Victorian Maidservant*. Ed. Liz Stanley. New Brunswick, N.J.: Rutgers University Press, 1984.

Darwin, Charles. *The Descent of Man, and Selection in Relation to Sex*. London: J. Murray, 1871.

———. *The Origins of Species by Means of Natural Selection of the Preservation of Favoured Races in the Struggle for Life*. London: Penguin Books, 1859.

———. *The Variation of Animals and Plants under Domestication*. London: J. Murray, 1868.

Defoe, Daniel. *A True-Born Englishman: A Satyr*. In *Poems and Affairs of State*, ed. Frank Ellis, vol. 6. New Haven, Conn.: Yale University Press, 1970. First published in 1708.

Dicey, Edward. *England and Egypt*. London: Darf, 1986. First published in 1881.

Dickens, Charles. *Bleak House*. Boston: Houghton Mifflin Co., 1956.

———. *Our Mutual Friend*. Harmondsworth: Penguin Books, 1978.

Dickinson, Emily. *The Complete Poems of Emily Dickinson*. Ed. Thomas Johnson. Boston: Little, Brown, and Co., 1960.

Disraeli, Benjamin. *Coningsby, or the New Generation*. London: Penguin Books, 1983.

Douglass, Frederick. *The Narrative of the Life of Frederick Douglass: An American Slave*. In *The Classic Slave Narratives*, ed. Henry Louis Gates Jr. New York: Mentor Books, 1987. First published in 1845.

Downes, Reverend P. *Woman: Her Charm and Her Power*. London: Charles Kelly, 1901.

DuBois, W. E. B. *Souls of Black Folk*. Chicago: A. C. McClurg and Co. 1903.

Dumas, Alexandre père. *The Black Tulip*. Trans. Marcel Girard. London: J. M. Dent, 1960. First published in 1850.

Dumas, Alexandre fils. *Camille*. In *Camille and Other Plays*, ed. Stephen Stanton. New York: Hill and Wang, 1957.

———. *La Dame aux Camellias*. Trans. David Coward. Oxford: Oxford University Press, 1986. First published in 1852.

———. *La Dame aux Camellias*. Trans. William Walton. Barrie and Sons, 1897. First published in 1852.

Eliot, George. *Daniel Deronda*. Harmondsworth: Penguin Books, 1967.

Freeman, Edward. *History of the Norman Conquest*. Oxford: Clarendon Press, 1870–79.

Galton, Frances. "Hereditary Improvement." *Fraser's Magazine* (1873): 116–30.

Gaskell, Elizabeth. *Ruth*. Ed. Alan Shelston. Oxford: Oxford University Press, 1985. First published in 1853.

Gissing, George. *The Odd Women*. New York: Macmillan Publishing Co., 1893.

Grand, Sarah. *The Beth Book*. London: Virago Press, 1980. First published in 1897.

Griffin, D. W. *Camille, an Ethiopian Interlude*. New York: Happy Hours Co., ca. 1880.

Haggard, Rider. *She*. New York: Dover Publications, 1953.

Hardy, Thomas. *Tess of the D'Urbervilles: A Pure Woman*. New York: New American Library, 1963. First published in 1891.

Harper, Frances Ellen Watkins. *Iola Leroy, or Shadows Uplifted*. Philadelphia: Garrigue Brothers, 1892. Reprinted with an introduction by Hazel Carby. Boston: Beacon, 1987.

H. G. Wells: The Critical Heritage. London: Routledge and Kegan Paul, 1972.

Hood, Thomas. *The Poetical Works of Thomas Hood.* 3 vols. Boston: Crosby and Nichols, 1864.

Hughes, Langston. *Mulatto,* in *Five Plays,* ed. Webster Smalley. Bloomington: Indiana University Press, 1963.

Hughes, Mary Vivian. *A London Child of the 1870's.* Oxford: Oxford University Press, 1934.

Johnson, James Weldon. *The Autobiography of an Ex-Colored Man.* Ed. William L. Andrews. New York: Penguin Books, 1990. First published in 1912.

Kipling, Rudyard. *Kim.* New York: Bantam Books, 1983.

Le Fanu, Sheridan. *Carmilla.* London: 1872.

Lewes, George Henry. *On Actors and the Art of Acting.* London: 1878.

Linton, Eliza Lynn. "A Social Sign of the Time." *Ladies Home Journal* (May 1896).

———. "The Wild Women as Social Insurgent." *Nineteenth Century* 30 (October 1891): 596–605.

Mann, Thomas. *Death in Venice.* Trans. David Luke. New York: Bantam Books, 1988. First published in 1911.

Mill, John Stuart. *Essays on Ethics, Religion, and Society.* Ed. J. M. Robson. Toronto: University of Toronto, 1969. First published in 1864.

Moore and Burgess Minstrels Programme and Words of Songs. London: Hill, Siffken and Company, 1896.

Moore, G. W. *The St. James's Hall Veritable and Legitimate Christy's Minstrels Christmas Annual.* London: *J. E. Allard,* 1868.

Norton, Caroline. *English Laws for Women.* London: 1854.

Nott, Josiah. *An essay on the natural history of mankind, viewed in connection with Negro slavery.* Mobile, Ala.: Dade, Thompson, 1851.

Oliphant, Margaret. "The Anti-Marriage League." *Blackwood's Magazine* (January 1896).

Parent-Duchâtelet, *De la prostitution de la ville de Paris.* 2 vols. Paris: J-B Balliere, 1836.

Pike, Luke Owen. *The English and Their Origin: A Prologue to Authentic English History.* London: Longmans, Green, and Co., 1866.

Pouchet, Georges. *The Plurality of the Human Race.* London: Longman, Green, Longman, and Roberts, 1864.

Prince, Mary. *The History of Mary Prince, a West Indian Slave.* Ed. Moira Ferguson. London: Pandora Books, 1987. First published in 1831.

Reade, Charles. "Androgynism, or Woman Playing at Man." *English Review* (1911): 10–29, 191–212.

———. *The Cloister and the Hearth.* London: Trubner, 1861.

———. *The Coming Man.* New York: Harper Brothers, 1878.

———. *It's Never Too Late to Mend.* London: Chatto and Windus, 1894.

———. *Peg Woffington.* London: Bradbury, Evans, and Co., 1868.

———. *Plays by Charles Reade.* Ed. Michael Hammet. Cambridge, England: Cambridge University Press, 1986.

———. Undated notebook, circa 1860. Parrish Collection, Firestone Library, Princeton University.

———. *The Wandering Heir.* Boston: James Osgood and Co., 1873.

———, and Tom Taylor. *Masks and Faces: or, Before and Behind the Curtain.* Parrish Collection, Firestone Library, Princeton University.

Scott, Sir Walter. *The Heart of Midlothian.* Edinburgh: A and C Black, 1887. First published in 1819.

Seacole, Mary. *Wonderful Adventures of Mrs. Seacole in Many Lands.* Eds. Ziggy Alexander and Audrey Dewjee. Bristol: Falling Wall Press, 1984. First published in 1857.

Shakespeare, William. *Othello the Moor of Venice.* Ed. Gerald Eades Bentley. Harmondsworth: 1970. First published in 1681.

———. *The Sonnets of William Shakespeare.* New York: Heritage Press, c. 1941.

Shaw, George Bernard. *Pygmalion.* Baltimore: Penguin Books, 1951.

Shelley, Mary. *Frankenstein.* London: Lockington, Hughes, Harding, Mavor, and Jones, 1818.

Smiles, Samuel. *Self-Help.* London: J. Murray, 1859.

Stevenson, Robert Louis. *The Strange Case of Dr. Jekyll and Mr. Hyde.* Ed. Jenny Calder. London: Penguin Press, 1979. First published in 1886.

Stoker, Bram. *Dracula.* Oxford: Oxford University Press, 1983.

———. *The Lair of the White Worm.* In *Bram Stoker's Dracula Omnibus,* ed. Fay Weldon. London: Orion Books, 1992. First published in 1911.

Stowe, Harriet Beecher. *The Key to Uncle Tom's Cabin.* Salem, New Hampshire: Arno Press, 1968. First published in 1854.

———. *Uncle Tom's Cabin, or, Life among the Lowly.* New York: Penguin Classics, 1986. First published in 1852.

Stratmann, Franz Heinrich. *A Middle-English Dictionary,* London: Oxford University Press, 1891.

Taine, Hippolyte. *The History of English Literature.* London, 1871. In *Criti-*

cal Theory since Plato, ed. Hazard Adams. New York: Harcourt Brace Jovanovich, 1971.

Talbot, Eugene. *Degeneracy: Its Causes, Signs, and Results.* London: Walter Cott, 1898.

Tennyson, Alfred. *In Memoriam.* Ed. Robert Ross. New York: W. W. Norton and Co., 1973. First published in 1842.

Thackeray, William Makepeace. *Vanity Fair.* Ed. and intro. John Sutherland. Oxford: Oxford University Press, 1983.

Thompson, Alexander. "Immortal Sewerage." In *Meloria.* 1883.

Tutchin, John. "The Foreigners." In *Poems and Affairs of State,* vol. 6, ed. Frank Ellis. New Haven, Conn.: Yale University Press, 1970.

Tylor, Edward. *Anthropology.* London: Macmillan Publishers, 1892.

Uncle Tom in England; Or, A Proof That Black's White. London: William Tyler, 1852.

Uzanne, Octave. "Notes on the Portraits of Alexandre Dumas the Elder." In *The Black Tulip,* trans. Richard Garnett. New York: Collier and Son, 1902.

Walsh, Townsend. *The Career of Dion Boucicault.* New York: Dunlop Books, 1915.

Weeks, Lyman. "Woman in Doublet and Hose." *Blackwood's Magazine* (1896): 88–102.

Wells, H. G. *Anticipations of the Reaction of Mechanical and Scientific Progress upon Human Life and Thought.* London: Chapman and Hill, 1901.

———. *The Island of Dr. Moreau.* New York: Lanser Books, 1968. First published in 1896.

Wells, Ida B. *Crusade for Justice: The Autobiography of Ida B. Wells.* Ed. Alfreda M. Duster. Chicago: University of Chicago Press, 1970.

Wilde, Oscar. *The Complete Works of Oscar Wilde.* New York: Harper and Row, 1966.

———. *The Picture of Dorian Gray.* In *The Portable Oscar Wilde,* eds. Richard Aldington and Stanley Weintraub. New York: Penguin Books, 1981. First published in 1890.

———. *The Plays of Oscar Wilde.* Intro. John Lahr. New York: Vintage Books, 1988.

The Woman of Colour: A Tale in Two Volumes. London: Black, Parry, and Kingsbury, 1808.

Yule, Colonel Henry, and A. C. Burnell. *Hobson-Jobson: A Glossary of Colloquial Anglo-Indian Words and Phrases, and of Kindred Terms, Etymological, Historical, Geographical, and Discursive.* London: J. Murray, 1903. First edition published in 1886.

Secondary Sources

Alexander, Adele. *Ambiguous Lives: Free Women of Color in Rural Georgia, 1789–1879.* Fayetteville: University of Arkansas Press, 1991.

Alexander, Ziggy. "Let It Lie upon the Table: The Status of Black Women's Biography in the UK." *Gender and History* 2, no. 1 1990 (spring): 22–33.

Altick, Richard. *The Shows of London.* Cambridge, Mass.: Belknap Press of Harvard University Press, 1978.

Anderson, Benedict. *Imagined Communities: Reflections on the Origin and Spread of Nationalism.* Baltimore, Md.: Johns Hopkins University Press, 1978.

Arac, Jonathan. *Commissioned Spirits: The Shaping of Social Motion in Dickens, Carlyle, Melville, and Hawthorne.* New York: Columbia University Press, 1979.

Armstrong, Nancy. "Why Daughters Die: The Racial Logic of American Sentimentalism." *Yale Journal of Criticism* 7, no. 2 (1994): 1–24.

Auerbach, Nina. *Ellen Terry: Player in Her Time.* New York: W. W. Norton, 1987.

———. *Private Theatricals: The Lives of the Victorians.* Cambridge, Mass.: Harvard University Press, 1990.

———. *Woman and the Demon: The Life of Victorian Myth.* Cambridge, Mass.: Harvard University Press, 1982.

August, Eugene, ed. *Thomas Carlyle, The Nigger Question; John Stuart Mill, The Negro Question.* New York: Meredith Corporation, 1971.

Baldwin, James. *The Evidence of Things Not Seen.* New York: Henry Holt and Company, 1985.

———. *Notes of a Native Son.* Boston: Beacon Press, 1984.

Banner, Lois. *American Beauty.* Chicago: University of Chicago Press, 1983.

Banton, Michael. *Racial Theories.* Cambridge: Cambridge University Press, 1987.

Barish, Jonas. *The Anti-Theatrical Prejudice.* Berkeley: University of California Press, 1981.

Barrett, Lindon. "In the Dark: Issues of Value, Evaluation, and Authority in Twentieth Century Critical Discourse." Ph.D. diss., University of Pennsylvania, 1991.

Barthelemy, Anthony Gerard. *Black Face, Maligned Race: The Representation of Blacks in English Drama from Shakespeare to Southerne.* Baton Rouge: Louisiana State University Press, 1987.

Barthes, Roland. *Mythologies*. Ed. and trans. Annette Lavers. New York: Hill and Wang Publishers, 1987.

Basch, Francoise. *Relative Creatures: Victorian Women in Society and the Novel*. New York: Schocken Books, 1974.

Baudrillard, Jean. *Simulations*. Trans. Paul Foss, Paul Patton, and Phillip Beitchman. New York: Semiotext(e), 1983.

Beckett, Jane, and Deborah Cherry, eds. *The Edwardian Era*. London: Phaidon Press and Barbican Art Gallery, 1987.

Beer, Gillian. *Darwin's Plots: Evolutionary Narrative in Darwin, George Eliot, and Nineteenth-Century Fiction*. London: Routledge, 1983.

———. "Origins and Oblivion in Victorian Narrative." In *Sex, Politics, and Science in the Nineteenth Century Novel*, ed. Ruth Yeazell. Baltimore, Md.: Johns Hopkins University Press, 1986.

Benjamin, Walter. "The Work of Art in the Age of Mechanical Reproduction." *Illuminations: Essays and Reflections*. New York: Schocken Books, 1968.

Bernheimer, Charles. *Figures of Ill Repute: Representing Prostitution in Nineteenth Century France*. Cambridge, Mass.: Harvard University Press, 1989.

Betterton, Rosemary. *Looking On: Images of Femininity in the Visual Arts and the Media*. London: Pandora Books, 1987.

Bhabha, Homi. "Interrogating Identities." In *The Anatomy of Racism*, ed. David Theo Goldberg. Minneapolis: University of Minnesota Press, 1990.

———. "Location, Intervention, Incommensurability: A Conversation with Homi Bhabha." *Emergencies* 1 (Fall 1989): 64–88.

———. *The Location of Culture*. London: Routledge, 1994.

———, ed. *Nation and Narration*. New York: Routledge, 1990.

Birdoff, Harry. *The World's Greatest Hit: Uncle Tom's Cabin*. New York: S. F. Vanni, 1947.

Bivona, Daniel. *Desire and Contradiction: Imperial Visions and Domestic Debates in Victorian Literature*. Manchester: Manchester University Press, 1990.

Bland, Lucy. "Sex and Morality: Sinning on a Tigerskin or Keeping the Beast at Bay." In *The Edwardian Era*, ed. Jane Beckett and Deborah Cherry. London: Phaidon Press and Barbican Art Gallery, 1987.

Bloom, Harold, ed. *Modern Critical Interpretations: Thackeray's "Vanity Fair."* New York: Chelsea House Publishers, 1987.

Booth, Michael R. *Prefaces to Nineteenth Century Theatre*. Manchester: Manchester University Press, 1979.

———. *Theatre in the Victorian Age*. Cambridge: Cambridge University Press, 1991.

Bowler, Peter. *The Mendelian Revolution: The Emergence of Hereditarian Concepts in Modern Science and Society*. Baltimore: Johns Hopkins University Press, 1989.

Boyle, Thomas. *Black Swine in the Sewers of Hampstead*. New York: Viking Press, 1989.

Brantlinger, Patrick. *Rule of Darkness: British Literature and Imperialism, 1830–1914*. Ithaca, N.Y.: Cornell University Press, 1988.

Bratton, Jacky S. *Acts of Supremacy: The British Empire and the Stage, 1790–1930*. Manchester: University of Manchester Press, 1991.

———. "English Ethiopians: British Audiences and Black-Face Acts, 1835–1865." *The Yearbook of English Studies* 11 (1981): 127–142.

Bridgeman, Harriet, and Elizabeth Drury, eds. *The Encyclopedia of Victoriana: A Sotheby's Publication*. New York: Macmillan, 1975.

Bristow, Joseph. *Empire Boys: Adventures in a Man's World*. London: Unwin Hyman, 1991.

Brown, Sterling. "Negro Character as Seen by White Authors." *Journal of Negro Education* 2 (January 1933).

Burns, Wayne. *Charles Reade: A Study in Victorian Authorship*. New York: Bookman Associates, 1961.

———. "More Reade Notebooks." *Studies in Philology* 42 (1945): 824–42.

———, and Emerson Grant Sutcliffe. "Uncle Tom and Charles Read." *American Literature* 17, no. 4 (January 1946): 334–47.

Butler, Judith. *Bodies That Matter: On the Discursive Limits of "Sex."* New York: Routledge, 1993.

———. *Gender Trouble: Feminism and the Subversion of Identity*. New York: Routledge, 1990.

Callaway, Helen. *Gender, Culture and Empire: European Women in Colonial Nigeria*. Urbana: University of Illinois Press, 1987.

Carby, Hazel. *Reconstructing Womanhood*. Oxford: Oxford University Press, 1987.

Carlson, Susan. *Women and Comedy: Rewriting the British Theatrical Tradition*. Ann Arbor: University of Michigan Press, 1991.

Case, Sue-Ellen, "Towards a Butch-Femme Aesthetic." In *Making a Spectacle*, ed. Lynda Hart. Ann Arbor: University of Michigan Press, 1989.

Casteras, Susan P. *The Substance and the Shadow: Images of Victorian Womanhood*. New Haven, Conn.: Yale Center for British Art, 1982.

Castronovo, Russ. *Fathering the Nation: American Genealogies of Slavery and Freedom*. Berkeley: University of California Press, 1995.

Chakrabarty, Dipesh. "Postcoloniality and the Artifice of History." *Representations* 37 (1992).

Clark, Timothy J. *The Painting of Modern Life: Paris in the Art of Manet and His Followers.* Princeton, N.J.: Princeton University Press, 1984.

Cohen, Richard. "Don't Laugh at Hugh." *Washington Post,* 4 July 1995.

Colley, Linda. *Britons: Forging the Nation, 1707–1837.* New Haven, Conn.: Yale University Press, 1992.

Cominos, Peter. "Late Victorian Sexuality, Respectability, and the Social System." *International Review of Social History* 8 (1963): 18–48.

Cook, Jim, and Christine Gledhill, eds. *Stage, Picture, Screen.* London: British Film Institute, 1994.

Cox, Richard, ed. *Sexuality and Victorian Literature.* Knoxville: University of Tennessee Press, 1984.

Cooper, Wendy. *Hair: Sex, Society, Symbolism.* New York: Stein and Day Publishers, 1971.

Creed, Barbara. *The Monstrous-Feminine: Film, Feminism, Psychoanalysis.* New York: Routledge, 1993.

Crenshaw, Kimberle. "Whose Story Is It Anyway? Feminist and Anti-racist Appropriations of Anita Hill." In *Rac-ing Justice, En-gendering Power,* ed. Toni Morrison. New York: Pantheon Books, 1992.

Cromwell, Adelaide M. *An African Victorian Feminist: The Life and Times of Adelaide Smith Casely Hayford, 1868–1960.* Washington, D.C.: Howard University Press, 1986.

Curtis, L. Perry. *Apes and Angels: The Irishman in Victorian Caricature.* Washington, D.C.: Smithsonian Institution Press, 1971.

Cvetkovich, Ann. *Mixed Feelings: Feminism, Mass Culture, and Victorian Sensationalism.* New Brunswick, N.J.: Rutgers University Press, 1992.

Davies, George P. "The Miscegenation Theme in the Works of Thackeray," *Modern Language Notes* 76 (April 1961): 326–31.

Davis, David Brion. *The Problem of Slavery in the Age of Revolution, 1770–1823.* Ithaca, N.Y.: Cornell University Press, 1975.

Davis, Tracy. *Actresses as Working Women: Their Social Identity in Victorian Culture.* London: Routledge, 1991.

Dayan, Joan. *Haiti, History, and the Gods.* Berkeley: University of California Press, 1995.

DeLauretis, Teresa. *Technologies of Gender.* Bloomington: Indiana University Press, 1987.

de Man, Paul. "Hypogram and Inscription." *The Resistance to Theory.* Minneapolis: University of Minnesota Press, 1986.

Diamond, Elin, ed. *Performance and Cultural Politics*. New York: Routledge, 1996.

Dijkstra, Bram. *Idols of Perversity*. New York: Oxford University Press, 1986.

Doane, Mary Ann. *Femmes Fatales: Feminism, Film Theory, and Psychoanalysis*. New York: Routledge, 1991.

Douglas, Mary. *Purity and Danger*. London: Routledge and Kegan Paul, 1966.

Dowling, Linda. "The Decadent and the New Woman in the 1890's." *Nineteenth Century Fiction* 33 (March 1979): 434–53.

Doyle, Brian. *English and Englishness*. London: Routledge, 1989.

Draper, Michael. *H. G. Wells*. New York: St. Martin's Press, 1982.

duCille, Ann. *The Coupling Convention: Sex, Text, and Tradition in Black Women's Fiction*. New York: Oxford University Press, 1993.

Dudden, Faye. *Women in the American Theater: Actresses and Audiences, 1790–1870*. New Haven, Conn.: Yale University Press, 1994.

Dukore, Bernard F. *Dramatic Theory and Criticism: Greeks to Grotowski*. New York: Holt, Reinehart and Winston, 1974.

Dyer, Richard. *White*. London: Routledge, 1997.

Dykes, Eva. *The Negro in English Romantic Thought*. Washington, D.C.: Associated Publishers, 1942.

Edwards, Paul, and James Walvin, eds. *Black Personalities in the Era of the Slave Trade*. Baton Rouge: Louisiana State University Press, 1983.

Eigner, Ed, ed. *Dickens and Pantomime*. Berkeley: University of California Press, 1987.

Ellison, Ralph. *Invisible Man*. New York: Random House, 1952.

Epstein, Julia, and Kristina Straub, eds. *Body Guards: The Cultural Politics of Gender Ambiguity*. New York: Routledge, 1991.

Erdman, Harley. "Caught in the Eye of the Eternal: Justice, Race, and the Camera, from *The Octoroon* to Rodney King." *Theatre Journal* 45 (1993): 333–48.

Erickson, Arvel. "Empire or Anarchy: The Jamaica Rebellion of 1865." *Journal of Negro History* 44, no. 2 (April 1959): 99–122.

Fanon, Frantz. *Black Skin, White Masks*. New York: Grove Wedenfeld Books, 1967.

Filmer, Kathy, ed. *The Victorian Fantasists*. New York: St. Martin's Press, 1991.

Fisch, Audrey. " 'Repetitious Accounts So Piteous and So Harrowing': The Ideological Work of American Slave Narratives in England." *Journal of Victorian Culture* (1994).

Fischer, Judith. "Image versus Text in the Illustrated Novels of William Makepeace Thackeray." In *Victorian Literature and the Victorian Visual Imagination*, ed. Carol Christ and John Jordan. Berkeley: University of California Press, 1995.

Forbes, Jack. *Black Africans and Native Americans: Color, Race, and Caste in the Evolution of Red-Black Peoples*. Oxford: Blackwell Publishers, 1988.

Foucault, Michel. *The History of Sexuality, Volume One*. Trans. Robert Hurley. New York: Random House, 1978.

———. *The Order of Things*. New York: Vintage, 1973.

———. *This Is Not a Pipe*. Trans. and ed. James Harkness. Berkeley: University of California Press, 1982.

Fryer, Peter. *Staying Power: The History of Black People in Britain*. London: Pluto Press, 1984.

Fuss, Diana, ed. *Human, All Too Human*. New York: Routledge, 1996.

Gagnier, Regina. *Idylls of the Marketplace: Oscar Wilde and the Victorian Public*. Stanford, Calif.: Stanford University Press, 1986.

Gallagher, Catherine. *The Industrial Reformation of English Fiction*. Chicago: University of Chicago Press, 1985.

———, and Thomas Laqueur, eds. *The Making of the Modern Body*. Berkeley: University of California Press, 1987.

Garber, Margorie. *Vested Interests: Cross-Dressing and Cultural Anxiety*. New York: Routledge, 1991.

Garrett, Stewart. *Death Sentences: Styles of Dying in British Fiction*. Cambridge, Mass.: Harvard University Press, 1984.

Gates, Henry Louis Jr. *Figures in Black: Words, Signs, and the Racial Self*. Oxford: Oxford University Press, 1987.

———, ed. *"Race," Writing, and Difference*. Chicago: University of Chicago Press, 1986.

Gay, Peter. *Education of the Senses, Volume I: Victorian to Freud*. New York: Oxford University Press, 1984.

Gerzina, Gretchen. *Black London: Life before Emancipation*. New Brunswick, N.J.: Rutgers University Press, 1995.

Gilbert, Sandra, and Susan Gubar. *The Madwoman in the Attic*. New Haven, Conn.: Yale University Press, 1980.

Gilman, Sander. *Difference and Pathology: Stereotypes of Sexuality, Race, and Madness*. Ithaca, N.Y.: Cornell University Press, 1985.

———. "I'm Down on Whores: Race and Gender in Victorian London." In *The Anatomy of Racism*, ed. David Goldberg. Minneapolis: University of Minnesota Press, 1990.

Gilroy, Paul. *Ain't No Black in the Union Jack.* London: Hutchinson Press, 1987.

———. *The Black Atlantic: Modernity and Double-Consciousness.* Cambridge, Mass.: Harvard University Press, 1993.

Ginsberg, Elaine K. *Passing and the Fictions of Identity.* Durham, N.C.: Duke University Press, 1996.

Gissing, George. *The Odd Women.* New York: Macmillan Publishing Co., 1893.

Glover, David. *Vampires, Mummies, and Liberals: Bram Stoker and the Politics of Popular Fiction.* Durham, N.C.: Duke University Press, 1996.

Goodman, Nelson. *The Languages of Art.* New York: Hackett Books, 1976.

Grewal, Inderpal. *Home and Harem.* Durham, N.C.: Duke University Press, 1996.

Guy-Sheftall, Beverly, ed. *Words of Fire: An Anthology of African-American Feminist Thought.* New York: New Press, 1995.

Halberstam, Judith. "Lesbian Masculinity; or Even Stone Butches Get the Blues." *Women and Performance* 8, no. 2 (1996): 61–73.

———. *Skin Shows: Gothic Horror and the Technology of Monsters.* Durham, N.C.: Duke University Press, 1995.

Hall, Catherine. "The Economy of Political Prestige: Thomas Carlyle, John Stuart Mill, and the Case of Governor Eyre." In *Cultural Studies*, ed. Lawrence Grossberg, Cary Nelson, and Paula A. Treichler. New York: Routledge, 1992.

———. *White, Male, and Middle-Class: Explorations in Feminism and History.* New York: Routledge, 1992.

Hall, Kim. "Reading What Isn't There: 'Black' Studies in Early Modern England." *Stanford Humanities Review* 3, no. 1 (winter 1993): 23–33.

———. *Things of Darkness: Economies of Race and Gender in Early Modern Culture.* Ithaca, N.Y.: Cornell University Press, 1995.

Hall, Stuart. "The After-life of Frantz Fanon: Why Fanon? Why Now? Why *Black Skin, White Masks?*" In *The Fact of Blackness: Frantz Fanon and Visual Representation.* London: Institute of Contemporary Arts, 1996.

Halperin, David. *One Hundred Years of Homosexuality, and Other Essays on Greek Love.* New York: Routledge, 1990.

Hanna, Ralph, ed. *The Awntyrs off Arthure at the Terne Wathelyn.* London: Manchester University Press, 1974.

Harper, Philip Brian. *Are We Not Men? Masculine Anxiety and the Problem of African-American Identity.* New York: Oxford University Press, 1996.

———. "Race, Sex, Property." In *Professions of Desire: Lesbian and Gay*

Studies in Literature, ed. George Haggerty and Bonnie Zimmerman. New York: Modern Language Association, 1994.

Harrison, Fraser. *The Dark Angel: Aspects of Victorian Sexuality*. London: Sheldon Press, 1977.

Hart, Lynda. *Fatal Women: Lesbian Sexuality and the Mark of Aggression*. Princeton, N.J.: Princeton University Press, 1994.

Harvey, John. *Victorian Novelists and Their Illustrators*. New York: New York University Press, 1971.

Hays, Michael. "Representing Empire: Class, Culture, and the Popular Theatre in the Nineteenth Century." *Theatre Journal* 47, no. 1 (1995): 65–82.

Helsinger, Elizabeth, Robin Sheets, and William Veeder, eds. *The Woman Question: Society and Literature in Britain and America*. Chicago: University of Chicago Press, 1983.

Hendrick, Joan D. *Harriet Beecher Stowe: A Life*. New York: Oxford University Press, 1994.

Henkle, Roger. *Comedy and Culture: 1820–1900*. Princeton, N.J.: Princeton University Press, 1980.

Higginbotham Jr., Leon. *In the Matter of Color: Race and the American Legal Process, the Colonial Period*. Oxford: Oxford University Press, 1978.

Hines, Reginald. *Hitchin Worthies: Four Centuries of English Life*. London: George Allen and Unwin, 1932.

Hobsbawn, E. J. *Nations and Nationalism since 1780*. New York: Canto Books, 1990.

Houghton, Walter. *The Victorian Frame of Mind: 1830–1870*. New Haven, Conn.: Yale University Press, 1957.

Howard, Christopher. *Splendid Isolation: A Study of Ideas Concerning Britain's International Position and Foreign Policy during the Later Years of the Third Marquis of Salisbury*. London: Macmillan, 1967.

Howard, Jean. "Cross-Dressing, the Theater, and Gender Struggle in Early Modern England." *Shakespeare Quarterly* 39 (1988).

Howell, Michael, and Peter Ford. *The True History of the Elephant Man*. London: Penguin Books, 1980.

Hudson, Lynton. *The English Stage: 1851–1950*. Westport, Conn.: Greenwood Press, 1951.

Hughes, Langston, and Milton Meltzer, eds. *Black Magic: A Pictorial History of African-American Performing Arts*. New York: Da Capo Press, 1990.

Husain, Asfar. *The Indianness of Rudyard Kipling: A Study in Stylistics*. London: Cosmis Press, 1983.

"Integrated but Unequal." *Economist* (8 February 1997): 58–60.

Jackson, Holbrook. *The 1890s*. London: Cresset Library, 1988. First published in 1913.

Jarrett-Macauley, Delia, ed. *Reconstructing Womanhood, Reconstructing Feminism* (London: Routledge, 1996).

Jenkins, Anthony. *The Making of Victorian Drama*. Cambridge: Cambridge University Press, 1991.

Jenkyns, Richard. *Dignity and Decadence: Victorian Art and the Classical Inheritance*. Cambridge, Mass.: Harvard University Press, 1992.

Johnson, Barbara. *The Critical Difference: Essays in the Contemporary Rhetoric of Reading*. Baltimore: Johns Hopkins University Press, 1980.

Jones, Ann Rosiland, and Peter Stallybrass. "Fetishizing Gender: Constructing the Hermaphrodite in Renaissance Europe." In *Body Guards: The Cultural Politics of Gender Ambiguity*, ed. Julia Epstein and Kristina Straub. New York: Routledge, 1991.

Jones, Bill T. *Last Supper at Uncle Tom's Cabin/The Promised Land*. VHS Recording, Bill T. Jones/Arnie Zane Dance Company, 1980.

Jordan, Winthrop. *White over Black: American Attitudes toward the Negro, 1550–1812*. Chapel Hill: University of North Carolina Press, 1968.

Judy, Ronald A. T. *(Dis)forming the American Canon: Afro-Arabic Slave Narratives and the Vernacular*. Minneapolis: University of Minnesota Press, 1993.

Kaplan, Cora. "The Thorn Birds: Fiction, Fantasy, Femininity." In *Formation of Fantasy*, ed. Victor Burgin, James Donald, and Cora Kaplan. London: Methuen Books, 1986.

Kaplan, Sidney. *American Studies in Black and White*. Amherst: University of Massachusetts Press, 1991.

Kasson, Joy S. "Narratives of the Female Body: *The Greek Slave*." In *The Culture of Sentiment: Race, Gender, and Sentimentality in Nineteenth-Century America*, ed. Shirley Samuels. New York: Oxford University Press, 1992.

Kennedy, Paul, and Anthony Nicolls, eds. *Nationalist and Racialist Movements in Britain and Germany before 1914*. London: Macmillan, 1981.

Kinney, James. *Amalgamation! Race, Sex, and Rhetoric in the Nineteenth Century American Novel*. Westport, Conn.: Greenwood Press, 1985.

Kutzinski, Vera. *Sugar's Secrets: Race and the Erotics of Cuban Nationalism*. Charlottesville: University Press of Virginia, 1993.

Lane, Christopher. *The Ruling Passion: British Colonial Allegory and the*

Paradox of Homosexual Desire. Durham, N.C.: Duke University Press, 1995.

Lansbury, Coral. "Gynecology, Pornography, and the Anti-Vivisection Movement." *Victorian Studies* 28, no. 3 (spring 1985).

Laqueur, Thomas. *Making Sex: The Body from the Greeks to Freud.* Cambridge, Mass.: Harvard University Press, 1990.

Larkin, Oliver W. *Art and Life in America,* rev. ed. New York: Holt, Rinehart, and Winston, 1960.

Leslie, Kent Anderson. *Woman of Color, Daughter of Privilege: Amanda America Dickson, 1849–1893.* Athens: University of Georgia Press, 1995.

Levine, George. *Darwin among the Novelists.* Cambridge, Mass.: Harvard University Press, 1988.

Litvak, Joseph. *Caught in the Act: Theatricality in the Nineteenth Century English Novel.* Berkeley: University of California Press, 1992.

Lorimar, Douglas. *Colour, Class, and the Victorians: English Attitudes to the Negro in the Mid–Nineteenth Century.* Leicester: Holmes and Meier Publishers, 1978.

Lott, Eric. *Love and Theft: Blackface Minstrelsy and the American Working Class.* New York: Oxford University Press, 1993.

Lowe, Lisa. *Critical Terrains: French and British Orientalisms.* Ithaca, N.Y.: Cornell University Press, 1991.

Lovejoy, Arthur. *The Great Chain of Being: The Study of the History of an Idea.* Cambridge, Mass.: Harvard University Press, 1966.

MacKay, Carol Hanberry. *Dramatic Dickens.* New York: St. Martin's Press, 1989.

MacKenzie, John, ed. *Propaganda and Empire: The Manipulation of British Public Opinion.* Manchester: Manchester University Press, 1984.

Malchow, Howard L. *Gothic Images of Race in Nineteenth-Century Britain.* Palo Alto, Calif.: Stanford University Press, 1996.

Malone, Jacqui. *Steppin' on the Blues: The Visible Rhythms of African American Dance.* Urbana: University of Illinois Press, 1996.

Mama, Amina. *Beyond the Masks: Race, Gender, and Subjectivity.* London: Routledge, 1995.

Mann, Judy. "Summer Seething." *Washington Post,* 21 July 1995, sec. E3.

Marcus, Steven. *The Other Victorians.* New York: Basic Books, 1964.

Marks, Edward. *They All Had Glamour: From the Swedish Nightingale to the Naked Lady.* New York: Messner Books, 1944.

Matlaw, Myron, ed. *Nineteenth-Century American Plays.* New York: Applause Theatre Book Publishers, 1967.

Mayer, David. "The Sexuality of Pantomime," *Theater Quarterly* 4 (1974): 55–65.

Mayhew, Henry. *London Labour and the London Poor.* Ed. Peter Quennell. London: Bracken Books, 1984.

McClintock, Ann. *Imperial Leather: Race, Gender, and Sexuality in the Colonial Contest.* New York: Routledge, 1995.

Meisel, Martin. "The Material Sublime: John Martin, Byron, Turner, and the Theater." In *Images of Romanticism: Verbal and Visual Affinities*, eds. Karl Kroebler and William Walling. New Haven, Conn.: Yale University Press, 1978.

———. *Realizations: Narrative, Pictorial, and Theatrical Arts in Nineteenth-Century England.* Princeton, N.J.: Princeton University Press, 1983.

Mencke, John. *Mulattoes and Race Mixture: Images, 1865–1918.* Ann Arbor: UMI Research Press, 1976.

Mercer, Kobena. "Black Hair/Style Politics." *New Formations*, no. 3 (winter 1987): 33–54.

———. "Skin Head Sex Thing." In *How Do We Look? Essays on Queer Film and Video*, ed. Bad Object Choices. Seattle, Wash.: Bay Press, 1991.

———. *Welcome to the Jungle: New Positions in Black Cultural Studies.* New York: Routledge, 1994.

Michie, Helena. *The Flesh Made Word.* Oxford: Oxford University Press, 1987.

———. *Outside the Pale.* Ithaca, N.Y.: Cornell University Press, 1993.

Miller, Christopher. *Blank Darkness: Africanist Discourse in French.* Chicago: University of Chicago Press, 1985.

Miller, D. A. *The Novel and the Police.* Berkeley: University of California Press, 1988.

Miller, J. Hillis. "The Critic as Host." In *Deconstruction and Criticism*, ed. Geoffrey Hartman. New York: Continuum Books, 1990.

Milling, Jill. "The Ambiguous Animal: Evolution of the Beast-Man in Scientific Creation Myths." In *The Fantastic in World Literature and the Arts: Selected Essays from the Fifth International Conference of the Fantastic in the Arts*, ed. Donald E. Morse. New York: Greenwood Press, 1987.

Mitchell, W. J. Thomas. *Iconology: Image, Text, Ideology.* Chicago: University of Chicago Press, 1988.

Mirza, Heidi Safia, ed. *Black British Feminism.* London: Routledge, 1997.

Montagu, Ashley, ed. *The Concept of Race.* London: Collier-Macmillan, 1964.

Morrison, Toni, and Lacour, Claudia Brodsky. *Birth of a Nation 'hood: Gaze, Script, and Spectacle in the O. J. Simpson Case.* New York: Pantheon, 1997.

———. *Playing in the Dark: Whiteness and the Literary Imagination.* Cambridge, Mass.: Harvard University Press, 1992.

———. *Rac-ing Justice, En-gendering Power.* New York: Pantheon, 1992.

———. *Sula.* New York: Plume Books, 1973.

———. "Unspeakable Things Unspoken: The Afro-American Presence in American Literature." *Michigan Quarterly Review* 28, no. 1 (1987): 1–34.

Mullen, Harryette. "Optic White: Blackness and the Production of Whiteness." *Diacritics* 24, nos. 2–3 (summer–fall 1994): 71–89.

Mullenix, Elizabeth Reitz. "Acting between the Spheres: Charlotte Cushman as Androgyne." *Theater Survey* 37 (1996): 22–65.

Mullin, David, ed. *Victorian Actors and Actresses in Review.* London: Greenwood Press, 1983.

Nicoll, Allardyce. *A History of the English Drama.* Cambridge: Cambridge University Press, 1955.

Nochlin, Linda. *Realism.* London: Penguin Books, 1971.

Nunokawa, Jeff. "For Your Eyes Only: Private Property and the Oriental Body in *Dombey and Son.*" In *The Macropolitics of Nineteenth Century Literature,* ed. Jonathan Arac and Harriet Ritvo. Philadelphia: University of Pennsylvania Press, 1991.

O'Farrell, Mary Ann. *Telling Complexions: The Nineteenth-Century English Novel and the Blush.* Durham, N.C.: Duke University Press, 1997.

O'Grady, Lorraine. "Olympia's Maid: Reclaiming Black Female Subjectivity." *Afterimage* (summer 1992): 12–16.

Otsuki, Jennifer. "Commodity Culture and the Hottentot Venus." Unpublished paper presented at the Interdisciplinary Nineteenth-Century Studies Conference, Santa Cruz, Calif., April 1995.

Pacteau, Francette. "The Impossible Referent: Representations of the Androgyne." in *Formations of Fantasy,* ed. Victor Burgin, James Donald, and Cora Kaplan. London: Methuen Books, 1986.

———. *The Symptom of Beauty.* Cambridge, Mass.: Harvard University Press, 1994.

Parrinder, Patrick, ed., *H. G. Wells: The Critical Heritage.* London: Routledge and Kegan Paul, 1972.

Peters, Catherine. *Thackeray's Universe.* Oxford: Oxford University Press, 1987.

Phelan, Peggy. *Unmarked: The Politics of Performance.* New York: Routledge, 1993.

Phillips, Caryl. *The European Tribe*. New York: Faber and Faber, 1987.

Phoenix, Ann, and Barbara Tizard. *Black, White, or Mixed Race? Race and Racism in the Lives of Young People of Mixed Parentage*. London: Routledge, 1993.

Pickering, Michael. "Mock Blacks and Racial Mockery: The 'Nigger' Minstrel and British Imperialism." In *Acts of Supremacy: The British Empire and the Stage, 1790–1930*, Jacky S. Bratton et al. Manchester, Manchester University Press, 1991.

Pollard, Arthur, ed. *Thackeray: "Vanity Fair," a Casebook*. London: Macmillan, 1978.

Pollock, Griselda. *Vision and Difference*. London: Routledge, 1988.

Poovey, Mary. *Uneven Developments: The Ideological Work of Gender in Mid-Victorian England*. Chicago: University of Chicago Press, 1989.

Powell, Richard. *Black Art and Culture in the Twentieth Century*. London: Thames and Hudson, 1997.

Quennell, Peter. *Victorian Panorama*. London: B. T. Batsford, 1937.

——, ed. *Mayhew's London*. London: Bracken Books, 1984.

Read, Alan, ed. *The Fact of Blackness: Frantz Fanon and Visual Representation*. Seattle, Wash.: Bay Press, 1996.

Reynolds, Graham. *Victorian Painting*. London: Studio Vista, 1966.

Reynolds, Harry. *Minstrel Memories: The Story of Burnt Cork Minstrelsy in Great Britain from 1836 to 1927*. London: A. Rivers, 1928.

Ritvo, Harriet. *The Animal Estate: The English and Other Creatures in the Victorian Age*. Cambridge, Mass.: Harvard University Press, 1987.

——. "Professional Scientists and Amateur Mermaids: Beating the Bounds of Nineteenth-Century Britain." *Victorian Literature and Culture* 19 (1991).

Roach, Joseph. *Cities of the Dead: Circum-Atlantic Performance*. New York: Columbia University Press, 1996.

——. "Darwin's Passion: The Language of Expression on Nature's Stage." *Discourse* 13, no. 1 (fall/winter 1990–91): 40–58.

Robinson, Amy. "Authority and the Public Display of Identity: *Wonderful Adventures of Mrs. Seacole in Many Lands*." *Feminist Studies* (fall 1994): 537–57.

Rogers, J. A. *Sex and Race: Negro-Caucasian Mixing in All Ages and Lands Volume 1*. Petersburg, Fla.: Helga M. Rogers, 1968.

Rony, Fatimah. *The Third Eye: Race, Cinema, and Ethnographic Spectacle*. Durham, N.C.: Duke University Press, 1996.

Rowell, George. *Nineteenth Century Theatre*. New York: Oxford University Press, 1956.

Rubin, Gayle. "The Traffic in Women: Notes on the Political Economy of Sex." In *Toward an Anthropology of Women,* ed. Rayna R. Reiter. New York: Monthly Review Press, 1975.

Rushdie, Salman. *The Satanic Verses.* Dover, U.K.: Consortium, 1992.

Said, Edward. *Culture and Imperialism.* New York: Vintage Books, 1993.

———. *Orientalism.* New York: Vintage Books, 1978.

Saks, Eva. "Representing Miscegenation Law." Raritan 8, no. 2 (fall 1988): 39–69.

Sanchez-Eppler, Karen. "Bodily Bonds: The Intersecting Rhetorics of Feminism and Abolition." In *The Culture of Sentiment: Race, Gender, and Sentimentality in Nineteenth-Century America,* ed. Shirley Samuels. New York: Oxford University Press, 1992.

Sandison, Alan. *The Wheel of Empire.* New York: St. Martin's Press, 1967.

Sartre, Jean-Paul. *Being and Nothingness.* New York: New York University Press, 1956.

Saxton, Alexander. *The Rise and Fall of the White Republic: Class Politics and Mass Culture in Nineteenth-Century America.* London: Verso, 1990.

Scarry, Elaine. *The Body in Pain: The Making and Unmaking of the World.* Oxford: Oxford University Press, 1985.

Sedgwick, Eve. *Between Men: English Literature and Male Homosocial Desire.* New York: Columbia University Press, 1985.

Semmel, Bernard. *The Governor Eyre Controversy.* London: Macgibbon and Kee, 1962.

Senelick, Laurence. "Boys and Girls Together: Subculture Origins of Glamour Drag and Male Impersonation on the Nineteenth-Century Stage," in *Crossing the Stage: Controversy on Cross-Dressing,* ed. Leslie Ferris, 80–95. New York: Routledge, 1993.

Sharpe, Jenny. *Allegories of Empire.* Minneapolis: University of Minnesota Press, 1993.

Showalter, Elaine. *Sexual Anarchy: Gender and Culture in the Fin de Siècle.* London: Penguin Books, 1990.

Shyllon, Folarin. *Black Slaves in Britain.* Oxford: Oxford University Press for the Institute of Race Relations, 1974.

Silverman, Kaja. *Male Subjectivity at the Margins.* New York: Routledge, 1992.

Small, Stephen. *Racialised Barriers: The Black Experience in the United States and England in the 1980s.* London: 1994.

Smith, Valerie. *Self-Discovery and Authority in Afro-American Narrative.* Cambridge, Mass.: Harvard University Press, 1987.

Smith-Rosenberg, Carroll. *Disorderly Conduct.* New York: Oxford University Press, 1985.

Sollers, Werner. *Neither Black Nor White Yet Both.* New York: Oxford University Press, 1997.

Spillers, Hortense I. "Interstices: A Small Drama of Words." In *Pleasure and Danger: Exploring Female Sexuality,* ed. Carol Vance. New York: Pandora Books, 1984.

———. "Mama's Baby, Papa's Maybe: An American Grammar Book." *Diacritics* 17, no. 2 (summer 1987): 65–80.

———. "Notes on an Alternative Model: Neither/Nor." In *The Difference Within: Feminism and Critical Theory,* ed. Elizabeth Meese and Alice Parker. Philadelphia: John Benjamin Publishing, 1989.

———. "The Permanent Obliquity: In the Time of Fathers and Daughters." In *Changing Our Own Words,* ed. Cheryl Wall. New Brunswick, N.J.: Rutgers University Press, 1989.

———, ed. *Comparative American Identities.* New York: Routledge, 1991.

Spivak, Gayatri Chakravorty. "Three Women's Texts and a Critique of Imperialism." In *"Race," Writing and Difference,* ed. Henry Louis Gates Jr. Chicago: University of Chicago Press, 1986.

Stallybrass, Peter, and Allon White. *The Politics and Poetics of Transgression.* Ithaca, N.Y.: Cornell University Press, 1986.

Stepan, Nancy Leys. *The Idea of Race in Science.* London: Macmillan, 1982.

———. "Race and Gender: The Role of Analogy in Science," *Isis* 77 (1986): 261–77.

Stocking, George. *Victorian Anthropology.* New York: Free Press, 1987.

Stoler, Ann. *Race and the Education of Desire: Foucault's "History of Sexuality" and the Colonial Order of Things.* Durham, N.C.: Duke University Press, 1996.

Stowell, Sheila. "Actors as Dramatic Personae: Nell Gwynne, Peg Woffington, and David Garrick on the Victorian Stage." *Theatre History Studies* 8 (1988): 117–36.

Straub, Kristina. *Sexual Suspects: Eighteenth Century Players and Sexual Ideology.* Princeton, N.J.: Princeton University Press, 1992.

Stubbs, Patricia. *Women and Fiction: Feminism and the Novel, 1880–1920.* London: Methuen Books, 1979.

Stuckey, Sterling. *Slave Culture.* New York: Oxford University Press, 1987.

Sundell, M. G., ed. *Twentieth Century Interpretations of "Vanity Fair."* Englewood Cliffs, N.J.: Prentice-Hall, 1969.

Sutherland, John, and Oscar Mandel. *Annotations to Vanity Fair.* Lanham: University Press of America, 1988.

Thomas, Keith. *Man and the Natural World.* New York: Pantheon Books, 1983.

Toll, Robert C. *Blacking Up: The Minstrel Show in Nineteenth Century America.* New York: Oxford University Press, 1974.

Tyler, Carole-Anne. "Boys Will Be Girls: The Politics of Gay Drag." In *Inside/Out: Gay and Lesbian Studies,* ed. Diana Fuss. New York: Routledge, 1994.

Vicinus, Martha. "The Adolescent Boy—Fin-de-Siècle Femme Fatale." *Journal for the History of Sexuality* 5, no. 1 (1994): 90–114.

———. *Independent Women.* Chicago: University of Chicago Press, 1985.

———, ed. *Suffer and Be Still: Women in the Victorian Period.* Bloomington: University of Indiana Press, 1972.

———, ed. *The Widening Sphere: Changing Roles of Victorian Women.* Bloomington: University of Indiana Press, 1977.

Walkowitz, Judith. *Cities of Dreadful Delight.* Chicago: University of Chicago Press, 1991.

———. *Prostitution and Victorian Society.* Cambridge: Cambridge University Press, 1980.

Walvin, James. *Black and White: The Negro and English Society, 1555–1945.* London: Orbach, 1975.

Watson, George. *The English Ideology: Studies in the Language of Victorian Politics.* London: Allen Lane, 1973.

Weeks, Jeffrey. *Sex, Politics, and Society: The Regulation of Sexuality since 1800.* London: Longman Group, 1981.

Weil, Kari. *Androgyny and the Denial of Difference.* Charlottesville: University Press of Virginia, 1992.

Wiegman, Robyn. *American Anatomies: Theorizing Race and Gender.* Durham, N.C.: Duke University Press, 1995.

Williams, Patricia. *The Alchemy of Race and Rights.* Cambridge, Mass.: Harvard University Press, 1991.

Williams, Raymond. *Culture and Society.* New York: Harper and Row, 1958.

Williamson, Joel. *New People: Miscegenation and Mulattoes in the United States.* New York: Free Press, 1980.

Wittke, Carl. *Tambo and Bones: A History of the American Minstrel Stage.* Durham, N.C.: Duke University Press, 1930.

Wohl, Anthony, ed. *The Victorian Family: Structure and Stresses.* London: Croom Helm, 1978.

Woodroffe, Martin. "Racial Theories of History and Politics: The Example of H. S. Chamberlain." In *Nationalist and Racialist Movements in Brit-*

ain and Germany before 1914, ed. Paul Kennedy and Anthony Nicolls. London: Macmillan, 1981.

Yeazell, Ruth, ed. *Sex, Politics, and Science in the Nineteenth Century Novel.* Baltimore, Md.: Johns Hopkins University Press, 1986.

Young, George M. *Portrait of an Age.* Oxford: Oxford University Press, 1983.

Young, Robert. *Colonial Desire: Hybridity in Theory, Culture and Race.* London: Routledge, 1995.

Index

Moore, G. W., 86, *87*
Moore and Burgess (minstrels), 86, *87*
Morant Bay, Jamaica, rebellion, 140
Morrison, Toni, 10–11, 33, 187 n.37, 207 n.92, 218 n.23
Mudie's Circulating Library, 108
Mulattaroons: as defined in this study, 16. *See also* Mulattas
Mulattas (mulattaroons): air of refinement of, 63; as associated with their fathers, 21, 54, 184 n.7; as barren, 97; desirability of, 22; and fancy girl auctions, 48; as iconic sign of miscegenation, 21; marrying white men, 18–19; as mediating device in literature, 187 n.33; as nineteenth-century phenomenon, 180 n.22; as preservers and threat to patriarchal family, 58; racially pure antecedents assumed for, 43; shifting cultural placement of, 18; as stock characters in African American fiction, 17; and Stowe's Eliza Harris, 63; as twice-owned property, 54; in *Uncle Tom in England*, 81; white complexion of, 12. *See also* Octoroons; Quadroons
Mulattoes: antagonistic relationships with their fathers, 184 n.7; and Creoles, 16, 56–57; as nineteenth-century phenomenon, 180 n.22; origin of term, 189 n.50. *See also* Mulattas
Mullen, Harryette, 12
Munby, Sir Arthur, 201 n.10

New woman, 162–64
Nochlin, Linda, 93
Nott, Josiah, 54

Occasional Discourse on the Nigger Question (Carlyle), 80–81
Octoroon, The, or Life in Louisiana (Boucicault), 46–58; the Christian characters as prevailing in, 55–56;

Dicks's plays cover, 52, *53*; incest allusions in, 55; the mulattaroon as represented in, 17; two versions of, 50–51, 190 n.63; and "The Yankee Hugging the Creole" parable, 56. *See also* Peyton, Zoe
Octoroons: adultery with, 46–47; defined, 47; equivocal position of, 47, 48; white complexion of, 12, 47, 48
Odd Women, The (Gissing), 162
O'Grady, Lorraine, 94
Olympia (Manet), 92–94, *93*, 199 n.69
"Only Leon" (performer), 86
On the Phenomena of Hybridity in the Genus Homo (Broca), 8
Originals: versus copies, 73
Osborne, George (*Vanity Fair*): on Amelia Sedley as the only lady, 38; on Amelia Sedley's slavish nature, 44; contempt for Rhoda Swartz, 36–37; marriage to Amelia Sedley, 35; as tainted by the values of the fair, 45; as third-rate hero, 33; yellow face of, 41
Othello the Moor of Venice (Shakespeare), 178 n.8, 203 n.38
Our Mutual Friend (Dickens), 32
Oxenberg, Catherine, 218 n.23

Pacteau, Francette, 118, 123–24
Pantomime, 115, 121, 206 n.79
Past and Present (Carlyle), 133–34
Peg Woffington (Reade), 107–11; and Coleman, 114; and dedication to Taylor, 101; on the hybrid, morbid, insane new truths of the era, 127; Irishness in, 109–10; and Mabel Vane, 110–11; Margaret Woffington as subject of, 98; *Masks and Faces* compared with, 107; Peg associated with low creatures in, 108; Peg as Lady Betty Modish in, 110; Peg's conversion to Christianity in, 111; and Pomander, 108, 109; and

being natural as a pose, 118, 127; *An Ideal Husband,* 103, 127; *Lady Windermere's Fan,* 110, 127–29; on a mask telling more than a face, 98; *The Picture of Dorian Gray,* 127, 129, 131, 160, 210 n.18; and Reade on proper place for poets, 125; as Reade's heir, 127; Wells's *The Island of Dr. Moreau* as response to trial of, 130–31

Williams, Basil, 144

Williams, Patricia, 13

Wilton, Marie, 116

Woffington, Margaret (Peg): Boucicault's play about, 99; in breeches roles, 101, 205 n.51; as Irish, 109–10; male roles played by, 100–101; in Reade's *Masks and Faces,* 98, 101–6; in Reade's *Peg Woffington,* 98, 107–11

Woman of Colour, The: A Tale in Two Volumes (novel): as abolitionist text, 26; black woman's body eroticized in, 22; and "Dialogue between the Editor and a Friend," 25–26; as opening in media res, 15. *See also* Fairfield, Olivia; Marcia

Woman of Colour, The, or Slavery in Freedom (play): as beckoning the octoroon to Britain, 185 n.13; and

Florida Brandon's rescue, 18–19; playbill, 18–19, *20*

Women: boy-women in pantomime, 115, 121; and divided skirts, 125, 162; fallen women as dead, 95–97, 199 n.72; falling from purity, 58; as ferocious and wild in Victorian discourse, 166; hardening of difference between men and, 59; as hybrid of resistance and compliance, 95; and lesbianism, 121–23, 207 n.90, 208 n.96; men-women, 103, 116; and the new woman, 162–64; playing a false part, 113; and prostitution, 90, 107; public women, 103, 114; pure versus passionate, 55; as vehicles of impurity, 4–5; in Wells's *The Island of Dr. Moreau,* 161–69. *See also* Femininity; White women; Women of color

Women of color, 14–58; rescue-fantasy scenarios for, 22. *See also* Black women; Mulattas

Woodroffe, Martin, 159

Wuthering Heights (Brontë), 204 n.38

Young, G. M., 153

Young, Robert, 67, 213 n.67

Jennifer DeVere Brody is assistant professor of English

at the University of California, Riverside.

Library of Congress Cataloging-in-Publication Data

Brody, Jennifer DeVere.
Impossible purities : blackness, femininity, and Victorian
culture / Jennifer DeVere Brody.
p. cm.
Includes bibliographical references and index.
ISBN 0-8223-2105-x (hardcover : alk. paper). — ISBN
0-8223-2120-3 (pbk. : alk. paper)
1. English literature—19th century—History and criticism.
2. Blacks—Great Britain—Public opinion—History—19th
century. 3. Race awareness—Great Britain—History—
19th century. 4. National characteristics, English, in
literature. 5. Great Britain—Civilization—19th century.
6. Women, Black, in literature. 7. Femininity in
literature. 8. Blacks in literature. 9. Race in literature.
10. Black race—Color. I. Title.
PR468.B53B76 1998
820.9'358—dc21   98-23196